"After reading *Falling Awake*, I feel clearer about almost everything. Even truths I thought I already knew, seem more natural and easily attainable. This book is a beautiful presentation of some wondrous thoughts about the things that matter most."

MARIANNE WILLIAMSON
Author of *Illuminata* and *The Healing of America*

"*Falling Awake* is a detailed, comprehensive invitation to the sweetness of possibility, so credible and compelling that you read it at your own risk. You simply will not be the same person nor lead the same life if you read and complete this book."

PAUL G. HAWKEN
Founder of Smith & Hawken
Author of *The Ecology of Commerce* and *Growing a Business*

"Anyone who is serious about actually creating the life of their dreams must read and follow the guidance of *Falling Awake*. It is the work of a master teacher, coach, and above all, inspirational encourager of each of us to go the whole way in this lifetime."

BARBARA MARX HUBBARD
Co-founder of Foundation for Conscious Evolution
Author of *Conscious Evolution: Awakening the power of our social potential*

"Dave Ellis lives the life he writes about. He genuinely brings qualities such as vitality, purpose, play, and authentic celebration to each day of his life. It is no wonder that when you read *Falling Awake*, you will discover a treasure chest filled with strategies for creating a more wonderful life."

DUANE ELGIN
Author of *Voluntary Simplicity* and *Promise Ahead*

"*Falling Awake* is the book for anyone who wants to trade sleep-walking through life for the life of their dreams. You deserve it and so does the world."

SAM DALEY-HARRIS
Founder of RESULTS, director of Microcredit Summit Campaign
Author of *Reclaiming Our Democracy*

(COMMENTS CONTINUED ON NEXT PAGE)

"You can have a wonderful life—whatever that means to you. Dave Ellis has collected powerful, common sense strategies that feel as natural as walking. Reading them, you wonder why you've made life so hard for yourself. Applying them, you find yourself flying towards your dreams. I highly recommend *Falling Awake.*"

VICKI ROBIN
Co-author with Joe Dominguez of *Your Money or Your Life*

"In writing *Falling Awake,* Dave Ellis has done a tremendous service to anyone or any organization that has the goal of producing breakthrough results while leading a balanced, enjoyable, and wonderful life. He shows how to do so in concrete, achievable steps without resorting to self-help jargon. Immediately after finishing *Falling Awake,* I ordered one copy for each of my staff so that they can read it before our next retreat. I expect to make reading this book part of every new employee's orientation."

ALEX COUNTS
President, Grameen Foundation USA

"Dave Ellis is a superb teacher, and this book will help millions seeking more positive, satisfying lives. Its simple and compelling wisdom will set you on the path."

HAZEL HENDERSON
Co-creator of the "Calvert-Henderson Quality-of-life Indicators"
with the Calvert Group of Mutual Funds
Author of *Beyond Globalization*

"*Falling Awake* is one of those treasures we constantly seek but seldom discover. It is a masterful combination of modern concepts and ancient wisdom. This book brilliantly leads us into a world where we find ourselves open to the limitless celebrations life truly offers. It is a roadmap to transforming our dreams into realities."

JOHN PERKINS
Founder of Dream Change Coalition,
Author of *Spirit of the Shuar* and *The World Is As You Dream it.*

"*Falling Awake* is a common sense and comprehensive guide to personal transformation. It contains a multitude of steps and strategies drawn from perennial wisdom that will help anyone become more effective."

STEVEN DONOVAN
Past president, Esalen Institute

FALLING AWAKE

creating the life of your dreams

DAVE ELLIS

This book is part of a complete system—an interactive multimedia project dedicated to assisting people to dramatically and permanently improve the quality of their lives. To find out more about this project, visit our web site at *www.FallingAwake.com* or write to:
Breakthrough Enterprises, Inc., PO Box 8396, Rapid City, SD 57709.

Printed in Korea on acid-free paper.

Library of Congress Catalog Card Number LCCN 00-135142

ISBN: 0-942456-18-1

Acknowledgments

I particularly thank Stan Lankowitz and Doug Toft, who are masters at organizing and expressing ideas. Their contributions were critical to the creation of this book. They served as fellow writers and editors.

The design and artwork of this book are key components to its message. For that work I appreciate the excellence of Bill Fleming along with the other people who have contributed so much to the design of this book, including Susan Turnbull, Amy Davis, and Neil Zetah. Copy editing and proofreading were expertly done by Ruth Hapgood and Shawn Kendrick.

During the last 20 years, I have worked day-to-day with dozens of people who, through their ideas, logistical support, and project management, have contributed significantly to the creation of this book. To all those people, I want you to know that this book would never have been produced without you. Several of my coworkers have made such a difference in this book that to leave them unnamed would be negligent. Therefore, I deeply thank and acknowledge the work of Bill Rentz, Robbie Murchison, Doane Robinson, Leonard Running, JoAnne Bangs, Richard Kiefer, and Jeff Swaim.

I am profoundly grateful to those who have enriched my life including: my parents Ken and Maryellen Ellis, my wife Trisha Waldron, and my daughters Snow, Berry, Sara, and Elizabeth.

I also acknowledge the thousands of others who have been my teachers— family members, friends, colleagues, authors, workshop leaders, people I have counseled, educators I have coached, and students I have taught.

Dave Ellis

Wanted: your ideas

Please help me write the next edition of this book. Sometimes, after a book has been written, rewritten, edited, designed, typeset, and printed, it is declared complete. That is not true of this book. *Falling Awake* is still in development.

In fact, this book will be in transition for many years. I will change it frequently as I learn more about what works to assist people to live the life of their dreams. For this reason, I want to hear from you. Please write to me to let me know about your experience with this book.

Most of the interactions I have had with others have been in workshops, classrooms, and coaching sessions. In these situations, feedback is usually frequent and complete. The communication takes place in two directions.

Communicating through a book is different. After publishing their ideas, authors get little feedback or none at all. Such one-way communication does not give me a chance to learn.

I want your feedback. When you see ways to improve this book, write to me. I want the next edition to reflect your experiences as a result of "doing" this book.

If an idea in this book doesn't work for you, let me know. If a technique is particularly effective, let me know that, too. If you particularly like or don't like a photo or part of the design, please tell me.

When you write to me, you are completing a communication loop. You are teaching me to be a more effective teacher.

Thanks for your help. Please write to me at:

Dave Ellis
PO Box 8396
Rapid City, SD 57709

or email me at *dave@FallingAwake.com*
or sign on to our web site at www.*FallingAwake.com*

This book is more than a book

This book reveals a time-tested, life-changing process. In addition to articles that explain the key concepts, there are exercises and journal entries to assist the reader in putting the core ideas to work in real life.

Additionally, you can request individualized support and feedback from me by visiting our *Falling Awake*™ web site at *www.FallingAwake.com.*

There, a community of staff and participants in the Falling Awake project is creating a broad network of support that would have been, until recently, simply impossible to sustain, due to limitations in technology.

If in reading this text, you have feedback or questions, or wish to be more deeply and individually assisted in the process of making your life

 exactly the way you want it to be, please log on. I'll do all I can to help you feel right at home.

A note about gender-fair language

To avoid awkward sentence constructions, I alternate the use of male and female pronouns throughout this book. My intent is to use language that is as inclusive and bias-free as possible.

Table of Contents

The purpose of the pictures…
and the design

The design of *Falling Awake* is intended to inspire both your creativity and your logic—to engage the left side of your brain and the right side. The pictures have been chosen to set a tone, evoke a mood, or arouse a passion—and to stimulate your thinking. Perhaps what you see will help your eyes and mind relax, feel comfortable, and linger just a few moments longer with the messages in the text.

This book is designed to have a different look and feel from other books. My purpose is to invite you to participate actively and to be the "co-author."

I have intentionally left a lot of white space in the margins. This is your space. You can use it to write notes, argue with me, doodle, or draw. As you think about the ideas presented in this book and explore new possibilities, you can use this white space to let your imagination soar, dream big dreams, and create a clear and compelling vision of a wonderful future.

This book has a format similar to that of a magazine. Each article stands alone and is presented as an individual unit. After reading an article and before moving on to the next one, I invite you to stop, think it over, interact with it, and consider how to integrate the ideas into your life.

Whenever you see an exercise, you'll notice a change in the typeface and a colorful, whimsical brush drawing. That's a signal for you to do something besides just read. You'll also notice pages that look like homemade paper. These are invitations for you to write. Doing exercises and writing are powerful ways to get the most value from this book.

LIFE
CAN BE
WONDERFUL

*There is a paradise
in and around you
right now, and to be there
you don't even have
to make a move,
not even lifting your eyes
from this page.*

THADDEUS GOLAS

An invitation

The simple experience of waking up from sleep is natural and easy. It requires no effort, struggle, or will power.

This book invites you to "fall awake" with similar ease. First, you can fall awake to a full awareness of what you really want in all areas of your life. You can invent new possibilities and unleash inspiring passions. You can fall awake to all of the amazing details that make up the life of your dreams.

Second, you can fall awake to what you already know. You can recognize all of your achievements and acknowledge how accomplished you've become. You can tap into your natural brilliance. You can become more fully aware of your ability to make things happen and to turn your visions into realities.

And third, you are invited to appreciate more fully how wonderful your life is right now. Even while wanting more and recognizing that some things could be different, you can celebrate all of the wonderful and abundant attributes of your current life.

By reading, writing, discovering, and taking actions, you can fall awake and create the life of your dreams.

The point of this book

The fundamental message of this book is outlandish: You can get what you want and create the life of your dreams—no matter what your history and no matter what your current circumstances.

And you can create the life of your dreams in a relatively short amount of time—within days, weeks, or maybe as much as a few months—no matter how much money or time you have.

"Creating the life of your dreams no matter what your circumstances in a short amount of time" might sound like a late-night television advertisement for an expensive self-help program or a new religion. But I'm not asking you to part with your money, and I'm not trying to start a cult.

However, I *am* selling something. I want to sell you on the idea of applying the twelve Success Strategies described in this book. You can use the Strategies to create a life full of deep intimacy, vibrant health, full celebration, daily ecstasy, or whatever else you want.

The purpose of this book is to help you raise the quality of your life—immediately, dramatically, and permanently. I want this book to make such a difference that it becomes one of the three most influential books you've ever read.

Open up to the possibility of joy

What if you *really could* create the life of your dreams within the next few weeks?

I think you can. And my best suggestions for creating the life of your dreams are the Success Strategies outlined in the chapters that follow.

Please be clear about what I'm suggesting here. I am not saying that you will create a life in which you feel bliss at every moment. And I am not saying that you will create a life that's problem-free.

I *am* saying that you can live a life that you can honestly label as wonderful—one that you can authentically describe as the life of your dreams. I do believe that it's possible for each of us to create lives filled with ecstasy that occurs on a daily basis; lives of celebration in which we are continuously being thankful; lives with health that allows us to do almost everything that we want to do; and lives filled with intimate and loving relationships.

If you think that this concept of creating the life of your dreams quickly is too outrageous, please practice a strategy I describe later in this book: Ask yourself *What if this is true?* Then, rather than arguing with the idea, you'll begin to consider what your life could be like if this unusual idea is accurate.

You may already have a life that works well. Once in a while, you might even tap into a sense of wonder, beauty, and ecstasy. And I'm guessing that you don't do this as often as you'd like.

The Success Strategies are practical suggestions that can repeatedly connect you with the life you want at any moment. These Strategies can

increase your happiness by helping you determine exactly what you want in life and then take focused, practical, and powerful action to get it.

Use the same strategies to meet <u>any</u> goal

Many self-help books focus on *content*—on getting what you want in specific areas of life. One book might suggest ways for you to achieve greater health. Another might recommend ways to create more loving relationships. Still another might list a series of steps you can take toward financial independence.

Falling Awake is different. This book offers a core set of strategies to help you achieve *any* specific goal.

The key word is *strategy*. A strategy is a general technique, method, habit, practice, transferable skill, or pattern of behavior. I suggest that the strategies for creating more loving relationships can also help you create more wealth. These same strategies can help you become healthier or accomplish anything else you want in life. *No matter what you want, you can use the same set of core strategies to get it.*

People in many disciplines recognize the power of any part to influence the whole. Biologists know that the chromosomes in each cell are the blueprints for that entire organism; careful study of any one cell will show a plan for the entire body. Sociologists study a few members of a group to discover how the entire group behaves. Pollsters can survey a few hundred people and determine how millions feel about an issue.

The same principle is at work in your life. When you carefully observe one part of your life, you gain insight into the way you conduct other parts of your life. And any change in behavior that produces new results in one area of your life can produce new results in any other area. For example, telling the truth can help you create more loving relationships. Truth telling can also help you get out of debt, exercise regularly, lose weight, and achieve just about anything else you want. The joy of this strategy is found in adopting one small change and then watching it expand throughout your whole life.

Success Strategies represent the "kernel"

The Success Strategies are based on several sources.

One is my own experience of creating the life of my dreams. I've applied the Success Strategies in many areas: career, friends, community, time, money, health, and that which is most precious to me—my family.

Another source is the coaching and teaching I have done to help others create the life of their dreams. I've presented these twelve Success Strategies to well over 11,000 workshop participants and clients.

A third source is my review of key works of literature, philosophy, education, psychology, religion, and spirituality.

I also work with a group of people who are constantly in conversation about the Success Strategies. As a self-funded think tank, we operate from the point of view that people are not broken and don't need to be fixed.

We affirm the fundamental genius of every human being. And we have an outlandish purpose—to dramatically improve the quality of life on Earth by inventing success strategies and ways to communicate those strategies. We've promised to test these strategies by applying them in our professional and personal lives. Our lives are our laboratory, and what you read in the following pages is largely the result of our collective experiments in creating wonderful lives.

Over the last 27 years, I've constantly asked *What's the kernel?* What are the core processes in creating the kind of life that most people say they want—and in creating that life as quickly as possible? My answer is the twelve Success Strategies described in this book.

The ideas and strategies that you can use to be happier, healthier, more loving, and more wealthy have been available for centuries. But they have often been explained in ways that are not easily understood and therefore not widely used. The aim of this book is to communicate powerful ideas, both old and new, so that you can put them into practice immediately.

The Success Strategies in a nutshell

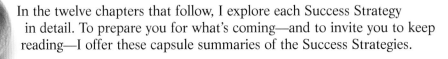

In the twelve chapters that follow, I explore each Success Strategy in detail. To prepare you for what's coming—and to invite you to keep reading—I offer these capsule summaries of the Success Strategies.

1. **Determine what you want.** Trust your desires and create a bold, detailed vision for the long-term future.

2. **Tell the truth.** Speak candidly, make promises, and align your actions with your words.

3. **Move toward love.** Be willing to release antagonism, and embrace problems as a step toward solving them.

4. **Take responsibility.** In any situation, ask *How did I create this?* and *How can I create a new result?*

5. **Lighten your load.** Move toward bliss by letting go of your attachments and expectations, and by choosing new ways to manage distress.

6. **Focus your awareness.** Release mental distractions and pay exquisite attention to moment-to-moment choices.

7. **Listen fully.** Open up to receiving any message—compliments, criticisms, or whatever the world is sending you in the moment.

8. **Choose your conversations.** Understand the role of conversations in creating your world, and enter conversations with care.

9. **Change your habits.** Take the mystery out of personal transformation by following three simple steps to make consistent changes in your behavior.

10. **Persist.** When faced with a problem, look beyond the first solutions that occur to you, and stay in action until you get what you want.

11. **Contribute.** As you get more of what you want in life, find added joy by assisting others to get what *they* want.

12. **Celebrate.** Constantly notice what you enjoy about your life right now, and go for fun.

Treat these ideas as tools

Human beings constantly filter the things they hear and see and feel. That's understandable. If we paid equal attention to every sight, sound, and sensation we experience, we'd quickly be overwhelmed. Filtering helps keep us sane.

When they enter the world of ideas, many people have long-standing filters, or judgments, already in place. Familiar ideas automatically become "right" or "good." And unfamiliar ideas become "wrong" or "bad."

These filters work well—so well, in fact, that they sometimes choke off *any* new ideas. People get stuck with the same old faded, wrinkled ideas for decades.

Imagine what our world would be like if people had filtered out all new ideas for the last 500 years or so: No electricity. No railroads. No skyscrapers. No notion of equal rights for women or people of color, to name just a few recent ideas. Not much fun.

Use the filter of application

There is another option: Put a new filter in place. Instead of reading this book through the filter of evaluation, read through the filter of application. Instead of asking whether an idea is right or wrong, or good or bad, ask *How can I use this idea? How could I be different? What could I do differently?*

Every concept and invention that we now take for granted was once a new idea. Remembering this, we can greet new ideas with friendly curiosity. Even the most "outlandish" or "dangerous" idea might have an element that we can use.

By the way, you don't have to postpone evaluation forever. Just save it for later—*after* you've experimented with an idea from this book and tested it in daily life.

See the Success Strategies as options

Some books offer beliefs that people cherish and defend to the death. *Falling Awake* has no such ideas. It only offers tools—ideas to try out and suggestions to apply.

I don't ask you to *believe* anything I write about the Success Strategies. I do ask that you *use* anything you find in these pages, just as you would experiment with a new tool in your workshop at home. Keep the ideas that work for you. Release those that don't work, or put them on the shelf for now and test them again later.

My intention is not to give you advice or final answers but rather to outline new possibilities that you can use to improve the quality of your life. I ask that you read these Success Strategies, test them, and question them. If need be, revise the Success Strategies so that they work for you.

The Success Strategies are not *the* way to live your life. Instead, they are just a set of options. They include ideas that have been around for years—in some cases for thousands of years—all expressed in modern language.

Think of yourself as a gardener. You're about to grow something called the life of your dreams. Your seeds, fertilizer, and groundbreaking tools are this book and your own natural experience. Happy planting.

Overview the book (EXERCISE)

Start participating actively with this book by previewing it. This could take anywhere from 15 to 30 minutes. Begin by reading the table of contents. Then turn page by page through the entire book, noticing whatever catches your eye—a picture here, a headline there. You can dip into this book at any page and receive something of value.

The benefit of this exercise is that it establishes a mental framework. With this framework in place, you are ready to absorb new ideas and information.

Think of this book as a house you're entering for the first time. Once you become familiar with the overall floor plan, you can find your way from room to room more easily. In this case, the "rooms" are the self-contained articles that make up this book.

To make this exercise more effective, be on the alert for techniques you can use right away, or for ideas that are particularly interesting. List each idea or technique in the space below, capturing it in a phrase or two and noting the page number.

Did you do the exercise?

If you did not do the previous exercise, please do it now. Exercises present you with an opportunity to actually "do" this book and actively create the life of your dreams. Your active involvement with this book is what makes it work. You're far more likely to remember and benefit from ideas if you *use* them.

I recommend that you do each of the exercises as you read them. And I realize this may not be your preference. You might want to read the entire book without doing any of the exercises, knowing that on some level your mind is absorbing and applying the ideas. You could choose to do some of the exercises but not all of them. Or you might want to read large portions of the book and then return to do many of the exercises, which have all been marked by a graphic in the style shown above on this page.

Keep a visible record of your dreams

Throughout *Falling Awake*, you'll find exercises and journal entries that ask you to write and to act on what you write.

Together, the journal entries and exercises invite you to experience three steps toward creating whatever you want in life:
- Summarizing your key discoveries (insights)
- Creating specific intentions (goals) based on those discoveries
- Acting on your intentions

Journal entries include discovery and intention statements that guide you through the first two steps. Exercises invite you to experience the third step by taking specific actions.

When writing discovery statements, you can note "where you are" in your life right now—your current strengths and areas for improvement. You can also use these statements to declare what you want for the future, to state your feelings, to transcribe your thoughts, and to chronicle your behavior. In order to get the most value from discovery statements, suspend self-judgment, tell the truth, and record specific details.

You can also do several things to increase the value of intention statements. For one, state your intentions positively—for example, say *I will stay smoke-free* instead of *I will not smoke.* Also be careful of intentions that depend on other people; if you delegate a task to someone else, then your success could hinge on that person's action. Another option is to break large intentions into smaller steps, setting deadlines for those steps when possible. And when you complete a step, reward yourself.

There are many ways to keep a written record of your discoveries, intentions, and actions.

One low-cost, flexible, and practical method is to use lots of 3x5 cards. I like to carry 3x5 cards with me and write on them (one idea per card). That way I can capture ideas quickly when I'm on the run. Later, I can easily sort, eliminate, prioritize, and store those ideas.

You can use 3x5s to remind yourself of strategies that you want to practice. Just write one strategy on a card. Then tape the card to a mirror, put it in your pocket, store it in your purse, or put it somewhere else where it's easily noticed.

You could also write on large Post-it® notes, in a bound journal, or with a computer. Many of the exercises and journal entries in this book suggest that you write on a separate sheet of paper; remember that you can use any medium that works for you. The important thing is to consistently keep a written record of what you want in life, the ways you intend to get it, and your experiences in taking action.

Create a personal time capsule (EXERCISE)

Before using this book to help you create the life of your dreams, take a few minutes to mark this moment in time. Write a letter to yourself that sums up who you are right now and who you wish to become. To get your letter started, you can complete any or all of the following sentences:

The most important thing I want to remember about this period of my life is …

_____

_____

The most significant struggles I've experienced so far in my life are …

_____

_____

The most important accomplishments I've experienced so far in my life are …

_____

_____

I'm becoming a person who …

_____

_____

The gift I most want to give myself is …

_____

_____

When you've finished this letter, date it and put it in a sealed, self-addressed, stamped envelope. Include some extra postage for good measure. Then give the letter to a trusted friend. Ask her to send it back to you in 15 months. Another option is to hide the letter and make a note in your calendar to retrieve it in 15 months.

Write your testimonial (EXERCISE)

This exercise includes an unusual request: Write a testimonial for this book. And do this now—even before you read the rest of the book.

Writing your own testimonial is based on a simple idea: You don't need to wait until you're finished reading this book to find out whether it's going to be valuable. You can choose up front—right now.

While the content of this book is important, what you choose to *do* with the content plays a far larger role in creating the quality of your life. Commitment is more important than content. Nothing that's written on these pages can equal your commitment to create value from the suggestions in this book. Writing a testimonial is one way to further your commitment.

Right now, on a separate sheet of paper write what you want to be able to say about this book once you've finished reading it.

After you have written several testimonials of your own, read the following sample testimonials to stimulate your imagination. (Note: These testimonials are pure fiction, but you, as a reader, can make them come true.)

The ideas in this book made significant life changes easy and joyful.

When reading this book, I discovered that I can be happy no matter what is going on in my life.

I saw for the first time that even when I feel sad or sick I can have a wonderful and joyous life.

Life is just wonderful! It always has been great, but I didn't realize it until I read this book.

Every hour of every day, I can make the choices to have my life continue to be outstanding.

Several years ago I read this book and made remarkable changes in my life. I haven't forgotten what I learned, and I continue to use the Success Strategies every day.

After reading this book, I transformed the quality of my life—dramatically—in just a few days.

I'm a skeptic, but the book showed me how to be happy almost every minute—and the ideas work, even though I still don't agree with all of them.

I've read dozens of self-help books, many of which were extremely helpful. This book did more than all of those books combined.

Like most people, I was doing pretty well and thought life couldn't get much better. Then I read this book and my life took an unbelievable leap forward. Now I realize that I didn't even need to read the book; I can just choose moment-to-moment happiness.

I thought I knew what transformation meant, then I read this book and realized that transformation means more than just improving. My life shifted dramatically for the better.

Unbelievable! I've never experienced anything like this book. It is possible to be happy no matter what happens in my life. And happiness is not equal to complacency.

Now that you've read the preceding examples, you might want to revise your testimonials. Taking a few minutes to do this now can make your experience of this book even more valuable.

Choose your way to use this book (EXERCISE)

Be specific about how you will use *Falling Awake* to produce the results you described in your testimonials from the previous exercise.

Read through the following list of statements and circle the one that best describes how you will participate with this book:

1. I will begin this book with an open mind. After I have some experience with it, I will choose my level of commitment to the book.

2. I will skim the book and consider using a suggestion or two.

3. I will read most of the book and apply some of its suggestions to my life.

4. I will read most of the book and apply many of its suggestions to my life.

5. I will read the entire book but I don't plan to do any of the exercises or journal entries.

6. I will read the entire book and will do some of the exercises and journal entries.

7. I will read the entire book and do a majority of the exercises and journal entries.

8. I will read the entire book and do all of the exercises and journal entries.

9. I will read the entire book, do all of the exercises and journal entries, and constantly search for ways to use its suggestions.

10. I will read the entire book and do all of the exercises and journal entries more than once, each time searching for new ways to use the ideas.

11. I will read this book and do all of the exercises and journal entries many times— as if the quality of my life depended on it.

12. I will read this book and do all of the exercises and journal entries many times— as if the quality of my life depended on it. And when I find an idea or an exercise or journal entry that I don't find valuable, I will rewrite that part of the book so that I can use it to create the life of my dreams.

An alternative is to write a statement that expresses your level of commitment in your own words. If you choose this option, please write your statement now in the space below.

_____

_____

_____

_____

_____

_____

_____

_____

_____

_____

_____

_____

_____

_____

_____

_____

_____

To get even more from this exercise, share your statement of commitment with at least one person. Making your commitment public allows others to support you and strengthens your intentions to act in ways that create the life of your dreams.

Getting the most from this book

My fundamental premise is that you are brilliant and can create dramatic new results in your life by using this book. Following are suggestions that you can use to maximize the value you create from *Falling Awake*.

Focus on purpose

The purpose of *Falling Awake* is to provide an opportunity for you to learn and adopt methods and ways of being that assist you in creating the life of your dreams.

Examining key words in the above sentence will help you make the purpose of this book come to life:

The purpose of Falling Awake is to *provide an opportunity*
(set the stage, enable, give a chance, not to force or guarantee)
for *you*
(this book is designed to be a personal experience)
to *learn*
(to acquire new skills and experiment with new ideas)
and *adopt*
(use, apply, put into practice, make part of your daily routine)
methods
(plans or actions based on plans)
and *ways of being*
(values, attitudes, basic principles of living, who you *are* beyond what you have and what you do)
that *assist* you
(this book can only offer suggestions; it's up to you to use them)
in *creating the life of your dreams*
(getting what *you* want, achieving levels of happiness, health, love, wealth, or whatever else *you* choose).

Please read the statement of purpose again while considering the definitions of the words in italics. A continuing awareness of your purpose keeps you on track and helps you achieve the results you desire.

Enjoy the benefits of a book

As a means of learning, books offer big advantages over a classroom, a workshop, or a television. You just experienced one of those advantages if you reread the purpose statement. With a book, you can review and reread that which you consider important.

If you didn't reread the purpose statement, then you experienced another advantage of a book: You have control. You get to choose what is interesting to you, what is helpful, and what is not. You can just scan the headlines—printed in bold type—to quickly get the main points of this book. Or you can slow down to study each word as you read. You can even take the time to look up key words in the dictionary. All these things are hard to do when you get information from another medium, such as a videotape or a lecture.

So take full advantage of this book. Skip around. Study what is useful. Reread what is unclear for you. Take the time to write about what you like. Ignore what you think is rubbish.

Be willing to change

It's been said that if you always do what you've always done, you'll always get what you've always gotten.

Many people expect to get different results in their lives without changing any of their thoughts or behaviors. That's not very probable.

There are periods in our lives when we grow significantly. There are times when we push to a breakthrough. There are moments of dizzying change when we make a choice that alters our lives forever. Your experience with *Falling Awake* might be such an occasion—especially if you're willing to adopt new attitudes and new actions.

Get a partner

Find an individual or small group who will do this book with you. Meet regularly to discuss and apply the ideas. Do the exercises and journal entries together.

Others can help you find new ways to create the life of your dreams, and you can do the same for them.

Remember that these techniques work—except when they don't

None of the Success Strategies are absolutes. A technique that works like magic in one area of your life might fail in another. Even the same strategy applied consistently in the same way might lose its effectiveness over time.

Consider these examples: You can be happy regardless of circumstances —except when you aren't. (Sometimes you will feel unhappy, and it pays to fully accept and experience your unhappiness.) Choose the career of your dreams and the money will follow—except when it doesn't. (Have some savings in the bank.) Learn to listen well and your relationships will improve— except when they don't. (Sometimes people need more than a sympathetic ear.)

When it comes to creating the life of your dreams, there are no sure-fire formulas that work every time. When your chosen plan or strategy doesn't work, just choose another.

Also consider how the *opposite* of a suggestion might be useful. For example, instead of simply accepting the preceding suggestion to do this book with a partner, you can explore the possible benefits of working through this book alone.

Apply the ideas to yourself

The Success Strategies are most effective when you apply them to yourself instead of wishing that other people would use them. After reading an idea, it's easy to say, "Wow, that is a great idea. I wish my spouse (or my kids, or my friends, or my boss) would do that." This type of thinking can rob you of the chance to apply the idea to yourself. And by insisting that others change their thinking and behavior, you risk alienating them and appearing judgmental.

You have far more influence on your own life than you do on the lives of others. Applying a powerful suggestion to your own behavior can be the fastest road to creating the life of your dreams.

Give it time

Be prepared to take time with this book. Some of the exercises, if you do them thoroughly, could take hours spread over several days or weeks. Remember that every minute you spend with this book is time invested in creating the life *you* want.

Do it

We have a way that we usually relate to books. We call it *reading*. That is not the only way to interact with this book. This book is meant to be *done*, not just *read*.

As you read about the Success Strategies, you might find ideas and suggestions that sound familiar. You might swear that you've already seen these ideas in fortune cookies, on bumper stickers, or in other self-help books.

If you're tempted to stop reading for this reason, then consider that people often *know* but don't *do*. They neglect to practice what they've heard, read, and already know.

One of the most important functions of any book or speaker is to present familiar ideas in a new way. Authors and speakers can create value by reminding us of what we already know— and inviting us to take action.

My goal is to present ideas in such a way that you move from "I know" to "I will" and "I do."

Don't do it

After giving thought to a particular idea or suggestion in this book, you might choose to do nothing about it right now. When this happens, you can write something in the margin like "No thanks— maybe later."

This statement can be as valuable as anything else you write. Deliberately choosing to take no action is far more effective than letting a suggestion slip by unconsciously. You can make thoughtful choices about what you will and will not do with *Falling Awake*.

This book is not for everyone

Human beings face a wide range of challenges. People deal with everything from short-term upsets and simple errors in communication to long-term problems and deep emotional wounds that cry to be healed.

Sometimes serious problems call for therapy, hospitalization, or medication. Such problems go far beyond the scope of this book.

Falling Awake is recommended for already successful people who want to be even more successful. This book is not intended to deal with mental disorders or to be a substitute for medical treatment. If you are severely depressed, overly anxious, or have suffered from poor physical or mental health for extended periods of time, please seek professional care.

People are unique, and books cannot fully take individual differences into account. Please view the content of this book solely as a starting point for creating your own options and solutions.

Success Strategy #1

DETERMINE WHAT YOU WANT

*A goal clearly defined
is a goal half attained.*

CARL JONES

Design your life—now (EXERCISE)

This chapter begins with an unusual request: Create a long-range, comprehensive vision for your life—right at the outset. Take a few minutes now to determine what you want for the rest of your life.

Write down what's really important for you to have, do, and be in this lifetime. If you're going to have a life of wonder and ecstasy—a life so wonderful that it brings tears of joy to your eyes—then one step is to figure out what *wonderful* means to you right now.

When I ask people what they want, they sometimes say "I don't know" or "I don't care." This exercise can help you move beyond both responses. Use the suggestions that follow if you're feeling "stuck." During the next few minutes, you can discover the passion and excitement involved in determining what you want.

Following are some suggested steps for designing the rest of your life.

- **Use a stack of unlined 3x5 cards.** Brainstorm as many goals for your life as you can. Write each goal on a separate 3x5 card, working quickly without stopping to rewrite. Just state something specific about what you want to have, do, or be in the future.

  Note: I recommend that you write each goal in the center of a card. Leave space in the corners so that items can be added later.

- **Think long-term.** The first goals you set might be short-term—things to accomplish within the next week, month, year, or five years. That's fine. While you're creating goals, also give some thought to the long-range future. Set goals to be accomplished within 10, 20, 50, or even 100 years from now. Be willing to create goals that extend beyond your lifetime, projects that others can take on when your life is over.

- **Don't worry about how to accomplish any of these goals.** You can create specific action plans later. Also, don't discard a goal just because it seems silly or unrealistic. The time for revising, refining, scaling back, or eliminating goals will come later.

- **Involve others.** If you want to have some extra fun, do this exercise with other people. Ask each person to generate her own goals and then share those goals with the other people present.

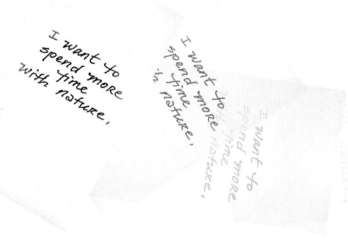

- **Just speak.** For another variation on this exercise, just speak your goals in the presence of another person. Ask that person to function as a supportive listener—one who will not interrupt, ask questions, or criticize any of your goals. Ask this person to write down your goals as you speak.

- **Safeguard your vision.** Put the goals you create in a safe, accessible place. One possibility is a file box for 3x5 cards.

Throughout this exercise, remember to write goals that will bring tears to your eyes and make your heart leap. Give up resignation—that idea that you might not be able to have what you want. For now, write down what you want even if you're *sure* you'll never get it. Write down what paradise would be for you.

Some sample goals are listed below. Remember that these are examples only—*not* necessarily goals for you to adopt.

Be a skilled listener.
Travel to India.
Start a consulting business.
Visit all the hot springs in the world.
Learn to play the piano.
Own a ranch in a beautiful valley.
Be more loving.
Be more physically fit.
Be funnier.
Help create an environment that will sustain life for the next 5,000 years.
Clean out my garage.
Clean out my neighbor's garage.

Stop at the store to pick up orange juice on my way home from work.
Eat a cheeseburger with coffee sometime before I die.
Build an athletic center on every Native American reservation.
Build a state-of-the-art recording studio and open it up to thousands of people for free.
Establish a foundation to give soccer scholarships to poor children.
Have a gourmet cook prepare my evening meals.
Pay for all my children's and grandchildren's education.
Give scholarships to women entering graduate school.
Grant money to people who start businesses that provide environmental or humanitarian benefits.
Have more toys.
Travel for a year throughout Africa.
Experience more sexual fulfillment.
Write full-time.
Paint full-time.
Work only six months each year.
Move to Bali and start a renewal center for social activists.
Sail around the world.
Start a buffalo ranch.
Breathe more deeply and slowly.
Start a revolving loan program for small business owners.
Create an institute for responsible fathering.
Create cars that produce no pollution.
Eliminate barriers to worldwide trade.

Trust your desires

You can create the life of your dreams without struggle, effort, self-discipline, or resisting your desires. You can trust your desires—in the process of determining what you want in life and ways to get it.

The common assumption in our culture is that in order to get what you want—more money, a more slender body, a better career, more education, or anything else—you have to live a life of self-discipline, effort, and struggle.

I reject that premise. I believe that we can let go of struggle and self-discipline. We can get what we want by following our passions—*not* by following other people's desires, doing what we "should" do, doing what we've always done in the past, or following any other external pressures. Instead, we can just trust our desires.

Go for pleasure

People who know me think that I'm disciplined about eating. I don't eat meat, dairy products, or hydrogenated oils. I eat only low-fat foods. And I eat only one bite of dessert per week.

But there's no discipline involved in my diet. I don't eat what I "should." I trust my desires and eat exactly what I want. For example, I don't want to eat more than one bite of dessert per week. To me, eating more than that means a sugar high followed by a "crash"—feeling tired and lethargic. That's not the way I want to feel.

I'm also smoke-free. But I don't stay smoke-free because it's hard. I do it because it's so *easy* not to smoke. I watched my mom and dad die of lung cancer—slow, long deaths. I don't want that, so there's no discipline involved in my choice to stay smoke-free.

I've even given away millions of dollars from a state of desire. I don't give away money because I should or because my grandparents or my minister told me to. I give money away because I can't think of anything that would make me feel better than giving it away.

Let your passions be your moral guide

I'm not writing to act as your moral guide. But I am suggesting an unusual possibility, which is to let your passions be your moral guide.

People will argue this idea to the death. "Life could be pandemonium if everybody did what they wanted instead of what they should be doing," a client said to me. "If I trusted my desires and acted on my passions, I'd go to bed with the next man I'm attracted to. My husband would leave me and my friends would desert me. I'd eat so much that I'd be 100 pounds overweight."

Well, you could find a new husband. You could also find

friends who want you to have what *you* want. And if you eat whatever you want and start gaining a lot of weight, you might not feel good. You might then desire to have a little less weight. You might even *want* to eat less.

If you want to have sex with that man you're not married to, you could even go for that. Of course, you might get into a lot of trouble. You might even lose your marriage. If that happens, you could get married again. Then, the next time you see a "hot" man and think about having sex outside your marriage, you'll probably realize that you really don't want that.

Your desires will mature and grow *if you let them*. But if you stuff your desires in a backpack or shove them in a closet, then your desires never get a chance to grow up. You stifle that part of your being that's filled with passion and moves you into action. Instead, you're pushed forward by your obligations.

If you let your desires be your moral guide, you might make mistakes initially—just as you would if you let your parents or your minister be your moral guide. No problem. When you follow desires that lead to something less than a wonderful life, you will naturally lose those desires or discover new ones.

When we thoughtfully choose what we enthusiastically want, perhaps there is no sin. Remember that the word *enthusiasm* is derived from a Greek word that means "God-filled." This implies that our ultimate passions are sacred, not sinful, and that we can trust that there is wisdom in our deepest wants.

In suggesting that your desires will change and evolve, I'm not saying that spirituality or philanthropy will be or should be your ultimate desire, or that you should follow a path from "selfish" desires to "unselfish" desires. Just follow your desires in any direction and trust where they lead you. When climbing the tree of desire, feel free to eat from the fruit of any branch.

Look at the big picture

Trusting your desires is not the same as being careless. When following the lead of your passions, you can make choices based on what you desire in all aspects of your life over the long run.

Recently, my oldest daughter experienced the power of considering comprehensive, long-term desires. She called me to talk about a new car she wanted. Although she wanted this vehicle, she acknowledged that it was small, perhaps a little unsafe, and probably too much for her budget. She asked for my coaching on whether to buy the car. I suggested that she keep looking at the issue, sleep on it, and trust her wants. "If you buy the car," I said, "after a few months you might like it so much that you decide it's worth cutting your other expenses or getting a second job to pay for it, and that it's worth taking some extra risk on the road."

As it turned out, she decided that she really didn't want that small, sporty, and impractical car. What she wanted more in the long run was a safe car and a budget that wasn't so tight.

Allow endless desire

When you follow your desires, you might find that your desires expand. You could satisfy one desire and find that another one comes to mind—and another one, and another one, with no end in sight. No matter how many you fulfill, there might always be more desires waiting to be satisfied.

That's fine. Living the life of your dreams is not just figuring out what you want, getting it, and then being done with desires. A wonderful life includes having desires that are not currently fulfilled. We can be totally satisfied while working to fulfill our desires. Perfection includes the possibility of change, and paradise includes the possibility of endless desires.

According to some teachings, the purpose of human life is to be free of desire. I disagree. Human beings are desire machines. We have infinite desire, and that's great. We can celebrate the desires we've already fulfilled—and create even more desires to fulfill in the future.

I've met people who worry about fulfilling too many desires too soon. They try to spread out the pleasures of life over several years for fear of burning out their happiness in a year or two. Other people argue that they don't want to get something that they've always yearned for. They fear that once they get it they will have nothing left to do and nothing left to look forward to.

I don't think either of these scenarios is likely to happen. Once people attain what they want, they'll find that they desire even more. And that just leaves the door open for even more achievement and more fulfillment.

Let your desires pull you forward

When you follow the path of creating the life of your dreams, then you can enjoy yourself even if the path is uphill. When you trust your desires, you can expend great energy and still feel like you're just playing. When you pursue a career you love and take on projects that you care passionately about, then you can work hard, even to the point of exhaustion at times, and do it happily.

That's the purpose of creating promises, plans, dreams, and goals to capture our vision of the future. A vision is not there to be followed blindly—it's there to pull us forward. If a vision is not compelling, then it's time to create a new vision. It's time to align our vision with what we truly want and return to trusting our desires.

Create boldly

Imagine paradise times four

One purpose of this chapter is to help you create your vision of paradise. Begin by creating enough goals so that you can honestly say, "If I achieved all these, I'd walk around for the rest of my life in ecstasy."

But don't stop there. Get in touch with even more desires. Create even more goals—twice as many—so that you have paradise times two. Then repeat the process again so that you end up with a vision of paradise times four.

There's a reason for creating this boldly: We won't get everything we want. When we determine in detail what we want, we often find that it doesn't show up in our lives quite like we expected. We don't get to control the universe. But we *do* get to create our vision of paradise—and then celebrate the results that actually take place.

So don't just write down what you want—write down at least four times *more* than you think you want right now. Then if you only get one-fourth of what you want, you will still end up with paradise.

Open up possibilities

Sometimes people stop in the middle of a creative spurt to ask *Can I ever achieve this goal?* That question can sink us back into the status quo and stop us from painting a bold vision of the future. Too often we end up thinking *Who am I kidding anyway? There's no way I can do this.* These are thoughts that erase dreams from the drawing board.

Many goals—from the invention of the airplane to the development of the computer chip—appeared ridiculous or unworkable when they were first proposed. These remarkable creations became realities because their creators kept lifting their eyes to the horizon and holding fast to a sense of possibility.

When determining what you want, *you* also can think big. You can write down any goal that comes to mind—even those that seem impossible to fulfill. You might discover ways to satisfy even the boldest, most "impractical" desires.

Acknowledge upset and keep determining what you want

If we don't get something that we want, we might feel upset. And this upset can stop us from determining what else we want.

This could happen when your desires include a large goal for the human race, such as ending world hunger. If you take on this goal, you'll soon discover that 35,000 people a day (18 million per year) die of hunger. Faced with that fact, you might feel miserable or deny your desire. Either choice does little to create the end of hunger.

A solution is to be in touch with your desire to end hunger, to know that it hasn't ended, and to celebrate the gains that *have* been made in solving this problem. You can even find ways to be happy while working like mad to end hunger once and for all. Those ways can include all of the Success Strategies explained in this book.

Turn jealousy into goals

For most of us, jealousy is a judgment against someone who has something we do not—anything from a new car to a new career or a fulfilling relationship. This emotion often turns into self-judgment as well: We put ourselves down for failing to acquire what other people have.

Instead of suffering when you experience jealousy, you can be creative. Write down what's missing from your life and develop action plans for getting it. Each time jealousy strikes, you can feel thankful rather than feeling a thorn in your side. Jealousy is just the universe's way of reminding you that you have a goal.

Express goals in many media

While it's common to express goals in writing, there are many other ways to keep a record of what you want. You might express your goals by drawing, painting, sculpting, writing a song, or making a video. You can also tell your plan to another person and tape-record the conversation. Any medium that gets you in touch with what you want in life will do nicely.

Imagine that time and money are no problem (EXERCISE)

One way to keep worries about money and time from cramping your creativity is to play with the following scenarios.

Scenario #1

Imagine that you've just won a lottery with a jackpot of $5 million. You now have all the money needed to sustain yourself for a lifetime. You have a steady stream of income extending decades into the future—enough to support any career or activity you want.

Once you've created this mental picture, describe what you want to have, do, and be during the rest of your life. Do this writing for five minutes, recording as many goals as you can on a separate sheet of paper or on 3x5 cards.

Scenario #2

Pretend that a philanthropist will pay you $500,000 per year plus benefits to do whatever you think will benefit your community most. What would you do? While writing, brainstorm as many answers to this question as you can.

Now imagine that a philanthropist will provide funds for you and 30 people you supervise to do something of value for the planet. You have a budget of $1 billion and 125 years to accomplish your project. What would you do? Again, write your responses.

Clarify what you want to have, do, *and* be

Most of our choices fall into three categories. We can:

- Increase our material wealth (what we *have*).

- Improve our skills and expand the range of our activities (what we *do*).

- Develop our being (who we *are*).

Most people devote an entire lifetime to the first two categories. For example, many act as if they are "human havings" instead of human beings. For them, the quality of life hinges on what they have, and they devote most of their waking hours to getting more—more clothes, more cars, more relationships, more degrees, and more trophies. Human havings define themselves by the *circumstances* of their lives.

Some people escape this materialist trap by adding another dimension to their identities. In addition to living as human havings, they also live as "human doings." Their goal is to do everything well. They define themselves by how well they do their jobs, how effectively they raise their children, and how active they are in clubs and organizations. Their thoughts and goals are constantly about *actions*—methods, techniques, and skills.

Of course, it is impossible to live our lives without having and doing things. This Success Strategy suggests that we also give lots of attention to our being—an aspect of our lives that goes beyond doing and having. We can call this aspect our soul, passion, purpose, or *values*. Our values describe how we see ourselves—our deepest commitments, the ground from which our actions spring. When we say that we want to be more loving, wise, or joyful, we are in a conversation about our values.

We can balance our wants in the domain of circumstances (what we want to *have*) with our wants in the domain of action (what we want to *do*) and the domain of values (who we want to *be*). We are more than just human havings or human doings. We are human beings.

clarify your values (JOURNAL ENTRY)

This journal entry provides you with an opportunity to clarify your commitment to various "ways of being." This is not a time to consider specific, attainable goals (things to do or have) but rather a time to reflect on more fundamental choices about who you are and who you want to be.

Please devote some thoughtful time for this activity. Complete the following sentence with several answers:

I discovered that I am committed to being …

_____

_____

_____

_____

_____

_____

_____

_____

_____

_____

Consider this journal entry to be a living document. Revisit it periodically as your life progresses and you gain more insight and experience.

One set of values

Values are our fundamental commitments, our highest principles, the things in life that we consider worthy for their own sake. Values influence and guide our choices. And our choices, even those that take place in an instant, ultimately determine the quality of our lives.

Some people have thoughtfully developed a set of well-defined values. Others are guided by values adopted uncritically from others, or by values that remain largely unconscious.

Investing time and energy to define your values and then align your actions with them is a pivotal suggestion in this book. *Falling Awake* offers many opportunities to define and refine your values, to experiment with a wide variety of strategies, and to adopt methods that bring you closer to what you want.

Following is a sample set of values. This list was intended to summarize core wisdom from the world's great traditions, both Eastern and Western.

Think of each value that appears in bold type as a way to complete the sentence *I value being....* Listed under each value is a set of words or a few sentences that further define its meaning. You can use these ideas as a starting point in developing your own list of values.

Accountable

This means being:
- Honest
- Reliable
- Trustworthy
- Dependable
- Responsible

Being accountable includes making and keeping agreements—operating with integrity.

Loving

This means being:
- Affectionate
- Dedicated
- Devoted
- Equitable
- Accepting

Being loving includes appreciating ourselves and others—being gentle, considerate, forgiving, respectful, friendly, and courteous. It also includes being nonantagonistic, nonresistant, inclusive, understanding, compassionate, fair, and ethical.

Self-generating

This means being:
- Self-responsible
- The creator of our internal experiences—regardless of our external circumstances

Being self-generating includes not being a victim and not blaming others. Instead, we choose to interpret and respond to all stimuli in ways that highlight our own role in creating our own lives.

Promotive

This means being:
- Nurturing
- Contributing—charitable; thrifty; generous with time, money, and possessions
- Frugal—achieving the best results with the fewest possible dollars
- Helpful
- Encouraging
- Reasonable
- Judicious
- Cooperative— working as a member of a team or a community
- Appreciative

Candid

This means being:
- Honest
- Authentic
- Genuine
- Self-expressed
- Frank
- Outspoken
- Spontaneous
- Sincere
- Free of deceit
- Free of both false modesty and arrogance
- Self-disclosing
- Open about strengths and weaknesses

Detached

This means being:
- Impartial
- Unbiased
- Experimental
- Satisfied
- Patient (not resigned)
- Open-minded
- Without distress
- Adaptable
- Trusting
- Tolerant
- Surrendering
- Joyful—fun-loving, humorous, lighthearted, and happy

Detachment includes being aware of and not identifying our true selves with our thoughts, emotions, body, health, accomplishments, relationships, desires, commitments, possessions, values, opinions, roles, and expectations.

The opposite of detachment is being addicted (physically or emotionally), dogmatic, bigoted, absolutely certain, prejudiced, anxious, grave, or somber.

Aware of the possible

This means being:
- Creative
- Imaginative
- Resourceful
- Inventive
- Foresighted
- Holistic
- Visionary
- Inquisitive
- Audacious
- Exploring

Being aware of the possible means expecting great things of ourselves and others.

Involved

This means being:
- Committed
- Participating
- Focused—precise and attentive to detail
- Enthusiastic—having intense or eager interest
- Enduring—persistent, persevering
- Courageous—vulnerable, willing to risk, trusting
- Energetic—displaying the capacity for action or accomplishment; being vigorous, robust, hardy, rugged, and strong
- Productive—putting yourself at risk, operating with something at stake, pursuing excellence, acting with a sense of urgency without panic, and allowing projects to matter

Live from a purpose

The American Heritage Dictionary *defines the word* purpose *as:*

> "… 1. The object toward which one strives or for which something exists; an aim or goal….
> 2. A result or an effect that is intended or desired; an intention…. 3. Determination, resolution.
> (From The American Heritage Dictionary of the English Language, *Third Edition, Houghton
> Mifflin Company, Boston, Mass.)*

Having a succinct statement of your overall purpose in life can be a huge help in determining
what you want. Your purpose is an umbrella, something that's big enough to include all that you
want in life—everything that you want to have, do, and be.

An effective purpose statement tells you when goals or behaviors are off-track. With your purpose firmly
in mind, you can make moment-to-moment choices with clarity and integrity.

Right now, writing in your journal or on a separate sheet of paper, spend five minutes drafting
a one-sentence statement of the purpose of your life. Following are some guidelines for getting started:

- Keep the above definition of the word purpose in mind. Or prompt yourself with questions based
  on that definition: What am I striving for? What is the aim or goal of my life? What is the main
  result I want in my life? What am I determined or resolved to achieve with my life?

- If you have no idea what to write, then just make up a purpose for now.
  You can change it later.

- Write several different versions of your life purpose.
  Later you can select one statement or combine several statements.

You could state your life purpose as a discovery statement or an intention statement.
Complete either of the following sentences:

I discovered that my purpose is to …

_____

_____

I intend to …

_____

_____

Once you've drafted a purpose statement, spend another 10 to 15 minutes revising it. See if your purpose can serve as an "umbrella" for everything you desire. If you find that your purpose statement excludes some of the important things you want, then you can revise it to create a bigger umbrella.

Repeat this journal entry several times. To gain more insight and creative input, do this journal entry with a group, giving people the option of reading their purpose statements out loud.

Following are some sample purpose statements:

> My purpose is to live, learn, love, and laugh.
> My purpose is to have a wonderful life and to dramatically contribute
> to the quality of life on earth.
> I intend to become financially independent and raise happy, healthy children.
> I intend to live in harmony with all creation.
> My purpose is to be a healing presence in the world.
> My purpose is to promote the well-being of my family.
> I intend to seek to release suffering and serve others.
> My purpose is to become a famous, accomplished pianist.
> My purpose is to serve.
> My purpose is to be loved and be loving.
> I intend to promote evolutionary change and be a catalyst for growth.
> My purpose is to have a great time and laugh a lot.

Besides writing a purpose for your life, you can write a purpose for each aspect of your life— your family, your career, your projects at work, your volunteer work, your vacation, or anything else. Ask What do I want from this relationship? Why is this project important to me? Experiment with living with a purpose, on purpose, moment-to-moment.

Create your life line (EXERCISE)

One powerful way to determine what you want is to consider what you'd like to see happen during your entire lifetime. You can even look beyond your lifetime, if you choose. Creating a life line offers one way to do this.

To get the most out of this exercise, be willing to let it move you. In my workshops, I've done this exercise with thousands of people. Many reported it to be an emotional and life-changing event. Some people even wept.

Following are some suggestions for making your life line:

1. Begin by taking a blank sheet of paper and orienting it horizontally. For ease in writing, you might want to use a larger-than-notebook size sheet, such as 11x17 inches. Using larger paper also adds significance to what you're about to create.

2. Draw a horizontal line across the middle of your paper. This is your life line. It represents the approximate number of years you'll be alive.

3. On the far left end of the line, draw a dot and label it with your date of birth.

4. Estimate how long you might live. Then place a dot about three-fourths of the way to the right and label it with your projected date of death. Remember that this step simply serves a useful function for this exercise and has no connection to reality. You're under no obligation to die on the date you write! The purpose of projecting a death date is just to remind you that you're mortal.

   Note: Do not place your date of death at the extreme right-hand edge of the line. Leave some space on the line for goals that exceed your life span.

5. Next, place a dot on your life line that represents the present. Label it with today's date.

6. At appropriate points to the left of today's date, plot some significant events in your life. Examples are graduations, marriages, career changes, children's birth dates, deaths of relatives, and the dates when you landed a new job or started a business. Take at least 10 minutes for this part of the exercise.

7. Now set goals for the time between today and when you might die. Do this by adding dots to the right of today's date. Label these dots with goals that represent what you'd like to have, do, or be in the future. Add a target date to meet each goal.

8. Finish your session by considering what could happen after you die. Here you can include predictable events, such as the retirement of your children or the death of a younger relative. Also think about what you want to occur after your life is done. Include goals for your family, friends, workplace, city, community, state, country, and world. Be willing to set goals that extend far into the future.

9. Write any insights, discoveries, or lessons that emerged as you did this exercise. Then generate new goals based on what you've learned.

You can repeat this exercise many times, ranging from once a month to once a decade. Each time you create a life line, you can gain new insights into the past and create a new vision for your future. Look at your life line as a living document—one that changes as you learn and grow.

At any time, you can get other people into the act. For example, create your life line and reveal it to your partner, family, and friends. Ask them to create a life line for themselves. Look for points of intersection, shared events, common goals, and similar values. It might also be useful to look for differences in what you consider significant about the past and in your visions for the future.

Each time you do this exercise, you can allow the artist within you to emerge. Use separate colors for different categories of goals. Put your life line on a long piece of paper or connect several pages together. Draw pictures that depict significant events—a diploma next to the day you graduated from high school, a heart next to the time of your first date.

Your life line does not have to be a straight line. Experiment with circles, arcs, slopes, rainbows, or waves. If you want to invest some extra time, make it three-dimensional. Express your life line in sculptures, collages, paintings, or mobiles. Make that life line come to life.

Start with what, where, when, *and* who

To unleash your desires and determine what you want, hold off asking *"How* will I achieve this goal?"* In the beginning, stick with *what, where, when,* and *who:*

- What do I want?
- Where do I want to be in the future?
- When will I make my desired future occur?
- Whom do I want to be with in the future?

There's nothing wrong with asking the *how* question. There's a time and place for choosing strategies to fulfill your goals. But that step comes later.

Avoid resignation

When we begin determining what we want, questions of strategy can easily be overdone, leaving us focused on how to *control* the future instead of how to *create* it. Focusing on *how* can even drive us into resignation and keep us from taking action: "I don't know how to meet that goal, so why even try?"

In 1960, President John F. Kennedy articulated a huge desire for his nation. He set a goal for Americans to land a person on the moon by 1970. Kennedy had a clear vision of *what* (a space landing), *where* (on the moon), *when* (by 1970), and *who* (the National Aeronautics and Space Administration) would work to meet the goal. However, in 1960 he did not know exactly *how* to achieve this long-term goal. And had he waited until NASA figured out how, he might never have spoken his vision.

When you're clear about *what* you want, you're more likely to discover an effective *how.* With a clear vision of the future, you can make spontaneous, moment-to-moment choices that bring you closer to your goals.

Add details

Another benefit of focusing on *what, where, when,* and *who* is that they add detail to your vision.

There's power in detail. Every time you eat in a restaurant, you draw on this power. When the server asks for your order, you don't just say, "I want dinner" or "Steak, please." You get more specific. When ordering a steak, you might say, "Rib-eye, 12-ounce, medium rare, please." And a good server won't let you stop there. He also asks, "Would you like salad or soup? And what would you like on your salad?" The more details you give when answering these questions, the more likely you'll get the dinner you want. This is what I'm suggesting you do when determining what you want: Put in your order for paradise with all the trimmings added. Serve yourself the life of your dreams by adding details to your vision for the future.

Ask two people what they want in life. One says, "I just hope to be happy, somehow." Not many details. Another says, "I want to become financially independent in 10 years so that I can devote my time to writing a novel and working with homeless people." It's not hard to guess who is more likely to realize her goals.

Right now, you can begin to bring your dreams into sharp focus.

Start by asking *what, where, when,* and *who.*

Expand your creations with how and why

Once you've gained some clarity about what you want, you can create even more details by asking two more questions:

- How will I achieve this goal?
- Why do I want to achieve this goal?

Caution: We can ask such questions in ways that erect obstacles to our goals and actually prevent us from getting what we want in life. I love to see people liberate themselves from these limiting options and discover more creative ways to ask *how* and *why*.

Ask "how" to create multiple pathways

Asking *how* assists you in developing action plans to meet your goals.

When asking *how*, we can avoid answers that lead us to a prescription—the idea that there is only *one* way to accomplish any goal. Most goals can be reached through multiple pathways. While generating more details about what we want, we can create more precise action plans—several of them—for satisfying any desire.

For example, you might determine that you want to earn $100,000 per year while working from your home as a freelance consultant. To meet that income goal, you could choose from several strategies. One is to charge $50 per hour and work 40 hours per week for 50 weeks per year. Another is to charge $100 per hour and work only 20 hours per week for the same number of weeks per year. You could also consider working more hours during the winter months so that you could take summers off and still earn $100,000 yearly. These are just a few examples.

Remember that strategies and techniques are not guarantees. They're just means to an end —moving you into action. Your clarity about what you want and your commitment to get it can be far more powerful than any action plan or technique.

Ask "why" to fulfill your "impossible" desires

Asking another question—*why*—can help you expand your list of desires and even fulfill those that seem impossible.

Suppose that I discover two contradictory desires: I love eating chocolate sweets, *and* I want to lose weight. Faced with these conflicting desires, I have at least two options.

One option is to look at *why* I desire chocolate sweets. If I'm not careful, this line of questioning can drive me into analyzing the past and making excuses: *I want to eat chocolate sweets because my mom baked a chocolate cake for me every week when I was a kid and sweets have become a source of comfort; I'd feel abandoned if I gave them up. Or I've become physiologically addicted to sugar and I just can't break the habit.*

Another option is to ask *why* in a way that creates more possibilities for the future and helps me discover the desires *behind* the current desire.

For example, I could say that I desire chocolate sweets because:

- I enjoy eating food that tastes exceptionally good.
- Eating dessert after meals is an effective way to spend more quality time with my family.
- I need the energy boosts from sugar to handle all the tasks I have to complete.

Once I discover these desires behind my desire for chocolate cake, I can then ask *how* to achieve them. I may even find a way to get all those desires fulfilled *without* eating chocolate sweets. For example, I could:

- Experiment with enjoying other kinds of foods that taste exceptionally good.
- Plan evening activities for my family that promote intimate time together.
- Talk to a professional health practitioner about how to maintain high energy without eating sweets.

Asking *why* in this manner grounds me in the realm of values—the things in life that I want most, including enjoyment, intimacy, and energy. This line of questioning greatly multiplies the options for fulfilling my purpose—creating a wonderful life.

Free the future from the past

For most people, the word *planning* means prediction. There's another option called *planning by creation*, and using it can change your whole experience of determining what you want.

Much of the goal setting that's done in business, government, and education is planning by prediction. In this type of planning, people carefully study what's happened in the past and use that data to predict what will happen in the future.

Planning by prediction is based on a few assumptions. One is that past events are the best predictors of what's yet to come. Another is that the forces now shaping our lives will continue to be at work in the future. In a sense, prediction is the past masquerading as the future.

Planning by creation means freeing the future from the past, and it involves a different set of working assumptions. For this second type of planning, you start from a blank slate—from nothing. Without considering the past, you state what you want to happen in the future. Then you ask how to achieve those goals. The underlying idea is that the past does not have to determine or limit what you can experience in the future.

I'm not saying that planning by creation is "better" than planning by prediction. Both types of planning have their uses. My suggestion is to know at any given moment what kind of planning you're doing—and to choose the type that suits your purpose.

To understand the differences between planning by prediction and planning by creation, look at two ways to create a budget.

For many companies, budgeting is an exercise in planning by prediction. The corporate planners predict next year's income and expenses based on this year's income and expenses. This amounts to taking the previous year's budget and "fixing" it.

An alternative is creating a budget from scratch. This means taking last year's budget, crumpling it up, and throwing it away. Instead of fixing last year's figures, the planners ask a lot of questions: What do we value? What do we want to be doing one year from now? How much money do we want to be making? How much do we want to be spending? What steps can we take to meet these goals?

Sometimes this approach is called *zero-based budgeting*. The same strategy could be applied to many areas of life and be called *zero-based planning*—or planning by creation. You can experiment with this strategy by doing the next exercise.

Create the future
from nothing (EXERCISE)

This exercise is an open inquiry into what's possible for the rest of your life—and beyond. During the exercise, you will experiment with totally erasing your personal history and current identity. You will start your life over again and then set goals.

Please be willing to stick with this process even if it sounds crazy. There is a logic hidden in this request to begin your life from nothing.

The point is that most of us live full lives, filled with a lot of "something." We carry around a detailed personal history: successes, failures, attachments, obligations, requirements, relationships, careers, thoughts, feelings, habits, and much more.

We can become so committed to preserving our personal history that we squash any possibility of change. Often history has such unrelenting momentum that we forget about alternatives. Our lives can get so "full" that we leave no room for something fresh—like a room that is so full that it has no place for a beautiful new painting.

So consider what it would be like to re-create your life from a clean slate. Imagine that you could wipe out the past and start over, fresh. What would you have? What would you do? Who would you choose to be?

To create a blank slate, start by relaxing. Take three deep slow breaths, release tension, and feel all parts of your body relax. Then continue reading and imagine doing the following:

- **Erase your current job.** Imagine that you have no job. Whether you love it, hate it, or feel neutral about it, the job's gone. Vanished. (Relax. You can have your job back at the end of this exercise.)

- **Erase your financial concerns.** Money problems are permanently behind you. Imagine that money is no longer used as a medium of exchange. Banks and credit cards no longer exist. There's no point in having money, and no one has any. You can get whatever you want without needing to have any money.

- **Erase your health problems.** Disease, chronic illness, and disability—whether real or imagined—are no longer issues for you.

- **Erase your friends.** Peers, colleagues, neighbors, acquaintances—all of them are gone. (Don't worry about being lonely. Your friends will still be there after this exercise.)

- **Erase your enemies.** Imagine that any people you resented or fought with are no longer part of your life.

- **Erase your family.** (Again, don't worry. These people are safe, and you can bring them back later.) For now, pretend that they are no longer around.

- **Erase your spouse or romantic partner.** Do this now, even if you have a wonderful relationship. Let this person go to the same place that your friends and family have gone.

- **Erase your house or apartment.** As of now, imagine that you have no place to live. No longer do you define yourself by the size, price, or location of your living space.

- **Erase your other possessions**, especially the big-ticket items such as cars or boats. And erase your precious possessions as well—the pictures, jewelry, old letters, and keepsakes.

- **Erase your community.** The town, city, or rural area where you grew up is gone. So is the town where you currently live.

- **Erase your memories.** All those accomplishments, those hurts, those mistakes, those successes—release them all.

- **Release your expectations.** Erase any thoughts about how future events should unfold.

- **Erase time.** Mentally toss your watch and clocks out the window. Then erase the window.

- **Erase your values.** Release any goal to be wise, healthy, creative, wealthy, passionate, punctual, or polite. Also let go of any goals about what you'd like to do or have in your lifetime.

- **Erase your religion.** For the moment, pretend there's no need for any special set of beliefs or practices.

- **Now notice anything about yourself that remains.** Is your body still there? Erase it. Are your clothes or glasses still there? Erase them, too. (Notice that you erased your body before you erased your clothes, so there's no need to feel embarrassed.) Also erase your emotions, opinions,and thoughts. If you have any worry about all that you've erased so far, just notice that worry and erase it also. Then erase anything else that's left.

- **Finally, notice any remaining thoughts about this exercise**—that it's silly, profound, boring, frightening, or anything else. Let those thoughts billow up and vanish like a bubble.

If these suggestions worked for you, you're at a blank slate.

Congratulations. You've arrived at a peak state of creativity. In fact, now that you're nobody, you may even be better company than when you were merely somebody. At this moment, you're free to make any choice whatsoever about what to have, do, and be. From the state of nothingness, you can call forth all possibilities.

Dwell in this state for at least five minutes. You could even extend this time to several hours. While in this state, ask yourself *What do I want? What's next for me?* Write your answers as goals on 3x5 cards or a separate sheet of paper.

After you've recorded these goals, slowly let yourself start to fill up again. Allow all your old roles, relationships, and possessions to *gradually* rejoin you. Return yourself to the present.

When you've fully come back to the present, review the goals you wrote back when you were nothing. Save those goals to review and refine as you read the rest of this book.

Create the distant future (EXERCISE)

Extending your goals outward in time—as far as you can possibly imagine—is one way to create a comprehensive global vision. There's no need to stop at setting goals for 10, 20, 50, or 100 years. Your goals can extend 500, 1,000, or even 10,000 years into the future.

If thinking so far ahead seems like an impossible or useless mental stretch, then keep a few things in mind:

• In the entire span of human history, a century is a very short period of time. Recall the history courses you took in school. There you probably reviewed entire decades in a matter of minutes. You can now preview the distant future in the same way that you reviewed the distant past.

• Many leaders have adopted the habit of looking decades or even centuries into the future. The people of ancient Egypt who designed the pyramids envisioned building projects that took several generations to complete. The people who drafted the Constitution of the United States created a document to guide the government for hundreds of years. When President Dwight D. Eisenhower announced his vision of an interstate highway system to blanket the country, he knew that this goal would take decades to complete. The fruit of this vision was perhaps the most successful public works project in human history.

• Goals for the distant future can represent highlights, not detailed agendas. When you set goals for the next decade or next century, you will mostly create the major events—the turning points in human affairs. These transformational events might take place over a period of many years.

• When you think 500 years or more into the future, it's easier to go beyond your short-term self-interests. In 500 years you will be gone from the earth. So will your children, your grandchildren, and their grandchildren. With a long-range perspective, you can be more objective and consider the fate of humanity as a whole.

• After thinking about long stretches of time, you might find it easier to think about shorter stretches. Once you've practiced thinking 100, 500, and even 10,000 years into the future, the notion of planning five years, 10 years, and even 20 years into the future can seem like child's play.

With the above points in mind, do the following:

1. Writing on a separate sheet of paper, describe the world you want to see in the year 2500. Remember that this is not an exercise in predicting the world of 2500. Rather, it's a statement about what you want humanity to have achieved by that time.

2. After you've played with creating the world of 2500, go even farther out in the future. Conceive the world you'd like to see in the year 3000 or 5000.

3. Now stretch your planning muscles even more and write goals for the year 10,000. Remember that 10,000 years ago, people were not yet farming, let alone writing. And in 8,000 years from now, people will likely be doing things that we can hardly imagine.

This concept of long-range goal setting might seem strange to you right now. If so, that's fine. Just experiment with the idea and see if it has any potential usefulness for you.

To spur your creativity, consider the following list of goals from one group of people who mentally stood in the year 10,000 and described what they saw.

We can decode natural communication systems. Now humans can communicate with rocks, plants, and all species of animals.

Eating is optional; we eat only for pleasure. It's a world of virtual cuisine.

Physical pain is erased with thought.

Bodies are optional, and we can live in the spiritual dimension at any time. There are "bodies-optional" beaches.

War has been absent from Earth for centuries. Now conflict is resolved by teams of skilled negotiators who can be dispatched to any place on the planet in a matter of seconds—before any dispute can involve weapons.

Cities are limited in size to 100,000 people at most. This, combined with nonpolluting, clean, and safe mass transit, makes traffic congestion and vehicle accidents a thing of the distant past.

Natural disasters are predicted with absolute accuracy, far enough in advance to make mass evacuations possible. No longer is anyone killed because of tornadoes, floods, or earthquakes.

Prioritize and categorize (EXERCISE)

Doing the exercises so far in this book probably left you with a large collection of goals, perhaps hundreds of them. Now you have an opportunity to gather all those ideas, organize them, and refine them.

Consider adding the following four items to each goal when appropriate:
• Priority
• Partners
• Timeline
• Categories

If you're writing goals in the center of 3x5 cards, as I suggested earlier, then you can note these items in a corner of each card. If you're writing goals on regular-sized paper or a computer, then find an appropriate place to add these items.

Add priorities

Rate each goal according to how important it is to you. I suggest writing a letter in the upper right-hand corner of your cards—A, B, C, D, or O. Each letter symbolizes a different level of priority.

I'll explain these by starting at the bottom of the scale with O. O's are obligations—things that you think you ought to do. It's okay to have some of those. And if you truly want to maximize your enjoyment and freedom, I recommend that you minimize the O's. See if you can eliminate these or raise them to one of the following priority levels.

D represents a below-average goal or a low-priority desire. You might not be sure you truly want it. Yet the goal aligns with your purpose, and you still want to keep it on file as a possibility.

If the goal is something you know you want, it's a C priority. This is an average desire—one that you plan to satisfy. It's important to you but not critical to achieve.

B-priority goals are things that tap into your passion. You're willing to create a written, detailed action plan to meet these goals. You're going to put time and money into satisfying these desires.

A-priority goals represent things that you absolutely intend to achieve. You're willing to promise that you'll get these things done, and you're willing to do whatever it takes. One caution: Don't make too many of your cards A's. If you have an abundance of A priorities, your vision could get top-heavy, fall over, and collapse. Your promises might feel like obligations since you have too many goals to achieve.

Add partners

In the lower right-hand corner of your cards, write the names of your partners—the people who can assist you in meeting each goal. There are plenty of people who will help you get what you want. In many cases, they'll be glad to lend a hand if you simply ask them.

Add timelines

In the upper left-hand corner of each card, give yourself a timeline for achieving each goal. You can note timelines in several different forms. For example, note a specific date, month, or year that you'd like to get what you want ("finish my novel by June 2003"). Or write a span of time that represents how long you'd like to do something ("spend two months in the Caribbean during the year 2005").

Perhaps you have no idea what the timeline is for a goal. That's fine. Just make something up for now and write it down. Remember that determining what you want is not about *knowing* your future—it's about *inventing* your future.

Also remember that some goals are probably better off without time limits. You probably wouldn't write "I want to be compassionate from 2001 to 2007." Some goals represent things you'd like to have, do, or be for your entire life.

Add categories

Your goals will naturally fall into certain categories such as *health, wealth, education, relationships, fun,* or *spirituality.* In the lower left-hand corner of your cards, note this category.

For even more precision, you can add subcategories. For example, the large category relationships can include the subcategories *family, friends,* and *colleagues.* If a goal pertains to your family, you could write *RELATIONSHIPS: Family* in the lower left corner.

Sort cards and add details

An advantage of adding these four items to your goals is that you can sort and re-sort your goals according to each item. If you first sort goals by timelines, for instance, you can later experiment with organizing them by priorities, partners, or categories. This can reveal gaps in your vision, such as an abundance of goals in the category of *work* and a lack of goals under *recreation.* Also, re-sorting your goals from time to time can give you fresh perspective on your vision and prompt you to discover or invent even more goals.

The process of adding priorities, partners, timelines, and categories will help you add specifics to your vision of paradise. Now that you've determined what you want at this level of detail, you can begin taking focused and powerful action to get it.

Success Strategy #2

TELL THE TRUTH

Candor is a compliment;
it implies equality.
It's how true friends talk.

PEGGY NOONAN

Perform an honest self-evaluation

If you want to change, then tell the truth.

When we're honest about which aspects of our lives are working well—and which are not—we're poised for growth. On the other hand, if we're out of touch with the truth, we can easily ignore pressing problems or come up with bogus solutions.

Alcoholics Anonymous offers one of the most popular and successful self-help programs around, and it begins with telling the truth. The first thing AA members do to change their behavior and transform their lives is to tell it like it really is. That's the idea behind Step One of the AA program: "We admitted that we were powerless over alcohol, that our lives had become unmanageable."

AA is just one example. People who join Weight Watchers begin by telling the truth about how much they weigh, and they repeat that ritual at the beginning of every meeting. Likewise, one of the first things that counselors do is to assess their clients—to learn the truth about what their clients are thinking, feeling, and doing. Physicians start their treatments only after a careful diagnosis. Coaches design a training program only after gaining a clear idea of their team's present capabilities. Supervisors, managers, and teachers do the same.

This strategy can be applied to tackling any problem. Talking straight about ourselves complements and enhances all other strategies in this book. When we tell the truth, we unleash the forces of positive change.

There is an added benefit to having the courage to tell the truth: We provide a model for others. After observing us, others might glimpse the power in this practice. People might see their potentials and take the first step toward solving a long-standing problem.

When we tell the truth, we contribute to ourselves and to others. Everybody wins. Our honesty may provide just the opening someone else needs to move forward.

Break through denial

Many people find it tough to admit to weaknesses. Often they're willing to go miles out of their way to avoid telling the truth.

To verify this, just ask any recovering addict. When the only way a person can get through the night is with a six-pack of beer, he'd probably rather keep the fact a secret—even to himself. When an executive fudges expense reports so that she can get cash for a gambling habit, she'll probably want to keep the fact hidden.

In the short run, denial might even work. It helps us avoid the pain that comes with telling the truth. It smoothes over the rough spots and makes things look all right for a while.

That benefit usually comes with a cost. Over the long run, denial limits the possibility of change. Denial stops us in our tracks and keeps us stuck waist deep in our problems. Denial cheats us out of happiness.

Denial also saps energy. Struggling to deny the truth can leave us exhausted. Struggle implies resistance. And the more we resist the truth, the more it fights back.

There is another option: We can break through deceptive layers of falsehood and open up to the truth. While telling the truth might hurt, it also takes us one step past the hurt. Telling the truth opens the door to strategies that we can use to make effective, enduring changes in our lives.

Approach evaluations without shame or blame

Many of us approach a frank evaluation of ourselves with the same amount of enthusiasm as we'd welcome an audit by the IRS.

The very word *evaluation* is often associated with negative experiences, such as incomprehensible essay tests, tense performance evaluations, and blood tests and rectal exams. Few people would list these as their favorite ways to spend an afternoon.

We can think about evaluations in another way. We could see evaluations as opportunities to solve problems and take charge of our lives. We could view evaluations as ways to get feedback, change behavior, and expand our happiness. We could greet evaluations with hopeful excitement and welcome them as gifts.

One step toward this goal is avoiding shame and blame. Some people believe that it's natural to judge their shortcomings and feel bad about them. Some people believe that blame is necessary to correct their errors. Others think that a healthy dose of shame is the only thing that can prevent the moral decay of our society.

As an alternative, we can discover ways to gain skill without feeling rotten. We can change the way things *are* without having to feel upset about the way things have been. We can learn to see shame or blame as excess baggage and just set them aside. Believe it or not, we can begin working with our list of weaknesses by celebrating them.

Consider the most loving, successful, enlightened, "together" people you know. If they were totally candid with us, we'd soon hear about their mistakes and regrets. The more successful people are, the more likely that they look openly at their flaws.

The point is simple: We can love ourselves and still work like mad to change ourselves. You can experiment with this idea by doing the exercises that follow.

Talk to a chair (EXERCISE)

One powerful way to practice telling the truth is to speak even when no one is listening.

The basic technique in this exercise is to place an empty chair across from you. In your imagination, see someone sitting in that chair. Then say out loud what you've been withholding from this person. Include both positive and negative feedback. Reveal all the things you've stopped yourself from saying to this person.

You have many options when choosing whom to "place" in that chair. If you're in conflict with someone, then imagine that person sitting across from you. You could also place someone you greatly admire in the chair, or a key person from your past. Or, imagine *yourself* in the chair and then coach yourself about ways to solve a sticky problem or meet a tricky goal.

You might feel strange when you first do this exercise. That's understandable. Simply notice that feeling without judgment. Then continue speaking.

Practice telling the truth when you're across from that chair. Give voice to your fears, your sadness, your anger, your celebrations, your conflicting desires, your darkest secrets, or whatever else comes to mind.

There's power in full self-expression even when the person you're addressing is not physically present. You might even choose to contact the person you "placed" in the chair and say some or all of the things you said during this exercise.

choose what not to examine (JOURNAL ENTRY)

While doing the exercises in this chapter, you may discover aspects of your life that you are not willing to examine. Perhaps you've raised issues that are too difficult or troublesome to face directly. That's fine for right now. You can simply tell the truth about what you choose not to examine. Consider scheduling a later time to examine these areas of your life.

Complete the following sentences:

I discovered that I am not willing to examine …

_____

_____

_____

_____

I intend to examine these areas of my life by the following dates …

_____

_____

_____

_____

_____

Take a First Step (EXERCISE)

This exercise gives you an opportunity to survey the entire expanse of your life and set in motion forces that can alter you forever. Prepare to admit your strengths and to write frankly about all the aspects of your thinking and behavior that you want to change.

This may be the most difficult exercise in *Falling Awake*. It can also be the most powerful. Doing this exercise thoroughly may be enough to fulfill your purpose in buying this book.

The idea is simple: Tell the truth about who you are and what you want.

End of exercise. Proceed to the next Success Strategy.

Just kidding. Actually, there is more to the self-survey, and the instructions below will guide you through the strategy step by step.

If you want to experience the full benefit of this exercise, do three things.

First, be concrete. Get down to specifics. Instead of writing "I'm unhappy," you could write "I feel isolated and have few people I can call on during times of crisis."

Second, be courageous. You may be looking at parts of yourself that you'd rather not face. If you start to feel uncomfortable, that's probably a clue that the exercise is working.

If this happens to you, acknowledge the discomfort fully. Then return to telling the truth. Remember that it's difficult—if not impossible—to change those aspects of our lives that hide in the shadows. When we shine a light on our shortcomings, we begin to rob them of their power.

Third, be complete. Many people think that telling the truth is a strategy that applies only to our weaknesses. In reality, this strategy is even more powerful when we admit our strengths and skills as well.

As you complete this exercise, you might reveal things that you don't want others to know—perhaps things that could get you into trouble.

For that reason, write your responses on a separate sheet of paper and consider destroying it when you're finished.

Allow about 30 minutes to complete the whole exercise.

Part 1

Set aside 10 minutes to complete the following sentence. Aim for at least 10 responses. And don't worry about whether your writing is wrong or silly. If an idea pops into your head, put it down. You can review and reflect on your responses later.

One of my strengths is that ...

Following are sample ways to finish this sentence. These are not prescriptions for what you should write—just examples:

I have a clear sense of the factors in life that I can control and also of the factors that I cannot control.

I periodically examine the quality of my thinking and choose beliefs that promote my happiness.

I take risks, even if it means making mistakes.

I use an effective set of strategies for responding to stress.

I listen attentively and with skill.

I communicate my thoughts and feelings without blaming others.

Part 2

Take another 10 minutes to complete the following sentence. List as many responses as you can—at least 10. This will be a rough draft, so don't worry about the quality of what you write. Just get as many ideas down on paper as you can.

Things don't work well when ...

Again, some examples follow:

I discover that my relationships are not working, and I avoid conflict with the people involved.

I spend more than I earn and accumulate large balances on my credit cards.

I break agreements with the people closest to me.

I think I'm unlovable.

I stop listening to people I dislike.

Part 3

Once you've finished the first two parts of this exercise, take a short breather. Also celebrate the difficult and potentially rewarding work you've done so far.

Now take another step to solidify your insights. Review the two lists you've created. Cross off any ideas that don't make sense. Add any new ideas that come to mind. Put an asterisk next to statements that really ring true. Look for ways to reword any of these statements to make them clearer or more accurate.

Part 4

Here's your chance follow up on what you've learned about yourself.

First, review your list of strengths regularly, especially when you feel discouraged or just plain stuck. You might want to post this list in a prominent place where you alone will see it often.

Next, look again at your list of problems from Part 2. Take your most limiting problems and rewrite them as goals. Move them from problems to possible solutions.

For example, *I run low on cash at the end of each month* can be transformed into *I intend to decrease my spending so that I have cash left over at the end of the month.*

If any of your intentions bring up outrageous possibilities or hold the promise of far-reaching change, that's great. Consider breaking these long-range goals down into simple, specific actions that you can start taking immediately.

There's only one step left, and it goes beyond writing: *Do what you intend.* Take action. Savor any positive new results in your life. Also, come back to this exercise periodically. Use it any time to spot-check for problems and take charge of your life again. You can make truth telling a habit.

Speak candidly

There are times in life when most of us think *I should have said something.*

Maybe we were angry when someone insulted us, and we were too frightened to stand up for ourselves.

Maybe we came up with an idea that would have been a great solution to a problem, but we were too embarrassed to share it.

Or maybe the timing was perfect for the hilarious comment we had in mind, but we were too self-conscious to say anything.

Being frightened, embarrassed, or self-conscious is just one of the ways we stop ourselves from speaking candidly. And in stopping ourselves, we might cheat ourselves and the people we love.

We always have another option—full self-expression. Instead of withholding our thoughts and feelings, we can share them. We can tell the truth—not *The Truth* (as in assuming that our ideas are always right) but *our* truth, the way we honestly think and feel.

Our ideas can be a source of nurturing feedback for others. Instead of using them to cut people down or diminish others, we could speak our thoughts in ways that help people experience success. Feedback is just a tool. And like any other tool, it can be used for harm or for good. Feedback can be given with the intent to hurt, or it can be given with love.

Ways we stop ourselves from speaking

There are many strategies we use to block our full self-expression. At times, these strategies are appropriate. Too often we use them as excuses to stop ourselves from speaking.

- Instead of simply starting to speak, we begin an internal dialogue:

  What if this idea sounds stupid?
  I'll probably just make a fool of myself.
  They know more about it than I do, anyway.
  What if I'm wrong?
  Nobody else really cares.
  Do I have any right to meddle?
  If I say this, I might create an ugly scene.

When this happens, we can easily get lost in a tangled web of doubt and confusion. We start to consider a lengthy list of issues unrelated to our original message. If we ever get around to speaking, our words are so measured and so cautious that the message is often lost.

- We keep silent with the intention to avoid forcing our values on others. We write off our opinions as value judgments that blame, demean, or find fault with others.

- We consider ourselves to be outstanding listeners. In fact, we listen so much that we hardly ever speak.

- We say to ourselves *I'm too busy right now to take the time to say what I really think.* Sometimes this is the truth. At other times, it's an excuse. People who are almost always too busy to talk may be choosing a full schedule to avoid communication.

- We avoid speaking in order to avoid our feelings: *If I don't talk about it, I won't have to feel it.* This approach is based on a faulty assumption—that hiding our emotions is the same as dealing with them.

- We remain silent because we don't want to get hurt. The less others know about us, the less ammunition they have to harm us. This line of reasoning assumes that other people are out to get us. Sometimes this is literally true, and then it's wise to avoid speaking. Most of the time, though, this is an unfounded assumption.

Withholding robs us of the chance to contribute

Refusing to speak our minds often cheats others of an opportunity to look at a problem with a fresh pair of eyes. Remember that other people always have the freedom to accept, modify, or even ignore our feedback. If they choose to ignore our ideas, we've still communicated the fact that we care. And if others use what we say to make a positive change in their lives, everyone wins.

Consider a woman who feels threatened and hurt every time her partner talks about his past romantic relationships. Her partner genuinely loves her and would feel terrible if he knew that she felt hurt. By keeping her feelings to herself, she denies her partner the opportunity to change his behavior. She also condemns herself to repeated pain. Instead, she can choose to reveal what she's really thinking and feeling, and break this self-defeating cycle.

More often than not, truthful speaking is useful speaking.

Ways to just speak

Build a bridge before walking the canyon

The emotional bond between two people is like a bridge between two sides of a deep canyon. A strong bond or emotional connection is like a sturdy bridge made of steel that can support heavy weights. If the emotional connection between two people is weak, then the bridge is more like a shaky footbridge made of wood and vines.

The messages people send to each other can be compared to materials we send across the bridge. A strong bridge can support tanks, large trucks, and other heavy equipment. Likewise, a strong bond between people can support the full weight of straightforward honesty. This assumes, of course, that the people speak with the intention to support each other and not with the intention to blame or hurt.

Before speaking candidly to another person, we can strengthen the emotional bridge first. We can do this in many ways. For example, we can be willing to listen as well as to speak. We can also make amends for our mistakes and release past resentments. These choices can transform a creaky emotional bridge into a superstructure that supports candid speaking.

Risk sounding foolish

When we speak candidly, we might say something that others find stupid or offensive. That risk is real. And a sure-fire way to avoid this risk is to avoid speaking. When we do, we rob ourselves of the opportunity to gain more skill at communication. We also rule out the possibility of truly getting to know others and letting them get to know us.

Speaking candidly calls for a willingness to risk sounding foolish. We can remain silent, avoid the risk, and cheat ourselves and others of feedback.

Or we can say what we think, risk sounding foolish, and be willing to make amends when needed. The reward is a life filled with more friendship and love.

Speak to the way people listen

When you talk to a bowler or make a speech to a group of bowlers, you might get nowhere if you talk about "shooting straight" or "hitting a bull's-eye." Instead, switch to "making a strike," "hitting the pocket" or "avoiding gutter balls." You'll probably connect with more people.

The suggestion here is to meet your audience where they are. Every group of people with a common interest has a particular set of preferred words, phrases, and images. Listen for their special language and tap into it. Then you can start broadcasting through channels that are already open. When in Rome, speak as the Romans do.

Think twice about advice

Other people might request your advice. Much of the time, an effective response is to turn down the request.

Giving advice can do more harm than good. Advice can imply that others lack the ability to see their own problems or discover their own solutions. Some people interpret advice as a recipe to follow blindly, and others might spend more time criticizing your ideas than generating their own solutions. At other times, people already know what they really want to do and feel offended if your advice contradicts what they think.

Often it is wise to withhold advice and let others work out their own problems. We can insult them by rushing in with an answer and doing what they can do for themselves.

Suggestions, on the other hand, can be empowering. A suggestion is an option, a possibility. Offering suggestions is like taking a friend to the deli. Though you point out your favorite dishes, your friend ultimately chooses what *she* will eat. In the same way, you can avoid giving advice, offer possibilities, and assist others to brainstorm their own options.

This advice about advice is not absolute. Sometimes advice works, especially when people take your ideas as possibilities and not prescriptions. When giving advice, share ideas only in your area of expertise, and be specific.

Preview, fill in the details, review

If your message is long or complex, remember an old adage that professional speakers use when they step in front of an audience: "First, tell 'em what you want to tell 'em. Second, tell 'em. Third, tell 'em what you told 'em."

Those three elements can be useful in telling your truth even when your audience is one person. When you speak, consider leading with your main points. Then add the details about each point. End by restating your main points.

This practice can be especially useful if you're in conflict with another person and your communication is emotionally charged. When you preview, add details, and review, you speak thoughtfully and slow down the pace of the conversation.

Say what you are <u>not</u> saying

Consider starting a conversation with what you are *not* saying. This strategy often works well in times of high emotion, when the conversation is generating lots of heat and little light: "I am not saying that I want you to move out. I am saying that I'd like you to respect my desire for privacy."

Speak assertively—not aggressively

Assertive does not mean *aggressive*. According to one dictionary, being assertive means that we "affirm positively or declare with assurance." To be aggressive means "to attack, assault, commit an act of hostility, or to begin a quarrel or controversy."

Aggressive acts happen when the operating rule is "win-lose." According to this rule, when one person wins or gets what she wants, another person loses.

Assertive acts take place when the context changes to "win-win." When we are assertive, we are confident *and* respectful of others. We ask directly for what we want without feeling embarrassed or inadequate. We can work hard to get what *we* want *and* work hard to help others get what *they* want. We can speak *and* listen. Getting what we want does not have to mean that others lose.

Avoid statements disguised as questions

Questions can be powerful. They can be liberating ways to learn. Knowledge is born of questions.

Questions can also be a disguise for assertions and requests that we're afraid to make. We can verify this by converting those questions into statements:

"What do you think you are doing?" becomes "Please don't do that."
"Do you like his new haircut?" becomes "I don't like his new haircut."
"Don't you think that's silly?" becomes "I think that's silly."

When we hide our opinions, desires, and requests behind questions, we do not take responsibility for them. Maybe it's just an unconscious habit. Maybe we feel it's too risky to be forthright and candid. Whatever the reason, we lose the chance to speak candidly.

We can be aware of questions that are really statements and practice speaking the truth. When we do this, others know they can trust us. People learn that they don't have to second-guess us or play mind reading games.

Now, really, don't you think this is a great idea and a better way to communicate?

Write a letter

Some of us are more comfortable writing a message than speaking it. This is often true when the message is emotionally charged. Writing helps us clarify our thoughts. We might discover that what we really have to say is not what we originally thought. Writing a letter can also include an invitation to talk further. The letter can offer suggestions that define and give structure to future conversations.

And we don't always have to send the letter. The act of writing in itself can have therapeutic value.

Ask these questions

No suggestion is absolute, including the suggestion to speak candidly. There are times when it is appropriate and effective *not* to speak—times when our speaking will hurt someone, spoil the punch line, or rob others of the opportunity to learn from their own experience.

Answering the following questions can help us decide when to speak and when to hold back for the moment:

- Is this statement really the truth from my point of view?
- Is this statement consistent with what I value and with who I say I am?
- Is this statement consistent with my promises and commitments?
- Would this statement hurt others unnecessarily?
- Am I saying this to get even or indirectly insult another person?
- Would this statement interfere with a conversation that is making progress?
- How much emotional energy (body sensations, knots in the stomach, headaches, heart pounding) is associated with my thoughts? Is there an underlying emotion that I want to discharge before I say what I'm about to say?
- What is the nature of my relationship with this person? (We probably don't need to tell the cashier at the grocery store that he has bad breath.)

We almost always have a choice about whether or not to say what's on our mind. Most of us err on the side of withholding our thoughts. But if we share all our thoughts in the moment they occur, we might go too far in the other extreme.

The idea is to speak in ways that serve ourselves while contributing to others.

Keep sending—or choose to stop

You might apply all the above suggestions and still not feel sure that your message is being fully received. If that happens, you have several options:

- **Speak more.** Keep speaking until you are confident that your message is being received.
- **Ask for active listening.** Stop periodically and request that your listeners summarize your message in their own words. This often reveals gaps in your message as well as misunderstandings.
- **If no one is listening, give up speaking for now.** You could even announce your intention: "I'm not sure that I'm being heard right now. I'd like to talk about this later."

Just say it

The idea behind this Success Strategy is to tell the truth—the whole truth and nothing but the truth.

You can practice telling the truth in every domain of life and with everyone who matters to you.

You can tell the truth to your friends and your loved ones. Tell them whatever you want. Tell them your fears and your hopes. Tell them your dreams and your aspirations.

You can even share your heart with your competitors and with your enemies. You can just shake off any façades and walk open-hearted into the world.

Now this is an uncommon idea—probably impractical, and maybe even strange. And there are potential costs. If you speak candidly, you could get in trouble. You might get into conflict with key people in your life. They might get offended or even stop talking to you.

You can also get into trouble when you withhold your thoughts and feelings. Instead of relating to you as *you,* people will relate to you as all the masks you wear.

Telling the truth is not practical. It's not easy. It's just life-altering. Talking about our feelings, whatever they are, is a path toward releasing them and healing our relationships. After expressing a tough emotion like anger, we might find out that there's fear or compassion underneath it. Saying "You jerk, I'm so angry at you" can lead to "I miss you" or even "I love you."

So don't rehearse. Don't wait for the right moment. Don't evaluate how you will look if you say it. Don't worry if the syntax isn't quite right. Don't always consider the outcome. Don't weigh your words, and don't speak in order to please someone else.

Just speak, and ask others to do the same.

Make and keep promises

Our promises create our lives.

Our promises give life to our purposes and goals. Our promises move us into action. Giving our word is a major step in creating a compelling future.

When we communicate our promises, we open up new possibilities. When we give our word and keep it, we are creating—literally. Through promises, our words can set the pace and invent the future. Promises are the forerunners of action. Our words float out into the universe bearing a vision of what is to come. When we align our behavior with those words, we turn intentions into reality.

Our promises make things happen. Circumstances fall into place. Information, resources, and help show up. All of these strategies start with giving our word. When we make a promise, our word inspires action.

Keeping promises creates a world that works

Life works to the degree that we keep our promises. When something goes wrong, the problem often goes back to a broken agreement.

Imagine how different life would be if all promises were kept. All marriages would be monogamous. All loans would be paid off when they were due. All treaties between nations would be respected.

If individuals, businesses, and nations kept their promises, tremendous resources would be freed to handle injustice and misery throughout the world. Problems in our homes, schools, businesses, and national governments would be minimized. Harmony would be maximized.

Align words and behaviors

There are two broad ways to keep promises.

One is to change our behavior so that it's consistent with our promises. For example, if we promise to start a regular exercise program or read for one hour daily, we can act on these intentions and live up to our word.

Another option is to change our promises so that they align with our behavior. Someone who's promised to change careers might study the options and conclude that her current job is the best fit for her right now. She can avoid making any promise to change positions. Using either strategy, we find that our words and our behaviors are consistent. Our promises are fulfilled.

When our words and behaviors are consistent, people generally feel more secure. They can be comfortable in knowing who we are. They feel they can trust the messages we send. Keeping promises also benefits us. When we give our word and keep it, we experience a sense of comfort, control, and freedom.

A promise is not to be made in order to saddle your life with another obligation. Promises are there to remind you of what you want. If a promise no longer sparks your enthusiasm or moves you into action, then it's time to create a new promise that's truly in tune with what you want.

Ways to keep a promise

Improving our ability to keep promises is a skill that can be learned. Experiment with the following strategies for aligning words and behaviors.

Make promises challenging and realistic

Promising is a daring adventure. Testing our skills and determination by making a promise can be enlivening. If the promise involves no risk, then it's not much of a promise.

We can monitor our promises by avoiding two extremes—laziness and outrageousness. Realistic promises are those we have a reasonable chance to accomplish, even as we stretch ourselves to meet them. If our promises are too audacious ("I'll become a world-class athlete in six months"), we set ourselves up for failure. If they are too easy ("I promise to *try* to get up five minutes earlier tomorrow morning"), we insult ourselves.

Effective promises move us to meet our potentials. At the same time, they represent results we can actually achieve.

Examine intentions

When we break a promise, we can examine our intentions. We might want to keep the promise ("Going back to school would be a good idea"), even while another part of us resists it ("Taking classes will strain my schedule and my budget").

When we genuinely and completely choose to do something, internal resistance often disappears. All aspects of ourselves—thoughts, feelings, and behaviors—stand ready to make good on the promise.

Include conditions of satisfaction

One way to increase the power of a promise is to clearly specify the conditions of satisfaction. When you meet these conditions, you and others know that you've fully kept your promise.

To prevent confusion, specify observable conditions. Compare the following two promises:
- "I promise to work harder."
- "I promise to contact at least three more potential clients each day and to keep a log of my contacts."

The first promise contains no conditions of satisfaction. The second specifies exactly what you'll do to keep the promise—observable behaviors that anyone could verify.

The first promise can easily lead to a wide variety of interpretations, questions, confusions, and disagreements. The second promise is clear. In making such a promise, you're far more likely to recognize and produce an effective outcome.

Prevent self-sabotage

When making promises, we can anticipate possible self-sabotage. The idea is to look for ways that we might consciously or unconsciously undermine our intentions. For example, I might promise to start keeping a personal journal on my laptop computer and to make daily entries in that journal at home, after work. I can look for a personal behavior that might sabotage that promise, such as my habit of leaving my laptop computer at work.

Be gentle with yourself

Everyone breaks promises. The only way to be absolutely certain we keep promises is not to make any—or to just make those we're certain we can keep. Either way leads to playing it safe.

We can choose to perceive broken promises as feedback, not failure. Until we stretch ourselves to the point of occasionally breaking a promise, we're probably missing our full potential.

Be gentle with others

At some point in our lives, nearly all of us will be on the receiving end of a broken promise. Examples are many: People fail to show up at key events. They leave us in the lurch when we count on their presence. They persist in an old habit, even after promising to quit it. They even leave us for good after promising to stay a lifetime.

Faced with such facts, we can keep score and stockpile resentments. That's sure to give us a lot of emotional baggage to drag around. Another option is to love and accept people who break their agreements. Caution: Forgiving broken promises does not mean setting ourselves up to repeatedly suffer broken promises. If there are people in our lives who consistently break promises, we can forgive them, release resentment, and still protect ourselves from repeated exposures to their lack of responsibility.

Examine consequences

Promises come with different stakes involved. Promising to go to a movie tonight is different from promising to pay taxes on time. The stakes become higher when we sign legal documents or when we declare marriage vows. Knowing the consequences of breaking a promise can help us choose whether or not to *make* the promise in the first place.

Ask other people to hold you accountable

Many of us are more likely to keep promises made to other people than promises we make only to ourselves. This points to a powerful strategy. We can ask people we trust to accept our promises and hold us accountable.

For example, you could ask key people in your life to accept your promise to exercise three times this week. These people can check on you periodically, and you can report to them when your promise is fulfilled.

Keep promises visible

There's probably some truth to the old saying "Out of sight, out of mind." Think of unusual ways to display your promises, and have fun with this strategy.

Some possibilities include:

- Write promises on 3x5 cards and put them on your desk.
- Tape the cards to a mirror in your home.
- Put notes on the dashboard of your car.
- Write promises in calligraphy on fancy paper and frame them.
- Create bookmarks that display your promises.
- List your promises in a letter to yourself and mail it. Or ask a friend to mail the letter back to you in two weeks (or two months or two years).

Design a detailed action plan

To reach a goal or fulfill a promise, break it down into smaller steps. Often you can divide a large goal into small actions to complete in one hour or less. List these actions on separate 3x5 cards and sort the cards by timeline or priority.

Chart your behavior

Charting your behavior can be one piece of a detailed action plan. If you promise to lose 25 pounds in the next 6 months, for example, then graph the number of pounds you lose each week. If you want to save up for next year's vacation, set aside some money each month and note the amount in your calendar. Creating ways to make our progress visible can help us generate enthusiasm, manage our efforts, and experience success.

Create a ceremony to make the promise

If the promise you are about to make is significant, you can honor it with a ceremony. Invite friends and relatives to a formal event during which you declare your promise.

We already use ceremonies to celebrate and give more significance to a wide variety of promises—weddings, confirmations, bar and batmitzvahs, and more. When rituals, ceremonies, and official public declarations accompany our promises, we are more likely to keep them.

Report breakdowns early

If you become aware of potential barriers to keeping a promise, report them early. This gives everyone time to adjust and to create strategies for helping you keep the promise.

Early reports also minimize the chances of unwelcome surprises: "What do you mean, you'll need another two weeks for that report?" "I thought you were planning to pick me up." "Aren't you taking care of the kids tonight, like we planned?" "Why didn't you tell me?"

Reporting that the promise will not be kept *as soon as we become aware of that likelihood* is key. Perhaps there are ways to minimize the damage. Then everyone involved can make alternative plans. And we can know that we handled the situation with integrity.

When appropriate, negotiate changes

After making a promise, you might want to change it. Perhaps you'll want to suggest a new timeline for a project you promised to complete. Perhaps you'll want to put the project on hold or cancel it altogether.

At any time, we can meet with the people involved and request to renegotiate a promise. We can point out that we are still willing to keep the original promise, and that new information suggests a modification. We can even ask to be released from the promise.

Make more promises

If we break a promise, we might be tempted to throw in the towel. That's not necessary. Even if we break long-term promises, we can acknowledge our mistake and recommit to the promise. While admitting that we've broken promises in the past, we can declare our intention to keep them in the future.

Practice total transparency (EXERCISE)

Brainstorm a list of important people in your life. Possibilities include coworkers, friends, family members, customers, competitors, and lovers (current or former).

Narrow this list down to five and brainstorm a list of secrets—things you've avoided telling these people. Then write each person a letter revealing the appropriate secret.

After making this list, you have several options. One is to send the letters. Another is to meet with each of the people involved and reveal your secrets. Or you can throw the letters away and continue to keep the secrets.

Please do not judge yourself if you choose the last alternative. There are no right or wrong choices in this exercise. If you have genuinely searched for the option that contributes most to yourself and others, trust your choice.

Please make your list in the space below and write your letters now.

Practice making and keeping a promise (JOURNAL ENTRY)

Make a promise that you can keep within the next 24 hours. Make it both challenging and realistic. After doing this, come back and write about your experience with promises.

Complete these sentences:

In doing this exercise, I discovered that I ...

_____

_____

I intend to ...

_____

_____

Keep a promises journal (JOURNAL ENTRY)

For one month, keep a written list of all the promises you make. Also set up regular times to review this list. Leave space for noting whether you fulfilled each promise. Add any comments about what stops you from keeping promises or what helps you fulfill them. After the month, return to your promises journal. Reflect on your experience with promises by completing the sentences below:

When reviewing my promises and record of keeping them, I discovered that I ...

_____

_____

_____

When it comes to making promises in the future, I intend to ...

_____

_____

_____

MOVE
TOWARD
LOVE

*Everything in life
that we really accept
undergoes change.*

KATHERINE MANSFIELD

Experiment with It's all OK!

We have a ticket to paradise. We hold that ticket right now, and we can use it any time. Whenever we use that ticket, we get a free replacement—one we can redeem anywhere.

This ticket is not a real ticket, one we actually hold in our hands. Instead, it's one we hold in our heads. This ticket to paradise is an attitude, a way of thinking, a style of seeing the world. This attitude means "loving it all" and permitting things to be the way they are—right now, in all their glorious imperfection and messiness.

"Move toward love" could be the most powerful, unusual, and indefensible Success Strategy in this book. It's also a Success Strategy with notable advocates throughout history. For example, Jesus suggested that we love our enemies as ourselves. And Gandhi said he wanted the British to leave India not as enemies but as friends.

When we practice moving toward love, we're willing to face our imperfections and those of others. We freely admit our weaknesses (as well as our strengths). We allow, permit, and even embrace our problems as chances to create new solutions and gain new skills.

Moving toward love does not mean that we let other people take advantage of us, or that we meekly put up with aggression. Instead, we let go of our *internal* resistance to our problems. *Love* in this context means full knowledge and full acceptance—seeing all the details about a problem and permitting it to be the way it is right now. While adopting this internal attitude, we can take whatever actions might be appropriate to change external circumstances.

When we move toward love, we acknowledge that life isn't perfect. And we accept all thoughts and feelings about that fact. Then we can discover solutions and take decisive action that's not tainted with hatred.

After using this Success Strategy for a while, we might be able to survey our whole lives and say "It's all OK!" We could see our circumstances and behaviors as perfect in the present moment—and that perfection includes the potential to change our circumstances and behaviors. Enjoying the perfection of the present means that we can celebrate the goals we've already met and look forward to accomplishing new goals. We can relish wanting as much as achieving.

Choose your place on the spectrum

You might not be able to love what's happening to you right now. Perhaps your current circumstances are confusing, disappointing, or even painful.

No problem. If you can't love it all, then just love as much as you can. See if you can just move *toward* love. And if you can't move toward love and acceptance, then see if you can at least move *away* from antagonism and resentment. While you do that, love yourself for not loving it all. If you find it hard to even *imagine* moving toward love, then just start from wherever you are and love as much as you can.

Think of this Success Strategy as a spectrum. If you can't move toward love 100 percent of the time, then practice it 50 percent of the time—or 25 percent, or 10 percent. Any movement you make toward full love can take your happiness to a whole new level.

Welcome chances to practice

When moving toward love becomes a habit, we find that we can freely observe things that once repulsed us.

For many years I've practiced moving toward love by seeking out things I routinely avoided. At one point I asked myself *What is the most repulsive sight I can imagine?* My answer was maggots. I figured that if I could love the sight of maggots, then I could love just about anything. So sometimes I would drive around until I saw road kill on the highway. Then I'd park the car, flip the road kill over, and say, "Aha! Maggots. Opportunity to practice!"

After doing this, I found it a lot easier to love the people and events in my life that were far less disgusting than maggots— everything from a flat tire to a passing driver who gave me the "finger." I could say, "Flat tire? Wow, I haven't changed a flat tire in years. It's time for me to brush up on this

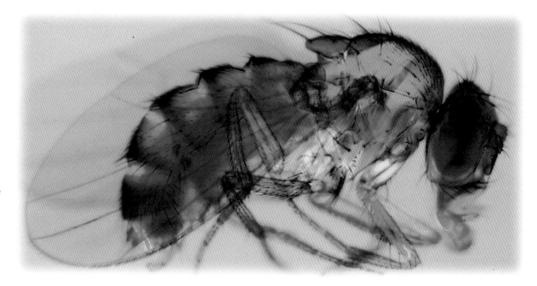

skill." And instead of taking that driver's gesture as a personal insult, I could take it as useful feedback about my driving.

Move from what should be to what is—and what's next

In moments of disappointment, when events don't turn out the way we expect, we might judge life to be awful. We feel the acute contradiction between the way things *are* and the way we think they *should* be.

"Move toward love" represents an alternative—noticing what *is* instead of what *should* be. And it's a path we can start on today—not next week, not tomorrow, but right now, before the next 60 seconds are up. And every step on the path involves the same strategy. We simply accept whatever is happening in the present moment—period. Then we can take appropriate action.

When we are willing to love our problems, we drain them of much of their energy. In addition, we often know exactly what to do next. If I learn that the fan belt on the family car is broken, then I know what to do: replace the belt. If my doctor tells me that my cholesterol level is too high, I also know what to do: alter my diet and exercise patterns to bring my cholesterol down.

We could take less effective approaches. Instead of replacing the fan belt, we could bewail the current state of fan belt technology ("Why can't they make fan belts that last forever?"). And we could complain endlessly about our lot in life ("Why did *I* end up with a body that cranks out cholesterol like it's going out of style?").

Those reactions are understandable. And the truth in this moment is that, for whatever reason, fan belts *do* break and cholesterol levels *can* get too high. Telling the truth about these facts and accepting them can lead to useful action. Complaining about them leads nowhere.

Experience fully to pave the way for full release

Moving toward love can reduce or eliminate many of the unpleasant experiences in our lives. When we totally experience discomfort, it often diminishes, and sometimes it disappears. This idea can apply to emotions, past traumas, and even physical pain.

You can use this technique the next time you have a headache. Make it your aim to love the pain—that is, to fully accept the pain and know all the details about it. Far from being solid, most pain has a wave-like quality: It rises, reaches a peak of intensity, and then subsides for a moment.

See if you can watch the waves come and go. Also notice if the pain has any "borders": Does it seem confined to one area or does it ripple throughout an area of the body? If you were to associate a color, texture, or word with the feeling, what would it be?

You can do this with any emotion at any moment. Just describe the body sensations that accompany the emotion— perhaps a tight stomach, tension in the jaw, or sweaty palms. As you experience sensations, no matter how unpleasant, simply notice them and let them go.

When we accept, allow, and permit discomfort at any level, we pave the way for its release. That's the power of moving toward love.

practice loving it—part one

One way to get the hang of "loving it all" is to start small. Take a small problem—
one that you may have decided you could live with for the rest of your life.
Then see if you can apply the Success Strategy "Move toward love."

First, describe the problem in detail without judging yourself or others.
Then see if this attitude helps you discover possible solutions.

In the space below, describe the problem you want to work with.
Then write about your experience in applying this Success Strategy.

The problem I have is ...

_____

_____

_____

_____

In moving toward loving this problem, I discovered that I ...

_____

_____

_____

_____

To solve this problem, I intend to ...

_____

_____

_____

_____

practice loving it—part two (JOURNAL ENTRY)

After doing the previous journal entry, apply the same process to a bigger problem. Again, in the space below describe that problem and how you choose to practice moving toward love.

The problem I have is …

_____

_____

_____

_____

_____

In moving toward loving this problem, I discovered that I …

_____

_____

_____

_____

_____

To solve this problem, I intend to …

_____

_____

_____

_____

_____

Practice loving yourself

Many of us find it easier to love others than to love ourselves. We may have come to believe that loving ourselves means that we are conceited, egocentric, or selfish. Or maybe while growing up we received messages, both overt and covert, that we were not lovable.

Consider an alternative line of reasoning: Perhaps we can love others only to the extent that we love ourselves. Perhaps we can give to others only that which we can give to ourselves. We cannot share water from a well that is dry.

Maybe the most unselfish and loving thing we can do for others is to first love and accept ourselves unconditionally. This kind of selfishness can be a virtue.

To practice moving toward love, we can begin by accepting and appreciating all aspects of ourselves. These aspects include our thoughts, emotions, and actions—especially the ones we'd rather not face.

Love your thoughts

Notice the content of your thoughts—the specific words and images that flash through your mind at any given moment. When you're feeling anxious or afraid, you might be mentally rehearsing a "worst case scenario." In your imagination, you might picture yourself doing something foolish in public, having an accident, or even making a mistake that leads to your death.

Then observe any judgmental statements that accompany these images, such as *This kind of thing always happens to me* or *I never come through when the chips are down.*

You can work with statements and images in exactly the same way: Move toward loving them. Just notice them and accept them, moment by moment.

When you do this, you gain freedom. Instead of experiencing blind terror or blind anger, you gain some clarity. Images lose some of their intensity. Judgments slow down and lose some of their grip. This not only provides relief but gives you a cooler head as you decide what action to take next.

Love your emotions

Being happy includes accepting and celebrating *all* of our emotions— especially those considered negative. These emotions, once fully experienced, have a tendency to disappear or dissipate. When that happens, we're free of any lingering residue. We don't need to carry around the excess baggage of suppressed emotions struggling to find an avenue for expression.

One way to be free of tough emotions is to love them and feel them without limitation. That means noticing them and totally accepting them for the moment. You can apply this strategy to sadness, anger, fear, or any other emotion. When you give emotions this kind of forgiving and focused attention, they often cease to be a problem.

In addition to fully experiencing an emotion, you have the option to fully express it. Unexpressed emotion is like static on a short-wave radio: It makes listening and speaking difficult. When we carry around suppressed emotions, we find it tough to be honest, open, and spontaneous.

Releasing emotions is something we do naturally. Emotions seek release. Laughter can release fear and embarrassment. Tears and sobbing release grief. Trembling releases fear. Yawning can release tension, and animated talk often releases boredom.

There are many safe and skillful ways to discharge our emotions. To begin with, we can simply talk about them in the moment we experience them. We can complete the sentence, "Right now I am feeling _____."

We can even set up environments in which we are free to scream, shout, cry, or laugh to the point of embarrassment—all without causing problems for anyone. For example, we can hit pillows or beat our beds with a rolled towel. And we can see a therapist or talk to a friend who's particularly skilled at listening.

Emotions are neither right nor wrong, good nor bad. Our only job is to permit them, fully experience them, and then choose ways to respond to them—if we choose to respond at all.

Love your actions

Whenever we set a big goal and move into action to meet it, we create the possibility of success. We also take on the risk of failure. The greater our capacity to contribute to other people and make a positive difference in the world, the bigger our potential for making mistakes that result in significant damage or loss.

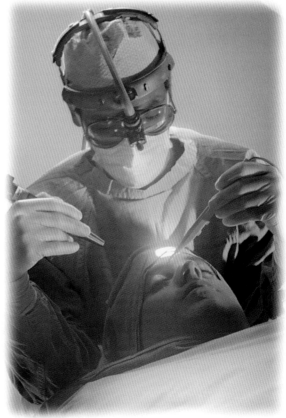

Look around and you'll find many examples. The chief executive of a corporation can make a decision that costs millions in lost revenue. The president of a country can make policy blunders that double the deficit or ignite a war leading to the death of thousands. Even a highly trained surgeon can make an error during an operation that leads to the loss of life.

There's a flip side to all this. The people in the previous examples can also be a force for good. A president can articulate a vision that unifies opposing political factions. Executives can lead their companies into prosperity, and surgeons can save lives. In each case, people with the power to succeed also have the potential to fail. The two possibilities are interwoven.

Whether our actions succeed or fail, we can move toward loving them—a path that can lead to even more effective action in the future.

Solving your problems won't hurt, either

(And it's easier when you drop resistance)

Throughout *Falling Awake* is the idea that we can create the life of our dreams no matter what our circumstances. We can have a great life even when we don't have all the money, time, relationships, or experiences we want. From this point of view, a great life is not about freedom from problems; it's about simply loving whatever problems arise.

This idea is powerful—except when it isn't.

Look, folks, this whole "having a wonderful life doesn't depend on circumstances" thing is just an idea. Life is larger than logic, and any idea has limits.

Yes, it's often true that we can be happy no matter what our circumstances and love our problems no matter what they are. And yet love may not be enough. Sometimes the most direct path to creating the life of our dreams is to move beyond loving a problem and start taking action.

Negative feelings are often a wake-up call, a pointer to something that needs doing or a circumstance that needs changing. For instance, regret is a natural accompaniment to breaking a promise, telling a lie, or doing something else that's inconsistent with our values. Depression might be linked to letting others take advantage of us. Irritability might be associated with harboring a grudge against another. Loneliness can be the result when we refuse to say what we're really thinking and feeling.

In each case, we can take some kind of action to clean up our circumstances. We may need to make amends, apologize, pay off a debt, or set personal boundaries and be more assertive. All these strategies can pave the way for more happiness.

Remember that loving a problem is not the same as being resigned to it. We can accept the faded and dirty siding on the outside of our house even as we paint it a new color. We can love our old job even as we change careers. We can remain friends with a former partner even as we seek a divorce. We can accept and love ourselves even as we work like mad to change our behavior.

While we're busy changing our circumstances, we can still drop our resistance to problems and practice moving toward love.

Be your own mentor (EXERCISE)

When we look back into the past and befriend our younger selves, we can find it easier to love ourselves in the present. In addition, we can learn lessons that can help guide our choices in the future.

Think back to a time in your life when you were faced with a problem. You might choose a time when you were young and afraid, or when you were struggling with a choice that was a major turning point in your life.

Now pretend that you can return to that time, and describe it in detail. How old were you? Who else was involved? Where did this event occur? What sights, sounds, smells, tastes, or physical sensations do you remember?

In your imagination, be who you are now, with all your hard-earned wisdom and experience. Then have a conversation with the person you were back then. Consider recording this dialogue on paper or an audiocassette. What insights or understandings can you share with your younger self? What can you teach yourself? How can you help your younger self have a different experience? Can you listen to your younger self in a way that nobody was able to at the time? What have you learned that will help your younger self get through this experience in a way that has a more favorable outcome?

In the space below, complete the following sentences.

In meeting my younger self, I discovered that I ...

_____

_____

_____

After coaching my younger self, I intend to ...

_____

_____

_____

Eight ways to keep a problem

Loving problems—telling the truth about them and seeing problems as opportunities to gain skills—is a key step toward solving them. Many people, however, are far more skilled at making problems stay in place. They often use the following strategies to keep a problem.

Deny it

Some people respond to a problem by denying that it exists. Not only does the problem continue, it's buried under an additional problem—denial. This makes the problem harder to uncover and more difficult to handle.

When we deny a problem, we navigate our way through life with a blind spot. Then we wonder why we keep bumping into things and getting bruised all the time. Denial helps to ensure that a problem will stay with us.

Avoid it

Even after we acknowledge a problem, we might still avoid it. Avoiding a problem is often nothing more than postponing an inevitable showdown. We might be able to avoid the direct experience of a problem for a while, but we can seldom escape the silent threat it poses.

The energy that it takes to avoid a problem can consume even more time and energy than tackling it head on. Avoiding problems can limit our full participation in life.

Resist it

Another possible response to a problem is to fight the unpleasant emotions associated with it. We can resist. We can struggle. Using will power and sheer determination, we can attempt to overpower our emotions and subdue them.

Sometimes this works. More often, the harder we fight against our emotions, the harder they fight back.

Resistance equals persistence. When we attempt to wrestle our emotions out of existence, they often end up winning the match.

Fix the blame for it

When faced with a problem, some people follow a simple rule: Fix the blame fast. Assigning blame helps some people feel better. They can experience self-righteous indignation about the source of the trouble and go to sleep at night with a clear conscience. But when they wake up in the morning, the problem is still there to greet them.

Explain it

To some people, explaining a problem can be as satisfying as solving it. Explanation often takes less work. Never mind that things aren't working. At least there's a good reason for it.

Be "right" about it

The desire to be "right" is a powerful force. Many people choose being right over being happy. These people might be willing to face a problem and even propose a solution. And they might insist that their solution is *the* right one—even if the problem persists.

Be resigned about it

To be resigned means to throw up our hands, shake our heads, turn away, and give up. When a problem is too big, too hard, or too hopeless, we sometimes admit defeat and quit.

In addition to feeling lousy when we quit, we lose the opportunity to fully explore a variety of possible solutions. When we're resigned, we take on the role of a victim when we could be taking responsibility for action instead.

Be a martyr about it

According to one definition, a martyr is a person who makes a great show of suffering in order to arouse sympathy and gain attention. Meanwhile, the original problem goes unresolved.

If enough sympathy and attention are forthcoming, some people would rather let a problem fester than find a solution. The person who complains about being alone every Saturday night is often avoiding the risk of picking up the phone and asking for a date.

Ask whether you're holding on to problems (EXERCISE)

The previous article explained eight strategies that people use to keep problems in place. Consider whether you're using any of these strategies. If you are, then admitting the truth about your behavior can be a step toward getting past the problem.

At first you might be not able to find any examples of these strategies in your own life. Give it some more thought. Ask friends or relatives if they can supply an example for you. It might be useful to keep examining your history or your current circumstances. It's likely that you can find a personal example of each strategy.

Sum up your insights on a separate sheet of paper. For each strategy, note specifically what you did to prolong the problem.

1. Denying a problem
2. Avoiding a problem
3. Resisting a problem
4. Fixing the blame for a problem
5. Explaining a problem
6. Being "right" about a problem
7. Being resigned about a problem
8. Being a martyr about a problem

Follow up by writing about ways you might be holding on to a current problem.

Embrace problems and dance with them

As an alternative to the eight strategies for keeping problems, consider some ways to embrace problems—and even dance with them—as steps toward releasing them.

The words *dance* and *embrace* might seem strange when talking about problems. Keep in mind that embracing or dancing with a problem does not mean seeking it out. Most of us already have more than enough trouble on hand without looking for more. Instead, this strategy suggests steps we can take when problems show up naturally.

Tell the truth

Embracing problems begins with telling the truth. This allows us to go to the heart of a problem without getting distracted or sidetracked. Usually, the most direct approach to a problem is to walk up to it and shake hands.

For example, if the truth is that we are afraid to speak in public, then we can start by admitting it. That simple truth can stand alone without evaluation, blame, justification, excuse, rationalization, or explanation. It can take on the status of a simple fact: Rocks are hard, water is wet, and we are afraid to speak in public.

Naturally, our feelings about public speaking are probably more charged than our feelings about rocks. Even so, we can tell the simple, factual truth about our fear.

Embrace problems

We can know that we're embracing a problem when we experience it and still feel reasonably comfortable.

It's unrealistic to expect that we'll feel comfortable with every problem we face. We can have happy, satisfying lives and still experience occasional fear, anger, upset, and frustration. The key is to not let our reactions reduce us to inaction or render us ineffective.

Here comes a tricky part: Embracing something does not necessarily mean agreeing with it. We can accept another person's statement of a problem, understand it, and even be relatively comfortable around it—all while disagreeing with that statement.

Move even closer

Standing squarely in front of our problems sometimes requires the courage to feel discomfort. Our unwillingness to deal with unpleasant feelings might tempt us to choose one of the eight ways to keep problems.

When that happens, we can face our discomfort and move in even closer. Even after telling the truth, we can observe in detail how the problem shows up, moment by moment, in our daily lives.

You can begin by paying close attention to physical sensations. When you feel fear, for example, you might experience sweaty palms, shortness of breath, dizziness, shaking knees, chest pains, nausea, or a host of other physical events. Greeting these sensations with nonjudgmental attention often decreases the discomfort.

Take the first step in the dance

Sometimes embracing a problem is all that's needed to solve it. More often, this is just the first step in a more intricate dance— the strategies we use to eventually resolve the problem. Our dance might include any of the Success Strategies described in this book. We can design and implement practical action plans to deal with our problems. If problems don't respond to our best efforts, then we can choose to seek help from a professional counselor.

Five reasons to celebrate mistakes

Mistakes are no reason for misery. Goof-ups do not need to result in teeth gnashing. Our mistakes can be the most powerful teachers we have.

If we truly realized the value of mistakes, we'd run the world much differently. We'd realize that mistakes are as important as successes. In addition to all the rewards and celebrations involving successes, our society would recognize and celebrate mistakes.

Politicians would wage campaigns by claiming that they made more mistakes than their opponents.

Job applicants would submit "failure résumés"—highlights of their most fascinating slip-ups and what they learned from those experiences. They could save tales of the truly *major* snafus for the job interview.

Marketing executives would brag about all the new products they pioneered—especially those that the public overwhelmingly rejected.

And athletes would fondly recall the times they got trounced by opposing teams.

I admit that this is an unusual attitude to take toward mistakes. And I can suggest at least five reasons for celebrating mistakes.

Mistakes get our attention

Mistakes have a way of focusing our attention and putting crucial problems right in our face. Mistakes light a path for us. When we own up to our mistakes, we often know exactly what's not working and what we can do to fix it.

Permitting mistakes allows us to take risks

There's one sure way to avoid making mistakes, and that's to avoid life. The writer who never finishes a book will never have to worry about getting negative reviews. The would-be center fielder who doesn't try out for the team is safe from making any errors. And the comedian who never performs in front of an audience is sure to avoid telling jokes that fall flat.

When we're comfortable with making mistakes, we're more likely to take risks and tackle projects.

Caution: Celebrating mistakes is not the same as setting out to make them. Celebrating mistakes involves wisdom; setting out to make them involves willful incompetence. Effective people don't set goals with the idea of making mistakes. Instead, they aim to reach those goals while accepting the risk of error.

Noticing mistakes shows our commitment to quality

Imagine working at a company that has no standards—where mistakes are not distinguished from successes and no one is held accountable for errors.

We could turn in the sloppiest, crudest pieces of work we'd ever done, and they would get treated the same as our best work.

We'd never be able to count on having the supplies we needed because no one would complain when vendors failed to deliver.

Projects could go perpetually unfinished, and no one would say anything.

Profit margins could fall through the floor, and no one would flinch.

The point is simple: In an atmosphere where there's no difference between failure and success, the word *mistake* would be without meaning. Mistakes can happen only when people are truly committed to making things work.

We can use mistakes to practice

Celebrating mistakes can enhance every suggestion in this book.

For example, take Success Strategy #1: "Determine what you want." The word *mistake* derives meaning only by comparison to what we desire. Mistakes are possible only when we're committed to lives that are filled with happiness, health, love, financial security, and whatever else we value. Noticing and admitting our mistakes reminds us of what we really want to have, do, and be.

Another example is Success Strategy #2: "Tell the truth." Mistakes offer us an opportunity to practice truth telling. With this act come the rewards of honesty and candor, including self-knowledge and the capacity for change.

Mistakes also offer a chance to apply Success Strategy #3: "Move toward love." As we tell the truth about our mistakes, we can benefit by releasing shame and blame. Fixing the mistake and preventing it from happening again are key goals.

These are just a few examples. You can use mistakes as an occasion to practice each of the Success Strategies.

Mistakes make powerful teachers

Mistakes are usually more instructive than successes—and often far more interesting. The lessons we learn from making mistakes often stick with us for a lifetime. We can translate those lessons into new values and behaviors that make a profound difference.

With all these potential benefits from mistakes, we have plenty of reasons to celebrate them.

Embrace a problem, then dance with it (JOURNAL ENTRY)

Choose a current problem in your life. Then, in the space below, describe in detail some ways that you will use the suggestions in this chapter to embrace and dance with that problem.

The problem I discovered is …

_____

_____

_____

_____

_____

_____

_____

To embrace this problem and dance with it, I could …

_____

_____

_____

_____

_____

_____

_____

Make mistakes your teacher (JOURNAL ENTRY)

Recall a mistake that you've made—the bigger, the better. In the space below, describe specifically what you did and the consequences of the mistake.

I discovered that my mistake was ...

_____

_____

Now interpret this mistake in several contrasting ways. Write three possible interpretations of this event and choose the most empowering one.

For example, if you were driving and ran out of gas, you could say to yourself:

- I'm stupid and forgetful.
  - If my boss would give me a raise, I'd be able to put more than a few dollars' worth in at a time.
  - I do not have the habit of regularly checking my gas gauge.

Now write three interpretations of your own mistake and circle one that you want to adopt.

_____

_____

_____

Next, choose what you will do differently in the future to avoid making the same mistake. In the example above, for instance, you could decide to tape a note that says "check auto gas" on your car dashboard.

I intend to ...

_____

Move from conflict toward love

Few things influence the quality of our lives more than the quality of our relationships. People often forget this and fail to approach this part of their lives thoughtfully.

When relationships work, life often seems wonderful. When relationships *don't* work, life can feel like a meaningless grind. Frustration and resentment can lead to pointless arguments with friends and family members. We might feel trapped, angry, and lost about what to do.

Sometimes people even avoid resolving conflict. They maintain their upset with someone in an attempt to force that person to change. However, living with continual upset is a high price to pay and often inconsistent with telling the truth.

When conflict with other people moves you toward tears or shouting, you can use the following suggestions to move toward love.

Go for win-win

The word *conflict* is defined as "a fight, battle, or struggle." In a battle, there is usually only one winner. Everyone else loses—the classic "win-lose" scenario. Going for "win-lose" is one way to deal with relationship conflict.

Another option is "win-win." When we pursue this option, we lay down our weapons, stop doing battle, and focus solely on solving problems. Using peaceful and creative approaches, we can create solutions that work for everyone involved.

With win-win in mind, we can stop playing the game of "us" versus "them." What's left is "we"—a mind-set that allows everyone to define the problem at hand and offer solutions.

Permit conflict

When we allow people to vent their feelings and bare their frustrations, we might feel that the conflict is just getting worse.

Often we can benefit by staying with the conflict a little while longer. Reversing an old saying, we could be witnessing the storm before the calm. Once people express and release their anger and fear, they might see how much they really care for each other and want a mutually beneficial solution.

Share your opinion without attachment

We can share our opinions without becoming married to them. If we adopt a firm opinion and invest our well-being in it, then we've gone beyond merely holding a point of view. We've become so attached to an idea that any disagreement about it raises our hackles.

Using certain phrases signals that our opinion is just that—an opinion, not a revelation of eternal truth from on high. Those phrases include: "I claim …," "I assert that …," "From my point of view …," "It looks to me like…."

Other suggestions for sharing an opinion without attachment are:

- Be open to challenges to your point of view.
- State the supporting facts along with your opinion. Provide evidence for your point of view.
- Stay in a discussion with the goal of reaching agreement.
- Be willing to leave a conversation with new opinion.

Consider interests, not positions

Usually there's only one way to satisfy a position. And often there are many ways to satisfy an interest.

For example, "This company needs to hire more people" is a position that can be satisfied only by hiring more people. "This company needs to improve overall productivity" is an interest that can be satisfied by exploring a wide variety of possible solutions.

When we broaden the discussion to include interests, we create more possibilities for resolving conflict.

Slow down

When you're listening to others express their opinions, let them lay all their cards on the table. Slow down the conversation and give people a chance to finish what they're saying before you respond. Ask, "Is there anything more you want to say?" Before you speak, allow a few moments of silence to digest what you've just heard.

Do it face to face

Conflict flourishes on third-party communication. Instead of talking directly *to* the people we disagree with, we find ourselves talking *about* them behind their backs.

Resolving conflict usually means doing just the opposite—going back to the key people involved and negotiating a solution that works for everyone.

Do it in writing

One way to prepare for negotiation is to put your thoughts in writing. Write a letter that sums up the points you want to make. Expressing your point of view in a series of complete sentences is a great way to clarify your thinking. You can enhance the power of this technique by summing up other points of view as well.

Look for diversity and find common ground

The meaning of a single word, phrase, or gesture can vary radically from one culture to another. Some Native Americans, for example, believe that looking people directly in the eye is disrespectful. When people avoid eye contact with us, we might interpret such behavior as a sign of apathy, dishonesty, or disrespect. The message we receive may be exactly the opposite of the one being sent. In all situations, we can stay open to diverse ways of interpreting any behavior.

We can also back up to common ground. Most human beings want similar things—happiness, health, love, and freedom from financial worry, to name a few. Even when we differ in our ways to get what we want, we can remind ourselves of our common desires.

Choose the freedom of forgiveness

Forgiveness has power.

Think about the costs of failing to forgive: retaliation, isolation, revenge, retribution, reprisal, vindictiveness. Holding on to resentment calls

for maintaining a constant supply of defensiveness, suspicion, and anger. And doing so takes up a lot of physical and emotional energy.

Ironically, some people complain about the amount of resentment they feel, yet they hesitate to give it up. They nurture their resentments like cherished pets. When they're angry, they feel most alive.

Resentment promotes a certain view of the world—the idea that we are objects mercilessly manipulated by circumstance and pushed around by other people. The problem with this viewpoint is that we see ourselves as victims. Our own choices seem to make little difference in the quality of our lives.

In addition, the people we resent come to dominate our minds. They take up much of the space inside our heads—rent-free. This can be true even for people who have moved away or who died years ago.

Sadness often relates to dwelling on times when someone really "stuck it to us." It's easy to replay these incidents mentally, reliving the same scene over and over again. Such thinking doesn't change the person we resent or resolve the problem; it only makes us miserable. At any moment, we can adopt new ways of responding to resentment that can lead us toward the freedom of forgiveness. Some options follow.

Notice resentments

When we feel resentment, we can simply be aware of it. We might make verbal or mental notes such as *I'm feeling resentment right now.* We can also write discovery statements in a journal each time we start nursing a grudge.

Simple awareness of how much resentment we feel and the circumstances in which we feel it can go a long way toward defusing the feeling. As we become aware, it's important not to judge ourselves. We can then just note the resentment and move on.

Consider the benefits of forgiveness

Forgiveness is not always easy. Reviewing the benefits of forgiving might help.

To begin with, forgiveness provides a path toward feeling lighter and freer. Releasing resentments can feel like unburdening ourselves of a 200-pound weight.

Through forgiveness, we might even gain some health. We don't know precisely how to measure it, but there's evidence that sustained anger relates to illness.

Forgiveness also contributes to others. Our forgiveness can help people forgive themselves. And that can help them make lifelong changes in their behavior.

We don't forgive just to benefit other people, even though that's a worthy goal in itself. Forgiveness is a selfish act in that it benefits *us* as much as anyone else.

Recognize the difference between forgiveness and absolution

Sometimes judgment masquerades as forgiveness, especially when we forgive with a holier-than-thou attitude: "You were a real jerk. But because you struggle with so many faults, I forgive you."

When forgiveness has this flavor, it becomes absolution. This attitude implies that we have the right to judge others. Instead of healing relationships, this approach to forgiveness alienates people.

When we forgive, we can practice releasing our judgments along with our resentments.

Replace resentment with a positive wish

Even in the midst of a resentment, we can say a prayer or make a positive wish for the person we resent: *I wish that she be released from her anger,* or *I wish that this person find a job he loves, along with deeply fulfilling relationships.*

Experiment with this strategy. You might find it impossible to sustain a resentful thought and a positive thought in the same moment. The positive thought literally crowds out the negative one.

Some people rebel against this suggestion at first. To them it seems unreal, uncomfortable, or dishonest. They feel like they're faking forgiveness when they don't really *feel* it.

If you feel this kind of resistance, that's fine. Just note it and keep replacing your resentments. Over time, notice what happens to your resentment.

You can also separate feelings from behavior: You can *act* in forgiving ways, even if you don't *feel* forgiving in the moment. That's real freedom.

We can look for the effects of resentment on our own happiness and then make a clear commitment to replace the habit of resentment with forgiveness.

List your resentments (EXERCISE)

One way to get started at forgiveness is to make a list of resentments.
Take some time with this and make it as complete as you can.

Making a list, even though it seems like a mechanical exercise, can promote forgiveness
for a couple of reasons. For one thing, people with a lot of resentments see that they have
a long list. They often get a clear sense of how much mental and emotional energy they
pour into their grudges. In addition, the simple act of writing can help us get perspective
and neutralize the negative feelings.

Get started with your list by drawing three columns on a separate sheet of paper. Label those
columns: *Person I resent, Action I resent, and My role in this situation*. Then fill in each column
as appropriate.

Pay special attention to the third column about your role. Ask yourself *Did I do anything
to help create the situations I resent?* For instance, the person who's recently been fired and
resents her employer can ask about the quality of her job performance. The person whose
spouse has moved out can ask what role he played in her decision to leave.

Sometimes, we play no role in what happens to us. Rape, incest, physical and psychological
abuse, and crimes are examples. Getting to forgiveness in these cases can be more challenging.
Perhaps learning to accept these events, with or without forgiveness, is the appropriate goal.
If we are facing these types of issues, professional help can be useful.

Promise to forgive (EXERCISE)

Describe the costs of holding on to the resentments you listed in the previous exercise, for example, "The person I resent dominates my thinking." Or "I never allow myself to visit my family because the person I resent might be there."

In the space below, write the names of the people you resent, along with the costs of holding on to the resentments.

_____

_____

_____

_____

_____

Now describe the benefits of forgiving each person, for example, "I get to forget about an incident that happened long ago and get on with my life." In the space below, write the names of the people you forgive and the benefits of forgiving these people.

_____

_____

_____

_____

Next, promise to forgive someone you've been resenting. Write the word _forgive_ on a 3x5 card (or wherever you record your intentions) followed by this person's name. Also give this goal a priority and a timeline, if that's appropriate.

You might be wondering whether you've already forgiven this person. If you choose to write the person's name on your card, then you haven't forgiven.

Don't worry about how to forgive. If you worry about _how_ to forgive, you might never commit to the _act_ of forgiving. Just make the commitment and trust your brilliance to create ways to forgive this person.

Give compliments

Most of us enjoy getting compliments—and we forget how much fun it is to *give* them.

Giving compliments can become a worthwhile practice in itself. The rewards are plain. Delivering a well-deserved compliment can defuse tension and make it easier to resolve conflict. Those who receive our compliments feel noticed and acknowledged.

Compliments change the giver

Compliments change the giver as well as the receiver. The next time you give a compliment, notice what happens. See if you release a little tension in your body. Notice whether you soften your resistance to another person or shed a resentment. See if your breathing becomes a little slower, a little deeper. Even many prescription drugs cannot deliver benefits like these. Granting compliments can be a healing gesture for others and ourselves.

Compliments create our world

Giving compliments is one way to create the world you live in. It's possible to wake up in the morning and notice everything that fails: the toaster that chars breakfast to a blackened crisp, the headlines about murder and mayhem, the fuel gauge that's sagging on empty.

You can also comment on how good the orange juice tastes, write a thank-you note to the person who delivers your paper each morning, and compliment the attendant who fills your gas tank. You can practice an "attitude of gratitude."

This is not a suggestion to put on rose-colored glasses or adopt a greeting card mentality. The idea is to balance our perspective and get the full picture. Effective, happy people are in touch with things that don't work well. They also notice when life is delivering the goods on time, in style.

Ways to give compliments

Compliments work best when they're genuine. We can sense when someone is "sugar coating"—giving a compliment that's insincere. People even use random compliments as a way to soften hard news: "I really like the way you perform your job.... By the way, your position is being eliminated today." This is not a way to become more credible with compliments.

Also, be specific. Point to actions. Give details. "You're so considerate" is pleasant. "I appreciate the way you clear the table after dinner each night" can be more powerful.

To get a head start, remember that you don't have to feel grateful before giving a compliment. Experiment with giving a compliment—one that is truly genuine and that you believe is accurate—even when you don't feel like doing it. Then observe your emotions. Giving thanks might create a feeling of thanksgiving.

According to a saying, "What goes around, comes around." Seize the next opportunity to float a compliment out into the world. Then see what comes back at you. The result might be a leap in your level of life satisfaction.

Bombard others with attention (EXERCISE)

This exercise is a gem to use at family meetings or at work.
Here are the basic steps:

1. Give one person a fixed amount of time to talk—two to five minutes.
2. When this person speaks, everyone else just pays attention and listens.
   This means no criticism and no piggybacking (adding to what the speaker says).
3. After the speaker finishes, other group members can offer appreciative comments.
   Those comments can focus on what the speaker said or the way she said it.

Give everyone in the group a turn to speak, following the steps listed above.

The logic behind this exercise is simple: The focused, nonjudgmental, and appreciative attention of a group can release fear and allow everyone involved to move toward love. The experience of being truly heard *and* affirmed can be liberating. This is a gift worth giving to the people we care about—and to ourselves.

Success Strategy #4

TAKE RESPONSIBILITY

…everything can be taken from a man but one thing: the last of the human freedoms—to choose one's own attitude in any given set of circumstances, to choose one's own way.

VIKTOR FRANKL

Pretend that you create it all.

Get ready for one of the most bizarre suggestions in this book. Here it is: Our lives work most effectively when we take total responsibility for all of our experiences.

We can take responsibility for our lazy, incompetent supervisor.

We can take responsibility for the cars in front of us that sputter and moan as we drive home on the freeway.

We can take responsibility for the neighbors who consistently play their CDs at volumes that could shatter glass.

We can take responsibility for the dogs that howl from midnight until 2 a.m.

Whenever we're tempted to blame someone or something for an unpleasant circumstance in our lives, we can do the opposite. We can take responsibility for it—*all* of it.

Check your first reactions to receiving this suggestion. Perhaps they went something like this: "No way! This idea is crazy. I will not take the blame for my rude, insensitive neighbor, or for that noxious dog, or for a boss who's so incompetent he can barely zip up his pants. If I start taking responsibility for things like these, pretty soon you'll ask me to start taking responsibility for poverty, war, and world hunger."

Good points. So stick around for some further clarification.

The first thing we can do to explore this idea is to lighten up. We can take this practice as a point of departure, a suggestive line of thinking. We can play with it and see where it leads. For now, we need not worry about proving or disproving it.

Another thing we can do is to be clear about what's really being suggested. As we hear the word *responsibility,* we can translate it into *response-ability.* Then this practice is not saying that we chose to have loud neighbors or an incompetent boss. We are not solely responsible for all the circumstances in our lives (though it's sometimes interesting and instructive to pretend that we are). "Take responsibility" really says that we can choose our *responses* to our neighbors, bosses, and anything else in our lives. And those responses play a huge role in creating our circumstances.

As we seek to take more responsibility for our experiences, we can benefit by asking two questions: *How did I create this?* and *How can I create a new result?*

Ask "How did I create this?"

Asking this first question prompts us to carefully examine the choices we made and to look at their consequences. In the process, we might discover that much of our frustration stems directly from what *we* did or failed to do. When our lives are not working, we can look first to the person standing in our own shoes.

This can be a particularly tough discovery when life isn't going well. That was my experience when I asked this question about my divorce. I was convinced that the end of my first marriage was not my responsibility. I was sure that I'd been an excellent husband, and I knew that I hadn't created my divorce any more than I had created the weather.

The problem lay in the fact that I was teaching the concept of self-responsibility in workshops across the United States. I felt a contradiction between my teaching and my life.

Finally, I chose to apply this concept to myself and look in detail for ways that I had created the end of my marriage. I started to make a list and came up with one item. Then I came up with another. The longer I thought, the more my list grew. Eventually I listed 30 of my behaviors that probably helped lead to my divorce. Of course, I still knew that my first wife had something to do with the end of our marriage. But now I saw my role more clearly than ever before.

Though it's not always gratifying to discover that we create some difficult circumstances, there is some welcome news. By asking *How did I create this?* we embrace our role as the author of our experience. We step out of the role of being a victim and into the role of taking responsibility for our life.

There's more news. If we have chosen our way into the present circumstances, we can often choose our way out again. Here is an opening to freedom. That's what the next question is about.

Ask "How can I create a new result?"

A second step in taking responsibility is asking *How can I create a new result?*

This question is pure magic. It refocuses our attention. It lifts us above the whole self-defeating arsenal of resentment, frustration, resignation, and fear. With this question we begin to move into a whole new dimension of life. By freely choosing our next response and moving into action, we start taking control of our lives again.

When I applied this question in relation to my first marriage, I moved from depression to excitement: *Wow! If I created a relationship that didn't work, I bet that I could create a relationship that* does *work.* So I took the list of behaviors that helped to end my first marriage and thought about how I could change each behavior during my second marriage. Since I knew 30 ways to create a divorce, I now knew 30 ways to create a great marriage.

Before making these discoveries, I viewed myself as the victim of my first wife. But by asking how I had created my divorce and what I could do to prevent another one, I became the co-creator of a second (and wonderful) marriage. I stepped out of the mud of victimhood onto the solid ground of self-responsibility.

Remember two more ideas

In summary, this Success Strategy says that "you create it all." That is, you choose how to interpret events and how to respond to them.

One way to enhance the power of this Success Strategy is to keep a couple of ideas in mind.

First, sometimes you *don't* create it. Floods, earthquakes, and other natural disasters happen. People experience mysterious medical conditions that have no known cause. And of course, none of us creates the weather.

Still, we can play a harmless game for a few moments and *pretend* that we do something to create situations like these. Then we can see where the inquiry takes us. Often the results are interesting.

For example, people who live with chronic pain might discover that the pain worsens when they forget to do their prescribed exercises. Though they don't create the pain, they are responsible for their treatment of the pain.

And while no one creates the weather, we create our *experience* of the weather. When the first snow falls, some people in northern climates say, "Yuck! Winter's coming." Other people say, "Wow! Winter's coming and the first snow is so beautiful." Now, these people all live in the same climatic zone. Yet they live in different worlds when it comes to their experience of the weather.

A second idea to remember is that you can apply this Success Strategy when something pleasant happens. On a sunny, 70-degree day in spring, ask yourself how you created that wonderful weather. Of course, you didn't make the sun rise, and you don't control the temperature. But other people might not notice the sun, or they might complain that the sun is too bright, or they might wish for warmer temperatures so they can go swimming, or … the list goes on. If you're enjoying the weather, then remember that you created that enjoyment.

Today I've got a phenomenal relationship with my children. I feel like I died and went to "dad heaven." Recently one of my daughters said to me, "There's nothing I like to do more than be in conversation with you." When she said this, my first thought was *Well, of course she's going to say things like that; she's a great kid.*

Well, she *is* a great kid. And I can give you a list of up to 50 ways that I helped create a wonderful relationship with her. I've worked on my relationship with my children more than I've worked at my career. I've invested time and drawn on many resources to enhance that relationship. While acknowledging how wonderful my daughters are, I can point to my role in creating our present relationship.

The difference in spelling between the words *victim* and *victor* is minor— just a matter of two letters. And the difference between being victors and victims in real life is initially quite small—just a matter of asking two questions: *How did I create this?* and *How can I create a new result?* Those two questions unleash the power of taking responsibility.

Practice taking responsibility (EXERCISE)

This is a problem solving exercise with three steps: describe, examine, and plan.

A. Describe the problem

Think of a current problem in your life. For purposes of this exercise, you might get the most insight from a long-lasting and perpetually unresolved problem.

Keep in mind one definition of a problem: a discrepancy between what you *want* and what you *have*. For instance, if you want a group of close friends and find that you have only a handful of passing acquaintances, that's a problem.

With this in mind, choose one problem in your life and describe it by writing on a separate sheet of paper.

B. Examine your role in the problem

Now brainstorm ways that you might be creating this problem.

Take the example of feeling isolated. A person with this problem might remember that it's been six months since he's thrown a party or invited anyone to his home for dinner. His problem and these habits could be connected.

Look for similar factors at work in your own problem.

Keep in mind that this list is a brainstorm. The goal for right now is to generate as many ideas as you can. Judging their quality or accuracy comes later.

Also remember that this list has nothing to do with shame or blame. You're merely diagnosing a problem the way a detective would—telling the truth in an objective, nonjudgmental way.

You might feel tempted to trace this problem to other people—what they're doing or failing to do for you. And in fact, other people may be a big part of the problem you're writing about. Even if this is true, look past this factor for now. Remember that other people's behavior is outside of your direct control anyway, and the purpose of this exercise is to discover *your* role in creating the problem.

Write a list of ways that you could be creating the problem you described in part A. Use additional paper if necessary. Then set aside your list for at least 24 hours.

C. Plan a solution

Now come back to your list with a fresh eye. Look over what you've written, considering it carefully. Choose one specific behavior—something you said or did—that seems to contribute the most to your problem.

State how you intend to change this behavior. Be specific and keep the focus on what *you* can do to solve the problem.

Practice this new behavior for a minimum of one month and determine whether or not it's helping to solve your problem. If not, go back to your original list of behaviors and choose another one to change. Then take action as before and evaluate the results. Even if the behavior change you originally made is helping, you still might want to review your list for others that could accelerate or strengthen your plan.

Cycle back through this exercise as often as you want. If you like, use it to tackle several problems. Doing this can be a significant step toward taking charge of your life.

Manage your interpretations

Imagine a person who wants to get away from it all for a while and take a relaxing vacation. But instead of booking plane tickets, he wallpapers his room with maps of Hawaii. Then he wonders why he's not feeling more relaxed.

Or picture a person who's hungry. In fact, he's so hungry that he walks into a restaurant and starts eating a menu with fancy pictures of food. Then he wonders why he's not enjoying the meal.

These people forget that the map is not the territory and the menu is not the meal.

We can laugh at these ridiculous examples. But many of us do something similar when it comes to using language. We act as if the *words* we use to describe something are the same as the *thing* itself. We forget that the word is not the thing, and that a description is not the thing described.

Take the word *fear*, for example. This word describes certain physical sensations that are different for each of us. Some people feel fear as a tightness in the chest that causes rapid, shallow breathing. Other people feel fear as a sinking feeling in the pit of the stomach and weakness in the knees. We use the same word for entirely different experiences. Perhaps we could each find a different description that's more true to our own personal experience of fear.

The sum total of the words we use to describe any experience is our *interpretation* of that experience. To a significant extent, our interpretations create our moment-to-moment experience of life. If we say that we're *exhausted* when we're really just *tired*, we might feel more drained than necessary. If we say that we're *terrified* instead of just *afraid*, we've probably increased our level of upset for the moment.

Happiness could have as much—or even more—to do with the way we *interpret* our circumstances as with those circumstances in themselves. By learning to manage the ways we interpret our experiences, we could dramatically increase our happiness without having to make the slightest change in our circumstances.

Notice your interpretations

One step toward managing our interpretations is simply noticing them. Just watch your interpretations arise, moment by moment, and remember that other interpretations are possible.

Suppose that you greet a friend on the street and she just walks by without saying hello. *What a rude person*, you say to yourself as you feel your anger start to swell.

But rudeness is just one possible interpretation of this person's behavior. Perhaps she was upset about an argument she had just had with her husband. Perhaps she was rushing to a meeting and just didn't hear you. Instead of interpreting her behavior as rude, you could interpret it as preoccupied and feel concerned instead of angry. The two interpretations could have very different consequences for your friendship.

When we interact with people, we make decisions or take actions based on our interpretations of them, which may be quite different from how they see themselves. If we're not careful, we could end up with a world full of rude and unfriendly people. And that's not much better than wallpapering a room with maps of Hawaii or eating a menu for lunch.

Choose useful interpretations

We can do more than simply notice our interpretations. We can also choose from among many alternative interpretations those that are most useful—interpretations that maximize our happiness and freedom. The way we interpret the world is just a habit, and we can change that habit in ways that help us create a more wonderful life.

When my children were younger, they sometimes said things like "I *hate* you! You're a terrible father." My first reaction when this happened was to feel like a victim. I saw only one interpretation of their statements: *I'm failing as a father.* That interpretation was often followed by an impulse to weep, which I sometimes did.

But that was just one possible interpretation of my children's speaking. I could have chosen another one, for example, *Even when I'm being an effective, loving father, my children will sometimes get angry with me.*

Now, I didn't know if this second interpretation was true. But I couldn't say that my first interpretation (*I'm failing as a father*) was any *more* true. So I chose the interpretation that gave me the possibility of more love in my live and more self-responsibility.

At any moment we can choose new and more useful interpretations.

We could interpret our children as sources of feedback on our parenting skills rather than people who want to make us feel terrible.

We could see human beings as potential friends, doing their best to be loved, searching for ways to become more intimate and connected with all other beings. Or we could see them as potential enemies who are out to win at our expense.

We could probably find hundreds of possible ways to interpret any single event. The point is to take responsibility for those interpretations and choose the interpretations that create the world we want to live in.

Remember four cautions

As you practice managing your interpretations, keep four helpful points in mind.

First, I'm not saying that interpretation is a problem or something to be eliminated. We need interpretations in order to make sense of the world. I *am* saying that at any time you are free to distinguish interpretations from facts, to choose useful interpretations, and then to act on those interpretations.

Second, be careful to choose interpretations that are both useful *and* accurate. We might be tempted to accept interpretations that seem useful because they get us off the hook, let us take the path of least resistance, or allow us to continue believing something we desperately want to believe. If those interpretations deny relevant facts, we are setting ourselves up for problems.

For example, some parents believe that their children can do no wrong. When their children misbehave, these parents find an interpretation that shelters the children from the natural consequences of their behavior. Having faith in children is wonderful. When this attribute includes distorting facts, children are robbed of the opportunity to learn.

A third caution is not to use this strategy as a substitute for appropriate action. A person who is in an abusive relationship can create dozens of ways to interpret that circumstance. In addition, she could improve the quality of her life and possibly save the relationship by leaving for a while and getting professional help for herself, while encouraging her partner to do so as well.

Finally, be careful of the need to find the "right" interpretation. I'm not sure we can ever know the most truthful or accurate interpretation of any circumstance. What we *can* do is to consider a variety of interpretations and choose those that are both accurate and useful—interpretations that will lead to the life of our dreams.

Separate behaviors from interpretations (EXERCISE)

As you play with this exercise, keep in mind the distinction between *behaviors* and *interpretations*.

Behaviors are observable actions, such as crying, breaking a vase, walking away, or slamming a door. Anybody in the immediate environment can observe these actions directly and report the same facts.

Interpretations are opinions or assumptions about the meaning of a behavior. The words *anger, frustration, rudeness,* and *jealousy* are examples of interpretations.

For instance, when you see someone shaking his fist, you're observing a behavior. You could interpret this behavior in a variety of ways: He might feel truly angry. He might be pretending to feel angry as part of an inside joke with friends. Perhaps he's simply trying to relax a tightened muscle in his forearm or loosen his watchband. And there are probably many more possible interpretations.

Interpretations cannot be directly observed. They belong to the private, inner world of each person's thinking.

Below are the steps to follow in this exercise.

1. Pick a specific situation in which to observe people. For example, you could observe customers standing in line at the grocery store or people waiting at a bus stop.
2. Writing on a separate sheet of paper, list some of the behaviors you observed in the situation you chose.
3. Now look back at your list and notice if some of the "behaviors" you listed are actually interpretations.

You can apply these steps in other situations. The idea is to spot the difference between behaviors and interpretations in any circumstance. When you notice this difference, you can choose a new and more useful interpretation to maximize your happiness.

Reconsider the reasons *for your behaviors*

Many people find it easier to accept themselves when they know *why* they behave the way they do. They look for explanations that might relieve their guilt or justify their anger. These people might say that they act the way they do because of the following:

Their parents made them do it.
Their parents didn't make them do it.
Their heredity made them do it.
Their heredity made them unable to do it.
Somebody else made them do it.
Nobody made them do it.
It's a habit.
It's not a habit.
They're not morning people.
They're not evening people.
It's what they learned when they were children.
The weather was just too terrible.
The moon was full last night.

These are just a few examples of the reasons that people give for their behavior. And there's a problem with each item on the list: Even when people settle on a *reason* for their behavior, that doesn't necessarily help them *change* the behavior.

When considering ways to be more successful, many people begin by analyzing their circumstances and searching for causes. They operate on a particular assumption—that until they know the reasons for their behaviors, it's impossible to change those behaviors.

Consider a different point of view: If we want to take responsibility for our lives, we might be more successful if we stop the search for causes. If we're poor, lonely, or depressed, we can just cross off all our reasons for being that way.

In using the principle of cause and effect to analyze our behavior, we can easily fool ourselves. Human beings are complex creatures, and life is complicated. When we consider all the variables at work in our lives, it's less clear that there is any one cause or group of causes that fully explains anything we do.

There's another problem. Even if we *could* figure out all the reasons for our behavior, we'd still be left with the same results in life. Even if we could talk with more sophistication about the causes of our misery, we might still be miserable.

When determining what we want in life and choosing ways to get it, we have a basic choice. We can trust our desires and look for ways to fulfill them. Or we can make a long list of reasons why we *haven't* fulfilled those desires. Sometimes creating "good" reasons for not creating the life of our dreams helps us tolerate the fact that we don't actually have what we want.

This does not mean we should throw the idea of cause and effect out the window. Thinking in terms of cause and effect provides a useful tool in making sense of our experience. But when we view cause and effect as the ultimate, all-purpose tool, we can get into trouble.

"Take responsibility" suggests that we minimize or avoid talking about cause and effect. Instead of asking *Why do I do that?* we can ask *How do I do that?* Instead of generating excuses, we can examine our current behaviors. Instead of searching for causes, we can take action. We can adopt new behaviors without knowing the reasons for our old behaviors.

So feel free to come up with a reason for doing the things you do— if that helps. And afterward, consider asking yourself this question: *What can I start doing differently right now?*

You might get so busy and so successful at creating new results in your life that you won't have time to consider the reasons for your behavior anymore.

Escaping victim mud–the power of your words

As a tool for rising out of the mud of victim-hood, we can use an imaginary "ladder of powerful speaking." On this ladder are six rungs running from bottom to top: *obligation, possibility, preference, passion, plan,* and *promise.* Each rung represents a certain type of speaking, from the least powerful (obligation) to the most powerful (promise).

At any point, we "stand" on a rung of the ladder of powerful speaking. That is, our speaking exists on one of these six levels. Moving "up" the ladder—speaking less about obligation and more about our promises—is a way to take responsibility and get more of what we want in life.

Listen for obligation

Obligation is the bottom rung of the ladder. When people say the following phrases, they're probably speaking out of obligation: *I should, I have to, I must, someone better, they made me, someone should, I had to, I couldn't help it, I ought to.* On this rung there's little freedom or opportunity to create the future. People who speak this way often perceive themselves as victims at the mercy of their circumstances.

Speak about possibility

The next step up the ladder of powerful speaking is *possibility.* When you use phrases such as *I might, I'll consider, I could, maybe I will,* or *I hope,* you make a small but significant step out of the mud of obligation.

Opening up possibilities is far more energizing and exciting than feeling obligated. Obligation puts other people or external circumstances in charge of our lives. Possibility, like all the rungs above it, puts you back in charge. When you speak at this level, you create an opening for new goals and new results in your life.

While possibility is more freeing than obligation, some cautions are appropriate. First, we can be careful not to fill up our speaking— and therefore our lives—only with possibilities. A person who is always talking about what he *might* accomplish some day may never get around to actually *doing* anything.

The second caution concerns hope. Many wonderful and inspiring stories revolve around people's hopes and dreams. However, when hope takes the place of planning, promising, or taking action, it becomes a deceptive, seductive narcotic.

Speak your preference

I prefer to and *I want to* are common expressions at the next level of powerful speaking—*preference.* Often it makes sense to move from declaring a goal as possible to declaring a clear preference for doing it.

Again, we can be cautious about overusing this rung of the ladder. People might constantly say that they prefer to do something but never get around to doing it.

Speak your passion

The next rung of the ladder, *passion,* is about energy. At this level, your words have more punch and your speaking is more animated. When people hear passion in your voice, they realize that you're enthusiastic about a goal you've created. *I'd love to, I'm excited about,* and *I can't wait to* are phrases that signal passion. When you are more passionate about a goal, you're more likely to take action to achieve it.

There is a catch. Enthusiasm is no substitute for action. Not much is likely to happen until we translate our energy into plans and promises, the next rungs on the ladder.

Speak your plan

You can bring your passion one step closer to reality by speaking about a *plan*. A plan, especially if it is written down, helps ensure that you'll back up your passions with action. A plan gives purpose and direction to your passions. Effective plans lay out the specific steps you'll take to achieve a goal.

Speak your promise

To reach the top of the ladder, you can make a *promise*. When you are absolutely committed to a goal, you can say: *I will, I do, I promise to achieve this.* Promises are plans backed by iron-clad commitment.

When it comes to promising, most of us do not even come close to our potentials. We are capable of far more than we've ever imagined. With promises we can free ourselves of the artificial barriers we've used to limit our participation in the world. One path to a rich, rewarding life is to make promises that stretch us to meet our potentials.

Choose your rung

If you look to your daily experience, you'll find examples of the ladder of powerful speaking.

Imagine going in to a bank to borrow money and saying, "Well, I know I probably *should* repay this loan." Your banker's going to get nervous. If you say, "Well, I *might* repay you," your banker will still get nervous. And if you say, "I *prefer* to repay the loan,"

or "I really *want* to repay it," you're probably still not going to get that loan. What the banker wants is a plan and a promise that you will repay the loan.

Or try using the language of obligation in your marriage. "Well, I know I really *should* be faithful" is not the language of romantic commitment. Neither is "I *ought* to be faithful," "I *might* be faithful," "I'd *like* to be faithful," or even "I really *want* to be faithful." None of that language brings much confidence in a marriage vow. Marriage is about promise and commitment: "I *will* be faithful."

Whenever we speak, we have the option of moving up the ladder of powerful speaking all the way to promising. At the same time, it's perfectly OK *not* to move up the ladder. It would be foolish to promise everything. As we listen to ourselves speak, we can pay attention to which rung of the ladder we're "standing" on. We can then move up the ladder for the purpose we choose, at the time we choose.

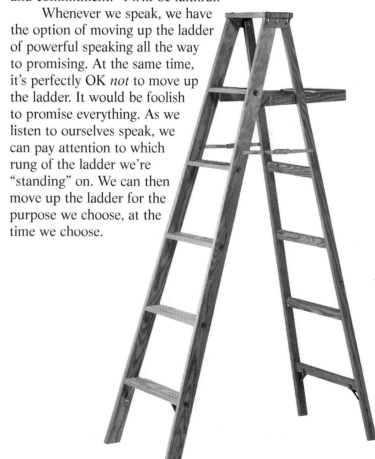

Speak from "I"

Trying to send a message to someone who feels under attack is like trying to chat about the weather with a person whose house is burning down. That person has other priorities. We might as well save our breath.

When people feel attacked, they instinctively become defensive. And when they're defensive, their first priority is to protect themselves. Most people find it tough to feel attacked and to listen at the same time.

In situations in which people are on the defensive, there are probably some "you" messages lingering in the air: "*You* always use that excuse." "*You* are a slob." "*You* make me feel like dirt."

"You" messages blame, shame, and label people.

There is a way to send messages that reduce defensiveness: Move from "you" to "I."

Experiment with the concept of an "I-message," originally developed by Thomas Gordon. This way of speaking is especially useful when tensions are running high and people are in conflict.

Besides reducing tension, I-messages help us focus on aspects of a situation that *we* can control. Using I-messages can help stop us from being victims of circumstance.

I find that it often helps to list the five basic elements of an I-message. The first three of these elements (observations, feelings, and wants) I consider to be essential. The last two (thoughts and intentions) I view as optional, and I recommend using them with caution.

Describe observations

We can start I-messages with a statement of what we observe— "just the facts, ma'am"—not an interpretation of the facts. For instance, "I left three messages for you yesterday and have not heard back from you" states a verifiable fact. "You don't care about me" is an interpretation of that fact, and it may not be the most accurate interpretation.

When stating observations, remember a useful guideline: Stick to what you see and hear. Think of observations as being what a video camera and microphone would record.

It's possible to send an I-message even when we don't have specific observations to offer. When this is true, we can state our interpretation or judgment and label it as such. For example, we can say, "My interpretation is that you're angry with me." Or "Right now I think that you're ready to fire me."

Describe feelings

Including the dimension of feelings adds emotional impact to an I-message. Yet many people who want to state their feelings actually end up sharing their thoughts and interpretations instead. Feelings include basic emotions such as anger, sadness, and fear. "I feel afraid" is part of an I-message that reveals a feeling.

Now consider the statement "I feel like we're not getting along." Because this statement starts with the words "I feel," it suggests that the following words will reveal an emotion. Actually, the words "we're not getting along" reveal an interpretation.

To increase your level of self-responsibility, consider leaving out the word *because* in reference to your feelings. This word tends to shift blame to others for the way we feel. An example is "I felt angry because you were late for our session." This statement blames another person for our anger. It can be more accurate and more self-empowering to say, "You were late for the session, *and* I'm feeling angry." This statement includes two facts without assigning any blame.

State what you want

A third useful element you can add to I-messages is a statement of what you want. Often this means including phrases such as *I want, I request that,* and *I'd like you to.*

Statements about what you want are usually more useful when you request an observable behavior. "Please be on time for the next meeting" is more effective than "Please change your attitude about being on time for meetings."

State thoughts and intentions cautiously

Stating what you think can sometimes enhance an I-message—for instance, "I fear for our relationship, and I think we could both gain from seeing a marriage counselor." Be careful, however, since the words *I think* can easily lead to judgment or interpretation, such as "I think our relationship is sick and that we need to see a therapist."

You could also state your intention: "I fear for our relationship, and I intend to get counseling." When used inappropriately, intentions can sound like threats and generate defensiveness in other people: "If you won't come with me o see a marriage counselor, then I intend to file for a divorce."

Remember that the main point in using I-messages is to reduce antagonism and increase your personal responsibility. With this purpose in mind, you can create I-messages that promote loving relationships and help you get more of what you want in life.

Practice saying "I" (JOURNAL ENTRY)

Think of a situation in your life right now that involves conflict with another person—
or the potential for conflict. Name that person and describe the conflict in the space below.

_____

_____

_____

Now practice your intention to use an I-message the next time you interact with this person.
Along with your intention, write at least three I-messages you could use the next time
you speak to this person. Feel free to write and rewrite until you create several effective
I-messages.

_____

_____

_____

_____

_____

_____

Come back to this journal entry whenever you find yourself in conflict with other people
and want more practice saying "I."

Teach people how to treat you (JOURNAL ENTRY)

You can "train" other people how to treat you. Say, for example, that another person consistently interrupts you. If you neglect to point this out, you are in effect sending a message that says "It's OK for you to interrupt me."

To illustrate this point, list two people who don't treat you well. Also describe at least two ways these people mistreat you. Be specific. Describe something that each person consistently says or does.

I discovered that _____ mistreats me by ...

_____

_____

I discovered that _____ mistreats me by ...

_____

_____

Now play with the idea that you taught these people to treat you in these ways. Know that you are a very clever person and you might have taught them without realizing it. Finish up by writing goals. Describe what you will do to "retrain" these people so that they will treat you differently.

When relating to _____ , I intend to ...

_____

_____

When relating to _____ , I intend to ...

_____

_____

Ask for what you want

Often we do not get results until we ask for something. Self-responsible human beings are "request machines." They know that one way to get what they want is to ask for it.

A request assumes that something is missing. Perhaps a task needs to be completed, a message needs to be delivered, an item needs to be found, or a solution needs to be discovered. If nothing is missing, if everything is complete, and if there are no problems, then requests are not needed.

A request also assumes that the person on the receiving end of the request has the ability to grant it. For example, we would be foolish to ask a lawyer to perform open heart surgery, or to ask a two-year-old to write a term paper.

Desire is like the flu—it's contagious. When you make a skillful request for what you want, other people can "catch" your desire. When that happens, they're often happy to grant your request.

When you ask for what you want, you also model a powerful strategy. By setting an effective example, you invite others to ask for what *they* want.

Include timelines

When appropriate, include a specific due date in your request: "Will you please deliver the report to me by 4 p.m. tomorrow?" Misunderstandings, hard feelings, and missed opportunities can be avoided when people agree on the timeline.

Look for effective responses

There are five effective responses to a request.

The first two are contained in a simple *yes* or *no*. In this case, others either grant the request or they do not. When they grant your request, they in effect promise that they will fulfill it to your conditions of satisfaction.

A third type of response is a *counteroffer*. They could commit to fulfilling part but not all of your request: "I will deliver the report to you tomorrow, but I am not willing to deliver it by a

specific time." With this information, you can choose to accept the modified outcome, negotiate another outcome, or stick with your original request.

If others are not clear about what you're requesting, they can use a fourth response and ask questions for *clarification*. For example, does delivering the report mean including a backup copy on computer disk?

A fifth effective response to a request is to *postpone* a response. Perhaps others need to check on the status of some other project before they know if they can fulfill your request. Maybe others just want to consider your request for a day or two before they answer. If so, ask when they can give you their response.

Notice that answering with "maybe" is not included in this list of effective responses. If someone responds to your request with "maybe," then consider asking someone else.

Ask cleanly and clearly

Most of us have grown up in a culture in which we're not supposed to feel proud about asking for what we want. Some people even have a habit of apologizing when doing so: "I'm sorry to bring this up, but would you mind not smoking while we're together? Of course, if you want to keep smoking, that's probably OK."

When we hedge a request like this, we clutter our message. Others may not understand what we're asking.

Another option is to trust your desires and make requests without qualification or apology. When you're proud of what you want, then you can ask cleanly and clearly. Compare the following two requests:

- "I was kinda thinking I might like to eat Vietnamese food tonight but I don't know for sure. You might like something different."
- "I want to go out to dinner at a Vietnamese restaurant. I'd like you to come along. How about it?"

It's easy for people to be on the receiving end of the second request. And many will find it easier to say yes.

Make authentic requests

Requests differ from demands. When we make an authentic request and it is declined, we can accept the refusal without becoming depressed, frustrated, or angry.

If we make a request of someone and react strongly when that person says no, then we didn't make a request. We made a demand. We're more likely to get what we want when we soften demands into requests.

Keep asking

Some people have a habit of making a request only when they're 99 percent sure that they'll get a yes in response. These people are cautious. They protect themselves against no's.

Another way to respond to a no is to ask again later, or to ask someone else for what you want. By making many requests of many people, you stand to get at least as many yes's as no's.

People might say no before they've fully understood or considered your request. Give them another chance. Keep asking with polite persistence.

Say thanks

Something wonderful happens when we make requests. Many of them get fulfilled. Often we end up creating the life of our dreams.

When that happens, say thanks. Share your joy and offer your gratitude when others grant your requests. Saying thanks or writing a thank-you note acknowledges the role that other people play in your success.

Giving thanks also reminds us that we live in a world where it's possible to determine what we want in life—and get it.

Climb the ladder of powerful speaking (EXERCISE)

Think of a problem in your life or something that you would like to change. On a separate sheet of paper, write about how you could describe this situation while "standing" on each rung of the ladder of powerful speaking.

Afterward, choose which rung is most comfortable for you.

Next, even if you feel some discomfort, move up the ladder to a higher rung. Practice speaking at this new level to a family member, friend, or someone directly affected by the problem.

For example, you might look at an unfinished project at work and say, "I can't finish projects on time because my boss sets totally unreasonable timelines." That's a case of dwelling on the rung of obligation. An alternative is to move up to the rung of possibility: "Instead of agreeing to the first schedule my boss proposes, I could lobby for extra time." You might even feel comfortable standing on this rung for a while.

LIGHTEN YOUR LOAD

*People are disturbed
not by things,
but by the views
which they take
of them.*

EPICTETUS

*Do everything
with a mind
that lets go.*

AJAHN CHAH

Bliss is our natural state—when we let go

Human beings tend to get attached. People say, "I'm really attached to my job." Or "I'm attached to my children." Often they use the word *attach* in a positive sense. When they say that they are attached to something, people mean that they care about it a lot.

It's also possible to carry attachment too far. Someone says, "I'm so attached to this job that I just can't imagine doing anything else." Or "Without my children, I'd be nothing."

These statements are clues that an attachment has gone beyond caring into a demand that must be met at any cost. In effect, people are saying that they *must* have certain people or certain circumstances in their lives before they can be happy—the right job, the right children, or whatever else wins their attachment.

This type of attachment is one of the biggest obstacles to creating the life of our dreams. The things we habitually attach ourselves to are often fleeting and impermanent, so they're bound to disappoint us. Jobs change or disappear. People leave or die. Fortunes are won, then lost.

The Success Strategy "Lighten your load" suggests that attachments are like baggage. If we lug two armfuls of suitcases with us wherever we go, we'll feel heavy, tired, and even sad. But if we let go of all that baggage, we'll lighten up and feel relieved.

We can treat our attachments like excess baggage. We can stop demanding that we have certain people or things in our lives before we can be happy. We can enjoy our jobs *and* be happy even if we're fired and forced to find a new one. We can love our children like mad *and* happily wave goodbye to them when they leave home. We can approach our accomplishments, relationships, skills, opinions, expectations, and just about anything else in life with the same willingness to let go.

Experience bliss

When we lighten our load of attachments, we can feel more than simple relief. We can start to experience a happiness that persists even when our circumstances change. This happiness can become so deep and so profound that some people call it *bliss*.

This Success Strategy suggests that bliss is the natural core of our being. Bliss is what's left when we let go.

People with a lot of attachments tend to take life pretty seriously. They're so afraid of losing something or someone that they feel stressed most of the time.

There is another option. We can stop being attached to circumstances. When it's time for them to change, we can simply let them go. We can also stop being attached to people. When it's time for them to leave, we can simply let them leave. We can even stop being attached to life when it's time to die.

This chapter mentions a number of things that people get attached to—their thoughts, feelings, bodies, roles, and more. While reading, look for any excess baggage that you might be carrying around. Then experiment with letting go. See what happens when you're willing to lighten your load, even just a little.

Let go—and work hard

The suggestion to lighten your load brings other suggestions to mind: Loosen up. Be lighthearted. Take it easy. Let go. Laugh about it all. Go with the flow. Just accept it. Stand back and let it happen. Detach.

These are all great ideas. And a different set of suggestions can be just as useful: Work as if your life depended on it. Live each day as if it will be your last. Get off the sidelines. Give it your all. Everything you do matters. Take it seriously. If you don't like it, change it. Play full out.

If you want to get more of what you want in all areas of your life, then practice both suggestions. You can let go *and* work hard. Take it seriously *and* laugh about it all. Change what you can *and* accept what you cannot change. Go with the flow *and* create the flow. Give it your all *and* don't worry about winning or losing the game.

The trick is to hold both sets of ideas in balance. There is a time to laugh and a time to cry, a time to work and a time to rest, a time to fight and a time to surrender, a time to zoom in and a time to step out. We can play life full out and at the same time not take it too seriously. While we loosen up and let go, we can work hard and play hard. We can be lighthearted even as we stay fully involved.

Taking things lightly and letting them go doesn't mean that we get lazy, stand contentedly on the sidelines, let work slide, or refuse to get involved. When we're lighthearted, we can still perform our roles with flawless efficiency. Some people are lighthearted without being involved, and we often describe them as being irresponsible or childish. That's not the kind of attitude this Success Strategy is meant to promote.

Remember to distinguish attachments from preferences. When we're attached to something, our well-being depends on having it. When we have a preference for something, however, we can enjoy having it while knowing that we can be happy even without it.

Having preferences is wonderful, and one purpose of this book is to help you get in touch with your preferences in every area of life. We can work hard to turn those preferences into realities. We can also remember that sometimes we'll get exactly what we prefer and sometimes we won't. That's hardly a profound statement, but it's easy to forget. And when we do forget, we transform our preferences into an armful of attachments.

So even as we make a full effort to get what we want in life, we can lighten up about the results. We can work hard—*and* let go.

Let go of your equations

One way to lighten up—to instantly experience more detachment, more fun, and more pleasure—is to notice your equations and let them go. Find out if there's anything you *think* you are that keeps you from lightening your load.

Notice your equations

An equation is any set of words or numbers joined by an equal sign (=) that forms a true statement. Most of us have seen equations with numbers, such as 2 + 2 = 4, and 156 × 237 = 36,972.

Equations also work with things other than numbers. In fact, our self-image is a collection of equations. Those equations tend to take a certain form: I = X. In place of the X, you can put anything that people identify with.

Many of us find it easy to identify with our bodies (I = MY BODY). The problem is that our bodies change constantly. Bodies experience different levels of health or sickness. Bodies start young and then get old. They lose hair, and they gain weight.

To preserve our bodies for a while, we give them drugs, food, sex, weight lifting workouts, cosmetic surgery, and more. Still, bodies never stay the same, and eventually they just wear out. When we identify exclusively with our bodies, we give up peace and security. We let our serenity rise and fall on the roller coaster of constant change.

Some people identify with their possessions. For example, somebody finds that her new car is scratched. She gets as upset about this fact as she would if someone had scratched *her*. She acts as if she *is* her car. Her equation is I = MY CAR. People with this equation tend to treat their cars with the utmost care. They might even treat their cars better than they treat their bodies. These people don't have their cars; their cars have *them*.

Other people identify with their money. If they lost their money, they might feel that they had lost themselves and that life wasn't worth living. Their equation is I = MY MONEY, and that equation might lead to suicide. These people don't have money; their money has *them*.

People can also identify with their thoughts. If you suggest that one of their ideas is wrong, these people think you're saying that *they* are wrong. In challenging their opinions, you challenge them. These people carry around the equation I = MY THOUGHTS.

Of course, they don't have to carry around this equation. People could have ideas and not *be* their ideas. They could have opinions and yet be willing to let them go when they discover a more accurate or useful opinion. Then they could have some great conversations with people who have different opinions.

Other people identify with their feelings (I = MY FEELINGS). When they feel sad, for example, they think sadness is more than just a feeling that comes and goes. They believe that they *are* their sadness. Or when they feel angry, they feel that they *are* their anger.

Any emotion, no matter what it is, seems to fill their entire being.

Many people identify with their roles. (I = MY ROLE) They accumulate roles like they accumulate clothes. Ask someone, "Who are you?" and chances are he'll respond with a list of roles:

"I'm a counselor."
"A teacher."
"A supervisor."
"A married man."
"A sports nut."
"The owner of a BMW."
"A good worker."

There's no harm in playing roles as long as we keep them in perspective. The problem comes when we let our roles take charge of us and define who we are. We can make our roles more important than our souls.

Parents sometimes identify with their children. These parents see their children as reflections of themselves (I = MY CHILDREN). They know exactly what they want their children to be and to do, and they believe that they can be happy only when their children live up to these expectations. Suddenly, the children become responsible for their parents' happiness. And that's a big burden for the children.

My parents avoided this equation, and I'm thankful they did. They let me go my own way at a young age and did not see me solely as a reflection of themselves. They let me define who I am on my own terms, and that was the biggest gift they ever gave me.

Release the equation

All this leads to a tool for working with our upsets: After noticing the equation, just release it. When we acknowledge the limits of our equations, we can let them go and lighten our load—and then watch our upsets start to disappear like puffs of passing smoke.

Several years ago I got a chance to practice this strategy in a major way. I bought into a business venture that went sour. It went so sour that I started losing $8,000 a day. Now at the time I bought this business, I had quite a bit of money. But money disappears fast when you're losing $8,000 every day. Eventually I lost all of the cash I had in the bank. Then I started going into debt $8,000 a day. In total, I lost over $4 million.

Fortunately, I remembered Success Strategy #5. I remembered that I *had* money (or at least I *used* to have money) but I *wasn't* my money. Even when I started losing $8,000 a day, I knew that I could eventually get another job and earn enough over time to pay off all that debt. During this period of my life I never lost sleep over all that debt, and I never missed a meal. I let go of the equation I = MY MONEY and stayed relatively happy.

Rewrite the equation

The question might arise that if we are not our roles, thoughts, feelings, possessions, or bodies, then who *are* we? When we talk about ourselves, what makes sense to put after the equal sign (I = ?)?

That's a great question. Philosophers and theologians have struggled for centuries to answer it.

My choice is to relate to people as if they are what they *say* they are. If someone says that his burning desire in life is to end hunger on the planet (I = END OF HUNGER), then that's how I interact with him. If another person says that her primary desire is to be loving (I = LOVE), then that's how I relate to her. And if someone says that his happiness depends on his athletic ability (I = ATHLETE), then that's how I treat him.

For me, the equation that makes the most sense is I = US. When I rewrite the equation this way, I realize that in some way I'm connected to everyone and everything in the world. And when I'm in touch with this connection, I usually experience the state that people call bliss, ecstasy, or heaven. My fear and upset are usually based on forgetting who I really am—on forgetting the equation I = US.

If you want to lighten up, then look for any hidden equations tucked away in your mind. And when you notice an equation, see if you're willing to release it or rewrite it. Change the habit of equating yourself with your thoughts, feelings, body, roles, car, money, or anything else.

When you do so, you'll notice a decrease in your level of upset and a sudden increase in your level of joy.

Release or rewrite the equation (EXERCISE)

The Success Strategy "Lighten your load" implies that we are not who we usually *think* we are.
We have ideas, and we are not our ideas. We have feelings, and we are not our feelings.
We have possessions, and we are not our possessions.

As suggested in the previous article, the challenge is to notice our equations and let them go.
Simply reminding ourselves with short phrases is a powerful tool. For example:

"I have a car, but I am not my car."
"I have a new couch, but I am not my couch."
"I have a job, but I am not my job."
"I have hair, but I am not my hair."

Writing in the space below, create some reminders that can help you release your equations. In
your reminders, mention some of the people, places, and things that are part of your daily life.

If you like, consider writing an equation that expresses your fundamental values—the person
you ultimately want to be. For example, if your primary value is to be loving, then your
equation could be I = LOVE.

Write several versions of your equation below.

unconditional happiness (JOURNAL ENTRY)

After reading about rewriting your equations, play with the idea a little more. In the space below, write 10 different endings to the following sentence:

I discovered that my happiness depended on …

_____

_____

_____

_____

_____

_____

_____

_____

_____

_____

Now I realize that happiness is a choice independent of my equations. I intend to be happy regardless of …

_____

_____

_____

_____

_____

Release your pictures

Most of us have pictures, or expectations, of what we want or need in order to be satisfied. For example, the person who wants to be rich doesn't just want a pile of money stashed in a bank vault. She probably has a specific mental picture of what riches can bring to her life: perhaps a new Mercedes loaded with chrome, or a 26-room mansion with an Olympic-sized swimming pool, or a 100-acre estate lined with tennis courts and lush flower gardens.

Of course, pictures can be about anything. The person who's hungry often has a vivid mental picture of the meal that would satisfy him: *Ahhh, I can just see that steaming, fresh bread and rich, creamy soup, that omelet smothered in cheese, and the mounds of gourmet ice cream for dessert....*

Discover your picture album

Just about any time we feel a need, we conjure up a picture of what will satisfy that need.

This habit starts early. A baby feels hunger pangs and starts to scream. Within seconds, her father appears with a bottle. The baby is satisfied. She now stores a mental picture of her father holding the bottle to her mouth. She connects that picture with stopping the pangs. Voila! She knows how to solve the hunger problem, and the picture goes on file. The picture becomes a powerful expectation that can guide her thinking, feeling, and behavior.

Keep in mind that the concept of "pictures" can involve all of our senses. Many pictures are visual, yet they can easily include tastes, sounds, smells, and physical sensations as well.

We could even say that our minds function like a huge photo album whose pages include pictures of all the ways we've satisfied our wants and needs in the past. Whenever we want something or feel dissatisfied, we mentally search the album for a picture of how to get what we want or how to make the dissatisfaction go away. With that picture firmly in mind, we behave to make the world outside our heads match the picture inside our heads.

Remember that pictures serve us— and hinder us

Pictures often serve us. We actually need them in order to survive.

Imagine trying to find your way to work without an accurate mental picture of the streets of your city. Or imagine trying to find a sock without a clear mental picture of the contents of your sock drawer.

The problem is that pictures can also get in our way. When our pictures become emotionally backed demands—attachments— we set ourselves up for trouble.

Sometimes pictures turn into demands when the outside world changes and the pictures in our heads stay the same.

As an example, take the college student who looks forward to returning home to see her parents at spring break. During the flight, she pictures her mother and father nestled in the living room by the fireplace like they always do after eating dinner. She also calls up a mental picture of her bedroom in which she can see the exact location of each object in that room—the easy chair, the stuffed animals, the compact disc player, and the stacks of her favorite recordings.

When she finally arrives at the airport, her parents greet her warmly. After some small talk, her father delivers the news: "Honey, your mother and I decided to sell the house and most of our belongings. Since we're retired now and you're almost done with school, we've decided to live the carefree life. We've bought a recreational vehicle big enough to sleep four.

Wait until you see it! It's got Naugahyde furnishings, bunk beds galore, two built-in porta-potties, and even an artificial fireplace."

Our student is crushed.

Gone is her room and all the resting places for those cherished stuffed animals. She starts conjuring up pictures of her parents' RV. In her mind she sees a cramped, clanky, gas-guzzling motor home that smells like burnt oil.

This is just one example of how pictures and reality can be in conflict—and the negative feelings that can result. Any time you feel depressed, anxious, or sad, check to see how reality is violating one of your prized mental pictures.

Release or replace your pictures

When pictures start to get in our way, there are two simple things we can do.

One is to just notice our pictures and release them. We can open up our mental photo albums and notice how the pictures stored there rule our thinking and behavior. Just becoming aware of what our pictures are and how they affect us can be a huge step toward decreasing their power.

A second thing we can do is to replace the old pictures with new ones. We stored those pictures in the first place. At any time, we can stock our albums with new pictures.

Return to our unhappy college student for a minute. She could take a second look at her mental pictures of her old house. When she's willing to tell the truth about that place, she remembers that her room had closet doors that never shut tight. Then there were those floorboards that creaked mercilessly on winter mornings. And even though the fireplace was pretty, it leaked a lot of cold air into the house.

Then she sees her parents' RV for the first time. She's pleasantly surprised. The motor home is more spacious than she expected. The furnishings are stylish and modern. The bunk beds are actually comfortable, and the

stereo system is a knockout. Even the porta-potties are spotless and exude a kind of rustic charm. Her old pictures of RVs as bulky, stuffy, and generally dorky just don't conform to reality anymore.

With this discovery, she creates a new mental picture of family bliss—one that's more in tune with the present. She sees herself lounging on a bunk bed, singing along with her parents to their favorite CD as they hit the highways to Malibu.

Keep in mind these things about pictures

Caution: The suggestion to release or replace pictures is not an invitation to practice denial or delusion. For example, many alcoholics choose a picture of themselves that says "I can choose to stop drinking at any time I want." This picture can be highly inaccurate. When releasing and replacing pictures, we can practice a Success Strategy explained earlier in this book: "Tell the truth."

When we gain skill at working with pictures, we remember a crucial fact about the world—things never stay the same. The only constant we can count on is constant change. When we try to negotiate life with a set of fixed mental pictures of the way things *ought* to be or the way they *used* to be, we're setting ourselves up for disappointment.

We always have another option: We can take charge of the images that float through our minds. We don't have to be ruled by an album of outdated pictures. Instead, we can keep releasing pictures and looking for more accurate ones. Ultimately, our pictures can become as fluid as reality itself.

Create an alternate picture (EXERCISE)

Think of some event that you anticipate with discomfort or even dread. Describe the pictures you associate with this event—the way you expect people to act and the way you expect things to turn out. If you've recently had an argument with your parents, for example, then you might expect to feel miserable at your next family reunion.

Write a description of your pictures in the space below. Feel free to do some drawing in the margins of the page as well; that might help you get pictures out of your mind and onto paper. If you like, continue writing or drawing on separate sheets of paper.

Now consider replacing the above pictures with pictures that are more realistic and more consistent with your happiness. For example, you could picture a family reunion in which you're willing to listen to your parents' point of view, even if you don't agree with it. In your picture, you and your parents communicate effectively and become even more intimate.

Describe your new pictures by drawing in the margins and/or writing in the space below. Again, use additional paper if needed.

Hello stress, goodbye distress

Stress has gotten bad press. The combination of thoughts and feelings that we label *stress* can often be valuable, even wonderful.

Stress is simply our gut response to any change. Physiologically, stress and excitement are almost the same. The stress response includes an extra surge of adrenaline, a heightened pulse rate, and an impulse to brace for sudden action.

We can have this experience in the face of events that are unpleasant—*and* with events that are pleasant. Stress can be our response to a dressing down from the boss—and to dressing up for a masquerade ball.

Stress can mean a power surge, an extra bolt of energy that moves us into action. Seeing an old friend for the first time in a year, embarking on a new career, going on vacation to a new part of the country—all these can trigger stress. These can be forms of stress that we actually enjoy.

Distinguish stress from distress

When it becomes too intense or lasts too long, stress becomes distress. That's when we start to notice it taking a toll on our health and our ability to solve problems.

Most people forget the distinction between stress and distress. When they use the word *stress*, people usually mean *distress*.

To get more of what you want in life, keep this distinction in mind. The basic idea is to seek out optimal levels of stress while avoiding crippling levels of distress.

We can choose to see distress as an invitation to change some aspect of our thinking or behavior. Distress is a signal that one of our current reactions is not serving us. We can relabel stress as the excitement and energy needed to make those changes.

Start with attitudes

If you want to say goodbye to distress, then start with your attitude toward it. Consider the possibility that distress is never the result of external circumstances. Nothing and no one "makes" you feel distressed—not even the supervisor who chews you out or the store clerk who insults you. No event is inherently distressful.

Instead, try on a new idea: Distress is a function of how we *respond* to other people and events. With some practice, we can learn to choose new responses—before stress cycles downward into distress.

If we adopt this attitude toward distress, then we don't have to rely only on fixing the circumstances that we usually see as the cause of our distress. We can first get relaxed, clear, and grounded. Then we can deal skillfully with our circumstances, whatever they are.

Take charge of your stress knob

Imagine that within your body-mind system is an old-fashioned radio knob that you can turn up or down. This is your stress knob—one that you can adjust to control your level of stress. When the knob is set too high, you feel distress. When responding to distress, we often give up control of the stress knob. We pretend that something or someone else causes our distress. In the process, we let other people and external circumstances take charge of our happiness.

By experimenting with the options explained in the next two articles, you can start taking charge of your stress knob by turning distress down into stress or even down into relaxation at almost any time you choose. Distress comes to us in many disguises, including anxiety, burnout, and boredom. Even though it can show up in a variety of ways, we can identify two basic types of distress—one that primarily affects the mind (worry) and another that centers on the body (physical tension). Some of the strategies described next work equally well for either kind of distress.

Release worry

It usually does little good to walk up to a stressed-out person and say, "Worried? There's no need. Just relax!" Often people want something more concrete.

The strategies listed below are places to start, especially when you deal with worry, the mental component of distress.

Let go of stressful self-talk

There's a conversation that goes on 24 hours each day and exerts a major influence on how we feel and behave. That conversation is the one inside our heads—the constant stream of words and images that our brains manufacture, even while we sleep.

When we're distressed, that stream cranks into high gear and starts looking and sounding like a low-budget horror movie. Thoughts such as *This is terrible* or *This is the worst thing that could ever happen to me* are accompanied by mental pictures of impending disaster. At these moments, we focus on the worst outcomes that could possibly happen.

Worry, goes the old saying, is a down payment on a debt we may never have to pay. Most of the catastrophic scenes we picture never come to pass. This offers a resounding argument for letting go of those pictures immediately.

Be rational

Rational Emotive Behavior Therapy (REBT), developed by Albert Ellis, offers a specific way to manage self-talk. Ellis bases this therapy on what he calls the ABC's of human emotion and behavior.

"A" stands for an activating event, such as getting fired or being diagnosed with a serious illness. "C" stands for the emotional consequences assumed to be caused by the activating event. Those consequences might include feeling depressed or getting angry.

Ellis claims that "A" does not directly result in "C." Instead, "B"—our belief about an activating event—is the real source of our emotional reaction.

Any belief can be rational or irrational. Rational beliefs lead to healthy responses that help us reach our goals. Irrational beliefs lead to unhealthy, distressful responses that block us from getting what we want in the long run.

Ellis points to three irrational beliefs in particular that can instantly undercut our happiness:

- Other people must always do exactly what we want them to do.
- Events must always turn out exactly as we want them to.
- We must never disappoint ourselves or act contrary to our expectations.

Good news. We can start to turn our internal conversations around by replacing these beliefs with beliefs that are more rational:

- Other people may or may not act the way we want them to. We don't have to invest our well-being in their behavior.
- Sometimes, despite our best efforts, events will turn out in ways that we don't like. We don't have to invest our well-being in how things turn out.
- We are likely to make mistakes now and then. We don't have to invest our well-being in being perfect.

Thinking rationally can change depression into mere disappointment and can upgrade debilitating devastation into manageable annoyance. By managing our beliefs about an activating event, we can reduce our levels of distress and respond to any circumstance in ways that help us get more of what we want.

Write about it

One way to manage distress is to simply become aware of what our minds are doing. Writing in journals—getting the conversation out of our heads and onto paper—is one way to defuse negative thoughts. When we translate our thoughts into words that sit right in front of us, it's easier to dispute irrational beliefs and replace them with more empowering thoughts.

Since the hand is slower than the mind, attempting to describe our distress on paper really puts the brakes on our thoughts. In addition, writing is a way to gain perspective. When our stressful thoughts are sitting obediently on a piece of paper, they often seem less forbidding.

Yell "Stop!" and fantasize

Thoughts can race faster than a speeding bullet. Sometimes a simple and dramatic way to calm a torrent of self-defeating thoughts is to give a direct order. Just yell "Stop!"

When appropriate, do this literally—yell the word out loud. If that's not wise, then do it mentally or just move your lips without making a sound.

Either way, notice what happens to your thoughts. An unusual response like this one can be just what you need to derail an unwelcome and stress-producing train of thought. Once the self-defeating thoughts stop or slow down, you can replace them with ones that are more pleasant and empowering.

For example, make a list of the ten most pleasant experiences you can imagine. Picture yourself walking barefoot on the beach on a mild summer day, or being with someone you love. Once you have put a halt to your stressful thoughts, then bring out your list and focus on one of the items.

Or instead of imagining how terribly things might turn out, take a few minutes to mentally rehearse success. Picture yourself sailing through IRS audits, work evaluations, or any other events you normally dread. Anticipating success can increase the chance that it will happen.

Zoom out

When you're in the middle of a situation and feel distressed, take a trip. You don't have to physically leave the scene; just do the traveling in your head.

Imagine that you're floating to the ceiling and looking down on the stressful situation as an outside, detached observer. If you want, let your imagination soar even farther. See yourself rising above the scene so that your whole community, city, nation, or planet is within view. From this larger perspective, ask yourself whether the situation is worth worrying about.

Another option is to zoom out in time. Imagine yourself one week, one month, one year, one decade, or even one century from today. Assess how important the current situation will seem to you when that time comes.

Recognize limits

Being a perfectionist means taking virtues, such as attention to detail and a passion for quality, to an extreme. Much distress results when we set ourselves up for failure by having expectations that are too high. The most powerful goals are those that both stretch us *and* engage us in a task we can actually accomplish—goals that are both high and realistic.

Talk about it

Finding a sympathetic ear can work wonders when we're distressed. Talking to a friend, family member, or counselor can be powerful. Unburdening our woes to a pet or even a plant might sound weird, but it can't hurt either.

If we're desperate, bereft of friends, or low on cash, we can remember that almost every major city offers toll-free hot lines for people in crisis to call. Through hot lines, we can gain immediate access to free counseling or an understanding listener. Ministers and community mental health centers can be powerful options, too. With all these resources, there's no reason to experience our pain alone, in silence.

Focus on today

This is a strategy well known to members of 12-step programs such as Alcoholics Anonymous. To a person recovering from alcoholism, the thought of a lifetime without alcohol can trigger feelings of despair. The thought of just getting through the next 24 hours without it seems a little more manageable.

We can apply the same strategy to any behavior or attitude we want to maintain or eliminate—take it one day at a time. Exercise just for today. Substitute fruit juice for dessert just for today. Postpone buying that luxury item just for today. Don't worry about how you're going to sustain a change for the rest of your life. Just focus on the next 24 hours.

Caution: Like any other strategy, this one can be misused. Some people use the idea of "one day at a time" to prolong an unacceptable situation. In harmful situations—such as an abusive relationship—we might resign ourselves to tolerating just one more day of suffering or humiliation. The problem comes when that "one more day" turns into weeks, months, and years.

The question we can ask when we find ourselves afraid to change, day after day, is *If not now, when?* Sometimes it takes a great deal of courage to change today. Telling the truth, finding support from others, and choosing to make a specific change can be the first steps toward more happiness.

Postpone worry

If you like to procrastinate, here's one situation in which this ability comes in handy. Instead of worrying now, put it off. Schedule a time to worry later, or tell yourself you'll get around to it if you feel like it. For now, give yourself permission to enjoy some peace of mind.

When we apply this strategy, a joyous discovery awaits us: Much of the time, the things we worry about never come to pass. By postponing worry, we save ourselves needless mental wear and tear.

Worry it to death

Sometimes we can manage distress by exaggerating the normal tendencies of a racing mind. If our minds want to imagine the worst, then we can let them. The trick is to be sure that we take this line of thought to the extreme of absurdity.

Example: "If I don't get this job, first I'll run out of money, then I'll have to go live with my parents, then everyone will laugh at me, then my parents will kick me out, then I'll be homeless and live in a cardboard box on the street, then I'll starve or freeze to death."

Once we imagine the very worst, we can backtrack and usually picture a more realistic possibility. Then we can start to devise workable plans that help us alleviate distress.

This is not a suggestion to ignore our problems. It is a suggestion to find a reasonable level of concern. When we've discovered that level, we can state the problem objectively and discover solutions.

Do something constructive

It's easy to live in our minds, trying to figure out why we feel the way we do. We can get so focused on ourselves that we become self-centered, forgetting that the outside world even exists.

Sometimes a simple change in our focus is all that's needed to lower distress. Instead of endlessly probing our own psyche, we can take an active interest in the world around us. We can shift our attention from *What am I feeling?* to *What needs doing?* This might lead us to vacuuming the living room, apologizing to a friend, or doing volunteer work. Upset has little room to maneuver when our attention is focused on accomplishing a task.

If this sounds like a suggestion to get distracted—well, it is. Distraction can be useful, especially when we've been mired in a problem for days or weeks and no solution is in sight. The change of pace that comes with refocusing our attention can actually give us a fresh perspective on the difficulty. This is not a suggestion to ignore or repress feelings. The point is to do something constructive *and* feel the feeling. While remaining fully in touch with an emotion, we can move into action.

Say no

Much of our distress results from our fear of a two-letter word—no. Uttering this simple word can work miracles. It can banish projects from our lives that serve no real purpose or that push us into overload. Most of the time, people will appreciate the honesty in a statement such as "My plate is full, and taking on one more task is more than I can handle."

Set priorities

When we try to cram ten hours' worth of activities into eight hours, we start out the day already two hours behind.

We can stop this form of self-sabotage by asking some questions: *What's my top priority for today? What's the worst that could happen if this didn't get done? If I could only get three things done today, what would I want them to be? What activities are most in line with my purposes and values?* The answers we get can help us separate the wheat from the chaff in our daily schedule.

Delegate

Often we can benefit by tackling only the projects that are uniquely suited to our own abilities. The other tasks we can handle in no time by giving them to someone else.

Coach yourself

When faced with a problem in your life, first put it into words. Describe the problem while talking out loud or by putting it in writing. Define the problem as carefully as you can.

Then pretend that someone else is having this problem—someone you care about deeply—and write down several suggestions for this person. Afterward, step back and ask if any of these suggestions might work for you. This is one way to start being your own coach.

Let the feeling pass

Feelings are dynamic, constantly in a state of flux. And they come in waves—a crest is always followed by a fall. What feels most intense at one moment can subside in the next. When all else fails, we can count on one thing: Our feelings are going to change.

When we accept our feelings—both pleasant and unpleasant—and allow them to pass, we climb off the emotional roller coaster. We can enjoy the highs without getting attached to them. And we can last through the lows without feeling trapped by them. In either case, we can rest on the flow of feelings, enjoying their richness and variety.

Ask for help

There are over six billion people on this planet. All of them are potential allies in creating the life of our dreams.

Distress multiplies needlessly when we try to solve problems alone. When other people know about the distress we feel, many are willing to lend a hand. Often the first thing they say is "How can I help?" Taking them up on the proposition is one way to defuse distress.

This is an obvious solution, and many people rule it out. They abide by some unworkable ideas, such as:

"It's a sign of weakness to ask for help."

"Other people aren't interested in my problems."

"They can't really help."

"They wouldn't help, even if they could."

We can release these thoughts before they compromise our happiness. The alternative is simple: Ask for help.

Release physical tension

While the mental aspect of distress manifests itself mainly as worry, the physical aspect often surfaces as tension in the body. Distress can register in the body as tight shoulders, stomach cramps, or cold, clammy palms. As the techniques explained below demonstrate, we can respond in kind by doing something different with our bodies.

Laugh

The physiological benefits of a belly laugh can be profound. Laughter affects our heart rate and breathing. It also softens muscles in various parts of the body. After a prolonged bout of laughter, we usually feel a wave of well-being and relaxation.

Learning to laugh on cue is a useful skill in managing stress. Keep a stash of jokes, cartoons, and humorous quotes. During times of stress, you can bring these goodies to mind and enjoy the results.

Relabel the sensation

We can discover alternative labels for various physical sensations—even those we associate with distress. For example, the sore muscles we used to complain about after a hard physical workout can now be enjoyed as "signs of getting into shape." We can experience effectiveness in finding new ways to code our sensations in words.

Set aside time for fun

We can lower distress by setting aside definite times each day and week when we're "off task"—freed of the expectation to compete, produce, or accomplish anything.

If we feel anxious or unsure about what to do during these times, we can forgive ourselves. With a little practice, we can remember ways to have fun. We can commit ourselves to having fun whether we like it or not.

Chant or sing

Words have the power to relax us. Sacred phrases and prayers are intoned by the adherents of many religions. These words offer ways to steady the mind and body that people have used for centuries.

We can use the same principle when confronted with distress. Bring to mind a favorite saying or prayer and repeat it several times. You can also speak these words out loud, write them down, or even sing them. Sometimes the sentiment expressed in these words is enough to restore our perspective. In addition, the sheer repetition of them can have a hypnotic, calming effect.

Breathe deeply

You do it naturally anyway; it's called sighing. Sighing is one way to deepen your breathing, and it's amazing how breathing deeply and slowly can relax you. When you're tense, remember that a different state of being is just one breath away.

Take care of your body

One of the most powerful things we can do when distressed is to take care of our bodies. That's just the opposite of what many people do. When they're under pressure at work or in the midst of strained relationships, they neglect sleep, exercise, and nutrition. Often they turn to junk foods or drugs for relief.

Our bodies can cope better with distress when we do just the opposite—stick to a regular meal schedule, get adequate sleep, and minimize or eliminate alcohol, sugar, caffeine, and other drugs. Cardiovascular exercise is a particularly potent antidote to stress.

Get physical

Hit a pillow with your hand or a tennis racket. Physically releasing pent-up energy can restore a level of calm. There are no advocacy groups for pillow rights, so go ahead and bang away. For added effect, shout at the pillow at the same time.

Get a massage

I would be willing to sell my house and move into a mobile home if that's what it took for me to afford a weekly therapeutic massage.

You can massage much distress right out of your life when you enlist the services of a skilled massage therapist. And don't forget that you can give yourself a massage. With your own hands, a massage vibrator, a foot massage machine, a vibrating chair, or a variety of other contraptions, you can do a pretty good job of relaxing yourself.

Do some hot water

People in almost every culture know the power of hot water in some form to de-stress the body. Experiment with anything from a hot bath to a sauna or sweat lodge.

Breathe to relax (EXERCISE)

Sometimes the simplest relaxation techniques are the most powerful. One is to purposefully slow down your breathing and take deeper breaths.

The speed of your thoughts and the level of tension in your body are frequently connected to the pace of your breath. By slowing down your breathing, you can often moderate thoughts and tension.

Practice slowing and deepening your breathing right now. Pay attention to any physical or emotional changes, and write your observations in the space below. Remember to practice this exercise and notice its effect on your level of distress.

_____

_____

_____

_____

_____

Scan your body to relax (EXERCISE)

One option to reduce distress is the body scan. To do it, lie down on a bed or carpeted floor and close your eyes. If possible, darken the lights in the room.

Next, systematically focus on each part of your body. You can start with your toes and move slowly up to your head. When you notice any spots of tension, mentally relax them. To accentuate the effect, you can tense each muscle group and then relax it.

With practice you can apply this technique in other positions, including sitting, standing, or walking. You can even learn to relax while going to the dentist, filling out tax forms, or boarding planes for transcontinental flights.

Practicing a body scan will improve your ability to relax. Use it several times in the next few days. Once you get better at it, you might choose to make it a regular habit.

choose new habits for managing distress

Complete the following sentences by writing in the space below.

When it comes to my overall effectiveness in managing distress, I describe myself as ...

_____

_____

_____

_____

Distress could get out of control in the following areas of my life:

_____

_____

_____

The most important thing I intend to do right now to effectively manage distress is ...

_____

_____

_____

_____

Surrender

This book is about taking charge of our lives. It's about taking responsibility for our choices. It's about ways to stop being the victim and start being the victor, no matter what life tosses our way.

With that in mind, it might sound illogical to include a suggestion to surrender.

That's right. It is illogical. But life is larger than logic. Sometimes one of the most powerful ways to deal with challenges is to stop our futile attempts to control events and other people. We can quit fighting what's happening. We can ride the horse in the direction it's already going.

There are times when life backs us into a corner and brings us to our knees. Someone we know is killed in a car accident by a drunken driver. Another person who has fastidiously taken care of her health is diagnosed with a terminal illness. Almost all of us have experienced times when our most valiant attempts to solve problems fell utterly flat.

At those times it's wise to bend. We can admit we're stumped. We can admit that we're hopelessly confused and overwhelmed, or that all our ideas and energy are spent. We can give up our old habits of thinking and acting like we have to be in control of everything. We can stop acting as general manager of the universe. And we can admit that we'll never make it by ourselves.

That's the moment of surrender.

Surrender to open up to help

There's magic in surrender. Once we admit we're at the end of our rope, we open ourselves to receiving help.

There are countless examples of this.

A student raises her hand in class and admits that she's totally lost, with no clue as to what the teacher is talking about. Now the teacher can help her frame a meaningful question.

A couple who want to have a child admit that they've been trying for years without success. After telling the truth about this, they're able to seek out support groups for infertile couples.

Someone else slowly develops an addiction to alcohol and vows to quit drinking scores of times. Each time, he fails. Finally, he surrenders. He admits that once he starts drinking, he can't stop. By entering a treatment center and joining a support group for recovering alcoholics, he gets the help he needs to keep from taking that first drink.

We can surrender knowing that an ultimate source of help is available for us. The name and nature of that help varies for people, depending on their beliefs, preferences, and spiritual practices. Names given to this power by different cultures include God, Allah, Higher Power, Jesus, Yahweh, the Creator, Mother Earth, the Tao, or simply the human community. The point is that there's always something or someone in life we can trust and count on during times of adversity.

Surrender in ordinary ways

Surrendering doesn't just work on life-and-death matters. In fact, we've probably experienced it in ordinary ways.

For example, you try to remember the name of someone you met at a party last week. For five minutes you rack your brain. No name. So you give up. Then, the next day when driving to work, the name suddenly pops into your head. When you stopped working so hard to remember, you let your subconscious mind deliver the name, with ease, in its own time.

Artists know that surrendering is one way to access the hidden reserves of the mind.

A person learning to play a Bach fugue on the piano worries about the fingering for a particularly difficult passage that's coming up. She starts to flounder at the keyboard until she remembers something her teacher said: "Practice hard and work out those fingerings before the performance. But while you're performing, forget all the technical stuff. Stop trying so hard and just let the music sing." Suddenly she relaxes into the composition, and the piece starts to play itself. She's surrendered to the music.

A writer is tackling the first chapter of his novel. He's painstakingly outlined the whole plot on 3x5 cards. Three sentences into the first draft, he's spending most of his time shuffling cards instead of putting words on paper. Finally, he puts the cards aside, forgets about the outline, and just tells the story. The words start to flow effortlessly, and he loses himself in the act of writing. The result is something far better than he could have imagined.

Surrender with care

It's easy to misunderstand what surrendering is all about. If you want this suggestion to work, then remember that surrender does not mean becoming resigned or inactive. We can surrender and, at the same time, continue to search for solutions and take decisive action. Some people surrender to a toothache. That strategy makes sense only if they're driving to the dentist's office.

When we choose to surrender to life's challenges and adventures, we can also choose to trust. We can trust dawn to follow darkness. We can trust sunshine to follow rain.

We can trust that we will come out on the other side of our problems with new strength and wisdom. We can trust the process.

We can surrender.

Practice surrendering (EXERCISE)

In the space below, describe a difficult problem in your life right now.
Look for a problem that persists despite your best efforts to solve it.

Now describe in writing how surrendering might help you deal with this problem.

practice asking for help (JOURNAL ENTRY)

Think of something in your life that is missing—a fact, skill, service, or resource that could solve a continuing problem.

Now think of someone else who could provide what you want. It could be simple (asking someone else to do the dishes tonight so that you can rest) or significant (asking someone to be your personal and professional coach).

Write about your request by completing the following sentence:

I intend to ask _____ to …

_____

_____

_____

_____

Success Strategy #6

FOCUS
YOUR
AWARENESS

*Excellence begins
with an act of attention.*

ANONYMOUS

Do what you do, be where you are

You've seen those late-night ads for fantastic gizmos that slice, dice, grind, chop, blend, and do everything except change the oil in your car. Those ads tout a product or service that promises to transform the quality of your life—all for just $19.95 plus shipping and handling charges.

Well, imagine that the article you're reading now is an ad for a skill that really *could* transform the quality of your life.

Also imagine that this skill is both inexpensive and free. In fact, imagine that it's a potential you've always had.

Well, this ability *is* already yours. It's a skill that you can develop even more without paying postage or C.O.D. charges.

This too-good-to-be-true offer is about something that's commonplace and extraordinary at the same time—your ability to focus your awareness.

Focus awareness to benefit all you do

Your ability to "be here now"— to focus your awareness—can boost the power and quality of all your activities. *Anything* you do benefits from receiving your full attention.

For instance, when you take a walk, you can just take a walk. You do not have to worry about making the rent or mortgage payment, or buying your child's next pair of shoes, or those unfinished projects at work. Or when you eat your favorite food—say, pizza—you can pour all of your attention into that mouth-watering concoction of cheese, tomato sauce, and freshly baked bread. You don't have to think about adding transmission fluid to your car, or that cutting remark your boss made a year ago, or any of the million other things that could distract you from the present moment. You can just eat that pizza, savoring every bite as if it were the first piece you'd ever eaten.

In summary, you could really start showing up for life. You could be where you are *when* you're there. You could do what you're doing *when* you're doing it. You could melt into the fullness and completeness of the present moment. Whenever this happens to us—while fishing, lying on the beach, cleaning house, working at our jobs, or listening to our favorite music—we feel fulfilled and complete.

The marvelous thing about focusing awareness is that we can do it any time, any place. Every second that we're awake, we can wake up and pay attention.

Consider this: Everything that's present in your life right now—your job, your relationships, your possessions, your home—results from where you've placed your attention in the past. You took focused action to gain these things, and to take any action at all you had to focus your awareness.

Perhaps the overall quality of your life is just a reflection of your ability to focus your awareness.

Just "be here now"

You've probably seen ads for self-help courses that promise to reveal the secret to great romance. Here's a shorter path to that goal: Focus your awareness.

Romance begins with the simple things: Noticing what our partners wear. Listening carefully to what they say. Seeing the kind things they do and offering thanks. All these actions require paying attention.

Marriages flounder when one or both partners say, "She hasn't heard a thing I've said for the last ten years," or "He never admits how hard I work." Long before problems reach this point, we can take preventive action. We can give our partners the gift of focused awareness.

You can use the same strategy to get something that many people say they want—a long-term, loving relationship that maintains sexual excitement. If you want to create new sparks, particularly in bed, then just be there in every single moment, with every single stroke, with every single look, every single smell, every single taste. Then you'll be with somebody new in every moment—the person right there in front of you, not some memory of who that person was in the past.

What works for great lovers also works for great performers and great athletes. They're present in the moment when they play music or dance or make a free throw—not thinking about something else.

The practice is to just "be here now" with each activity. Be here now while working … while reading … while talking … while listening … while doing anything at all.

Inevitably our minds will wander. Seeing this, we can gently bring them back again … and again … and again. Though we may find this difficult to do at first, we'll also find that our ability improves with practice. With patience and forgiveness, we can return our awareness to the present moment now … and now … and now.

Four ways to "be here now"

We can use many methods to practice focusing our awareness. Each method involves taking a few minutes daily to dwell fully in the present moment.

Some techniques you can apply right away are: making mental notes, using tick marks, involving your body in the process, and handling distractions.

Make mental notes

To practice making mental notes, just choose one activity to do with total attention—fishing, walking the dog, reading the paper, or anything else. Each time your attention wanders away from that activity to a distracting thought, just make a mental note of this fact. You can even say to yourself *distraction,* then gently return your mind to the task at hand.

While you're making mental notes, remember to release any self-judgments about getting distracted in the first place.

For example, if the lyrics to a song start to bubble up while you're reading this book, just say to yourself *music distraction* or *song distraction.* Then return your attention to this book. The specific words you use for mental notes are not that important; the act of noticing distractions and refocusing your awareness is.

Make tick marks

Another effective way to focus your awareness is to create a visible record of your distractions.

Say that you notice your attention wandering while you're taking notes at a meeting. When that happens, make a small tick mark in the margin of your paper. Add another mark each time that you start daydreaming about going to the beach, picturing what you're going to eat for dinner, or going on any other mental trip that removes you from the meeting.

The purpose of making tick marks is not to give yourself a grade for concentration. Rather, you can use the physical act of putting pen to paper to re-engage your attention.

Bring your attention to your body—or your body to attention

When your mind is drifting, you can engage an old and reliable friend—your body. There are at least two ways to do this.

One is to momentarily bring attention to the state of your body. You can do this as a step to refocus your attention on the task at hand. Scan your body and notice physical sensations. Noticing these sensations as they arise and pass in the present moment is a way to return to the here and now. Once your awareness is focused on the present state of your body, you can redirect it in any way you choose.

A second option is to bring your body to attention. Assume the posture of someone who is fully engaged, active, and alert. Instead of slumping in a chair, move up to the edge of your seat and straighten your spine. Act as if you're waiting for someone to yell "Fire!" Be fully prepared to leap off your seat. Notice what happens to your wandering mind.

Handle the distraction fully, now

Say that you're reading a book and your mind keeps drifting to an argument you had earlier in the day with a coworker.

Faced with this situation, you could apply one of the three techniques mentioned above. Another option is to put down the book, call your coworker, talk it out, and resolve the conflict.

Sometimes a wandering mind is a sign that's worth heeding—a reminder that a problem in the world outside our heads needs to be resolved. What we first label a distraction could be a call to action from a wiser part of ourselves.

"Be" with an orange (EXERCISE)

When we slow down and "be here now" with simple things, we can experience the ordinary in extraordinary ways.

You can begin with something as simple as eating an orange:

- Notice the color, shape, and surface of the orange. Take three minutes (a full 180 seconds) to observe these characteristics in great detail.
- Now spend another few minutes feeling the orange with your eyes closed. Use your fingers, your forehead, your cheek, your tongue, and the back of your neck. Roll it between your palms. Throw it from one hand to another. (You might want to open your eyes for this part.) Feel its weight and mass. Squeeze it. Will it explode if you squeeze hard enough? What temperature is it? Warm the orange up on your stomach. Does it feel different now? Can you balance it on the top of your head? Will it roll in a straight line?
- Listen to your orange. No kidding. What is the sound of one orange peeling? Are you sure there are no sounds inside your orange? Just put it up to your ear and listen carefully. Will the orange make a sound if you squeeze it? Tap on it with your finger, then with a spoon, then with other objects that are nearby. Compare the sounds. How are they alike and how are they different? How else can you use an orange to make sounds? Will oranges of different sizes make different sounds?
- Without using any type of instrument or utensil, begin dissecting your orange. Will you start at the top, the bottom, or in the middle? How do you know which end is the "top"? Do you use your fingernails or your teeth? Can you peel an orange and keep the entire skin in one piece?
- Use the same strategies you used on the outside of the orange to explore the inside of the peel. The inside is a different color than the outside. Exactly where does the color change? Does it change closer to the outside or inside edge of the peel? How is the inside texture different from the outside texture? Exactly where does this change take place? How many different uses for the peel can you create?
- Now examine what most of us think of as the most important characteristic of an orange: its taste. What does a little piece of that white stuff that we usually try to avoid taste like? What would a whole bunch of it taste like? Put a slice of the orange in your mouth. Will it "melt"? What does it feel like under your tongue? With a slice between your tongue and the roof of your mouth, very slowly squeeze some juice out. Does it squirt, ooze, or do both in different directions?

And just think—we haven't even begun to consider the growth cycles, chemistry, economics, nutrition, advertising, or politics of oranges. If we look closely enough, we might discover secrets of the universe hidden in a simple orange.

If you get tired of oranges—and have the courage—eat a bowl of cereal this way.

Become a camcorder (EXERCISE)

You may have used a camcorder—a portable video camera with a built-in microphone. These gadgets have a simple function: to record the sights and sounds that occur in the spot that the lens and microphone are pointed. Camcorders do this without editorializing or making any judgments. Wherever we point them, they just register the details.

There are times when we can benefit by functioning in the same way. Just registering the sights, sounds, smells, tastes, and textures in our immediate environment can help us relax in a matter of seconds. And like the camcorder, we can just register the details in a neutral, objective, nonjudgmental way.

Experiment with becoming a camcorder. Following are some specific details about the outside world for you to "record." Expand the list with your own ideas.

* The number of steps between your front door and the sidewalk
* Colors of the clothes that your spouse, partner, or children wear
* Locations of objects in a room
* Plants, flowers, and trees in your neighborhood
* Varieties of sound in your environment: traffic, birds, voices, air conditioners, furnaces, machines, and so on
* Smells, colors, textures, and tastes of foods that you eat often
* Colors of the sky and shapes of clouds
* The feeling of your fingers on the keys on a computer keyboard
* The sensation of your clothes touching your skin

Meditate

The word *meditate* comes from the Sanskrit word *medha,* which means "locating your center, your inner wisdom."

Meditation is now taught and endorsed by people ranging from gurus to physicians. Our contemporary ills—tension headaches, high blood pressure, insomnia, anxiety, irritability, lack of self-confidence, blocked creativity—have made the benefits of meditation more attractive than ever.

Meditation can provide a deeper form of relaxation than sleep. During meditation, pulse rate and oxygen consumption may drop as much as 20 percent. This form of focused awareness can restore energy and promote healing. Meditation also offers a way to promote inner peace, the value of which can be easily overlooked as we scramble toward other goals.

Meditation is a technique, not a doctrine.

It need not conflict with your religious beliefs. In fact, meditating might enhance your current religious practices. You can also meditate in the midst of an active life.

Meditation need not be a limiting or isolating activity.

Consider three aspects of meditation

At the heart of meditation are three practices.

One is learning to focus attention. Human beings are famous for their ability to be in several places at once, at least in their minds. Meditators remind us that approaching life in such a mentally scattered fashion forces us to miss many moments of joy. Instead, we could view many activities as ends in themselves. Walking, working in a garden, talking to friends, eating delicious food, and even washing the dishes can become fulfilling activities in their own right. The key is to do them with focused awareness.

A second meditation practice helps us gain precise understanding about what goes on in our minds and bodies. Often we go through life with only a dim awareness of the nature of our thoughts and feelings. Through paying close attention we learn that feelings and thoughts are constantly changing, that we don't have to become attached to any individual pleasure or desperately try to avoid any discomfort. While paying close attention to constantly changing pleasure or pain, we can experience a sense of spaciousness and freedom. The highs are sweeter, the lows don't last as long.

Third, meditation involves an attitude of acceptance. While meditating, we don't have to censor any thought or resist any feeling. Events taking place in the mind and body simply float to our awareness. We can assist the process by refusing to judge them or repress them. There are many different ways to meditate. Any of them can open the door to a wonderful new dimension in our lives. Following are a few guidelines.

Make a commitment

Most of the benefits of meditation come from doing it *regularly*. The fragmented schedules and general hustle and bustle of life can make it difficult to do anything regularly.

Write your intention down. Be specific about when and where you will meditate. Practice for at least 20 minutes a day.

Pay attention to your breathing

Sit in a comfortable position with your spine erect. Notice your breath as it flows gently in and out of your body. Imagine yourself breathing *in* calmness, relaxation, and well-being. Visualize yourself breathing *out* frustrations, tensions, and negative emotions.

Notice thoughts

Thoughts will continue to pop into your head as you meditate. Notice them and let them go. You also can concentrate on something to lessen distractions. Silently repeat a word or phrase that has special meaning for you. Stare at a candle flame or at a point on the wall or floor. Each time a thought enters, let it float away like a stray cloud in an endless sky.

Notice feelings

Some people think that meditation is all about feeling good, getting blissfully spaced out, or dozing off. Actually, the essence of meditation is learning to become fully aware and to bring any feeling into sharp focus.

While you meditate, you might feel strong, negative emotions. Anger, sadness, anxiety, or fear may come to the surface. That's fine. The idea is to fully allow and experience any feeling, pleasant or unpleasant.

As we do this over time, compulsions and other negative emotions start to lose their grip on us. We discover that the very habit of repressing certain thoughts and feelings gives them a kind of power. We begin to free up a lot of energy when we change this habit.

Meditate at the same time and place

When you're consistent about doing an activity in one location, at one time of day, your body and mind know what to expect. If you don't have a special place to meditate, then set up other signals: Wear a special shirt, light a candle, burn incense, or play certain music.

Consider taking a class

Local spiritual organizations, meditation centers, YMCA's, and community education programs teach a variety of meditation styles, which can involve additional elements such as movement or prayer. Meditating with other people gives you a powerful incentive to learn and practice this valuable technique.

Focus your awareness (JOURNAL ENTRY)

To say that focusing awareness is simple does not mean that it's easy.
You can verify this for yourself.

Tell yourself that for the next two minutes you will close your eyes
and pay attention to nothing but the feeling of your clothing on your body.
You won't think about sex, or about calling your cousin in Des Moines,
or about all the things you need to get done today.

Go ahead. Do this right now.

Follow up by writing in the space below what you just learned
about your ability to focus your attention.

I discovered that I …

_____

_____

_____

Genius is in the details

Life often hinges on the little things.

A one-hundred-mile hike begins with one step.

Friendships are developed one small interaction at a time.

Books are written word by word, sentence by sentence, page by page.

A mansion is built board by board, brick by brick, and a massive garden begins with a single flower.

Corporate dynasties are built on one decision and one action at a time. Managing even the largest enterprise involves attending to the smallest details with consummate care.

Create your life with moment-to-moment choices

Maybe one shortcoming of many self-improvement schemes is that they concentrate on huge goals—such as happiness, health, love, or wealth—while forgetting how we do the little things: the way we sweep the floor, the way we shut the door when leaving the house, the way we set down a bag of groceries on the kitchen counter, the way we hold our face muscles when listening to another person.

The smallest choices can be as powerful and far-reaching as the largest choices. For example, the way we breathe when feeling distressed, the words we choose to describe a problem, the gestures we make when speaking to a lover—all of these are small choices that we may not even realize we're making in the moment. Yet when added together, all those micro-choices gain the force of a tidal wave that affects everything we have, do, and become.

Major choices in our lives, like who we marry (if we marry) or what career we pursue, can make a huge difference in the quality of our lives. But such big choices are made rarely, while every few minutes we make many small choices.

We can make such choices thoughtfully, in ways that are consistent with what we want in life. The way we choose to live the next moment is the way we live the rest of our lives.

Start small and reap big rewards

Valuable lessons can be learned when we closely examine our moment-to-moment choices. Each day we can take some time to step back and watch ourselves as an outside observer would. We can see our lives played back as films projected on a screen and place ourselves in the audience. From that vantage point, we can take a microscope to everything we say and do.

To use any idea in this book, start with the smallest choices you make every day. If you want to gain better health, for example, then start by changing one small habit such as flossing your teeth daily. If you want to become a better listener, then just listen with full attention to the next person you meet. If you want to practice eating all your food more slowly (so that you eat less at each meal and enjoy it more), then start by eating one bite of food slowly with focused awareness.

If you apply this suggestion, you might notice that small changes start to echo throughout your whole life. If you start by noticing the color of your spouse's shoes, then you might also get better at noticing typos in memos. If you choose to show up at your next meeting a few minutes early, then you might start showing up at all your appointments with time to spare.

When we pay exquisite attention to the small choices as well as the larger ones, our lives can be more in tune with our values. By handling the details with  care, we increase our experience of happiness, health, love, financial security, or whatever else we want in life. By taking baby steps, we can make transformational leaps.

Small change, big difference (JOURNAL ENTRY)

In the space below, describe a routine activity you perform and what it might reveal about how you approach other activities in your life. For example, if you balance your checkbook regularly, you might notice that you faithfully complete other maintenance tasks (such as changing the oil in your car) on a regular schedule.

Complete the following sentences:

The routine activity I perform is …

_____

_____

When comparing this activity to other activities in my life, I discovered that I …

_____

_____

Now describe a small behavior you will change immediately—one that might pave the way for larger changes in your life.

I intend to …

_____

_____

Pay attention to time

Time is the original equal opportunity employer. All of us, regardless of race, creed, or color, get the same amount of time to work with—24 hours per day, 168 hours per week. Time is no more scarce for us than it is for anyone else. Everyone gets the same time "salary."

It's often said that time is money. This statement overlooks a major difference between the two: Money that's lost can often be returned or re-earned. In contrast, time is a nonrenewable resource. Each hour that ticks away is lost, never to be regained. We can deposit money in a bank and store it there to withdraw later. Not so with time.

Imagine a drive-up teller who could dispense time as well as cash. You could speed up to the window and plead for extra time: "I need four more hours to meet a deadline; I'd like to make a withdrawal from my account, please." It won't happen.

So time is valuable. Every moment of time is unique and unrepeatable—a gift that literally comes only once in a lifetime.

The closer attention we pay to time, the more we realize the benefits of managing it. For many, the phrase *time management* calls up images of people on rigid schedules that are planned down to the minute. They fear that managing time will kill their spontaneity and rob them of flexibility.

Actually, using time-management techniques can be a ball. Time management is about freeing up more time for the things that matter most to you, including time for fun and being with the people you love. Few things feel as good as spending your life energy in the ways that you choose.

Begin with being willing to take charge of your time. Ironically, some people are not. They'd rather blame their frustrations, lack of productivity, and unrealized dreams on the demands of others: "I'd have gotten that done a long time ago, but my boss keeps dumping

work on me." "When you have children, you give up having any time for yourself." "I just was born without any skill at time management."

An alternative is to stop blaming others and start taking charge of time. We can learn to say no to the demands of others and to negotiate more realistic expectations. We can choose to free up extra minutes and hours each day. We can distinguish between what merits our time and attention and what's not worth doing at all. With these ideas in mind, we can have the time of our lives.

Following is a cycle of regular activity you can use to get the most out of this precious gift we call time. The cycle includes three steps: monitor, plan, and revise. Taking each step can help you apply the principles of focused awareness and moment-to-moment choice to your experience of time.

Monitor

If you want to take charge of your time, then get a detailed picture of how you currently spend this nonrenewable resource. Many people spend a lifetime without getting this picture. Years and even decades pass, leaving them only to guess where all the time went.

With an accurate account of how we spend our time, we can spot any recurring problems we have with managing time and diagnose them with pinpoint accuracy. Armed with that baseline data, we can make changes in our schedule that free up time for high-priority activities.

For example, someone complains about not having enough time for reading books. After monitoring his activities for several days, he discovers that he spends at least two hours every day watching television. He decides to cut television back to one hour so that he can spend an extra hour reading a book.

Choose a method for monitoring your time that works for you. One option is to summarize your entire day on a single 3x5 card. Simply note the starting and ending times for each major activity.

Other options are to list your daily activities on a calendar or to use computer software that's designed for time management.

Track your time for at least two days. You can learn even more by doing this exercise for a week.

After collecting specific data about

how you use your time, summarize it. Create a list of categories that describe your typical activities: sleeping, eating, grooming, working, watching television, reading, and so on. Then total up the number of hours you spent in each category.

Plan

Imagine the woodcutter who constantly claims that she's too busy to sharpen her axe. She may get a lot of work done in the short term. However, her productivity will eventually drop to zero unless she takes the time to care for her equipment.

Many people cut furiously at the "trees" nearest them without taking the time to get an overall view of the forest or take care of their tools. They spend the bulk of their time reacting to crises, urgent phone calls, and other species of disaster. In the process, they forget about important but nonurgent activities such as exercise, cooking nutritious meals, meditation, prayer, or spending time with the people they love.

We can avoid this fate by creating a comprehensive vision for our lives—by writing a life purpose, choosing our values, and setting long-range goals. Then we can practice planning the short-term future by creating daily or weekly to-do lists that align with our vision. Planning from the long-term to the short-term helps us stop putting out fires and start living the life we choose.

Revise

When mid-week rolls around, you might find that your weekly plan needs to be changed. Perhaps some activities are taking twice as long as you expected. Or maybe a scheduled event was canceled. When these things happen, feel free to revise your plan.

Some people are afraid to do this. To them, revising a plan feels like admitting they've made a mistake. What's actually involved here is *updating* your plan based on the latest feedback. Plans that are regularly fine-tuned can be the most useful.

This fine-tuning is a strategy that you can practice for a lifetime. As you do, play with the following options.

Expand, then contract. Regularly ask yourself *What do I want to accomplish in the next two weeks?* You'll probably come up with a long to-do list. To avoid being overwhelmed, first estimate the number of hours each task will take. (Be realistic.) Then narrow your list down to the items that are the most urgent and most important.

You might want to block some time in your calendar for handling your "A+ activities"—those with the highest priority. Remember to make dates with yourself for recreation, reading, exercising, and other self-renewing activities. These activities are as important as anything else you put on your calendar.

Schedule fixed commitments first. Sleep, work, housework—such activities tend to concentrate themselves in blocks of time. These activities can become so routine that we take them for granted and fail to account for them in our plans. When planning, allow adequate time for regular, fixed commitments. Then schedule other tasks around them.

Expect the unexpected. Include time for errands, travel, and surprises. Errands include low-visibility and easy-to-forget activities—runs to the post office to buy stamps, last-minute trips to the grocery store, and commuting time between appointments. To avoid being rushed, leave breathing space in your schedule for these events.

Get it done, one task at a time. The loftiest long-term goals are accomplished in the same way as your goals for next week: completing one task after another. As you plan, convert any ambitious goal into a list of small steps—simple activities that you can add to a daily to-do list.

Put your activities into "containers." Activities tend to fill up whatever space is allotted to them. By allowing less space for them on our calendars, we can often increase our efficiency.

Set clear starting and stopping times for each task. Sometimes a task that normally takes three hours can be completed in two.

Get back to your purpose. If you did the "Live from a purpose" journal entry earlier in this book, you have in hand a powerful tool for sane scheduling.

Use your purpose as a device for screening out activities and commitments that are out of alignment with your values and deepest desires. For example, if your life purpose is to practice and promote health, then schedule time for exercise. You might choose to bump or eliminate a lower-priority activity (such as watching television) in order to do this.

That's fine. You're demonstrating the power of a life purpose.

At any point in the day, you can recall your purpose statement and major life goals. Then ask *What would a person with this mission do this month? This week? Today?* You might get answers that are not on your to-do lists.

That's fine. You're not a robot that's programmed to blindly follow orders.

With your long-term vision firmly in mind, you can make moment-to-moment choices that bring you most directly to the life of your dreams.

Match your values and time (JOURNAL ENTRY)

This journal entry is designed to help you discover whether you're satisfied with the way you currently spend time. You can make a distinction between tasks you freely choose to do and tasks that represent obligations imposed by others.

This journal entry has several parts, each to be completed at certain points during a single day. On a separate sheet of paper, write your responses to each numbered item below.

1. When you awake for the day, ask yourself if you really want to get up. Quickly list the things you look forward to doing—the activities that make it worthwhile for you to get out of bed.
2. Ask a few questions as you sit down to each meal. Are you truly hungry and ready to eat? Do you want to eat the food that's in front of you? Will you feel energized by the food you're about to eat?
3. As you go about your daily activities, ask "Would I choose to do this if I was financially independent, free of the need to work for a living?"
4. After conversing with someone, ask yourself "Did I truly want to be with this person? If I could have spent time with someone else, who would that person be?"
5. After work, review your plans for the rest of the day. Ask "Do I consider the activities I'm about to engage in to be worthwhile? If I had only six months to live, would I do anything different with the remaining time in my day?"

Next, sum up your responses by completing the following sentences:

When thinking about the degree of alignment between my values and my activities today, I discovered that I ...

_____

_____

In order to bring my activities more in line with my values, I intend to ...

_____

_____

Come back to this journal entry periodically and note how your responses change over time.

Pay attention to money

One purpose of learning about personal finance is to manage your money instead of letting money manage you.

It's totally appropriate to have money, but many people let money have *them*. For these people, worries about money take up an inordinate amount of time and emotional energy.

To get past those worries, pay attention. This means knowing down to the penny how much money you earn, spend, and invest. With this knowledge you can make moment-to-moment choices about finances that align with your values.

As you start managing the details of your money life, you can also start waving goodbye to many money worries. You might even discover—as have some people interested in voluntary simplicity—that you can live on one-half your income or even less.

The same three-step cycle that helps you pay attention to your time can also help you pay attention to your money. Those steps—monitor, plan, and revise—are explained next.

Monitor

If you want to manage money effectively, then begin by telling the truth. Discover exactly how much money you spend and make every month. Befriend the data.

The important thing is not how much money you *earn*—it's how much you truly *need* to live the life of your dreams. And that might be far less than you imagine at first. Solutions begin to appear when you practice honesty about your current income and expenses—whatever they are.

Create specific categories for keeping track of how much you spend and earn each month. Track your expenses in categories such as housing, groceries, restaurants, entertainment, gifts, and interest payments. Also record your income in categories—for example, wages, salaries, tips, inheritances, interest payments from bonds, stock dividends, and capital gains.

As you gain skill in monitoring income and expenses, watch the fog roll out of your money life. There's power in knowing the details.

Plan

For many people, the phrase "mastery of money" means learning fabulous and fool-proof ways to increase their income. This is the "more money in" school of thought about personal finance.

Increasing income might seem to offer a final solution to money worries, at least for a while. But people often discover that their expenses increase to meet—or even exceed—their increased income. Hello again, debt city.

An alternative is to practice the "less money out" school of thought by reducing or eliminating expenses that contribute little or nothing to your purpose, values, and goals.

It's not rocket science. If you spend less while maintaining a steady income, you'll have more money on hand. You can even remain fulfilled and satisfied with your life as your spending decreases. A pared-down lifestyle offers many potential joys: fewer possessions to maintain, fewer loan payments with crippling interest charges, and less pressure to work at a job that pays well but scores high on the misery index. Add to that the pleasure of having a comfortable cushion of cash savings, and you just might sleep better, too.

One way to spend less money is to develop a plan for spending your money, also called a budget. Create one budget for the short-term (usually the next month) and another one for the long-term (a year or more from now). Determine in advance how much money you'll want for major, periodic expenses such as insurance premiums or income taxes. Budget for the routine expenses—things like housing, food, and clothing. Also budget for unexpected expenses, such as prescription medications or car repairs.

Once you predict in advance how much money you need, you can begin setting that amount aside. Budgets offer one way to avoid unpleasant surprises.

Revise

If you're determined to revise your spending habits, you'll find plenty of ways to do so. Remember that changing money habits is an ongoing process, so give it time. In addition to budgeting, you can experiment with the following strategies.

Weed out expenses that fail the "values test." Clarify exactly what you want to gain from working and having money to spend. Each month, review what you earn and spend. Get the specific figures.

Then ask *Does money flow in and out of my life in ways that are consistent with my values? Does the way I earn and spend money allow me time for the activities I consider most worthwhile?*

Go after the big fish first. If you want to make a real dent in your expenses, look to the big-ticket items. Notice what you spend the most money on each month.

Many people write their biggest checks for car payments and rent or mortgage payments. See what you can do to reduce these expenses.

If you own two cars, consider getting along with one. You can use public transportation, take cabs, walk, ride a bike, or even rent a car when you're in a crunch.

When looking for a place to live, consider a more modest house or apartment. Shy away from major urban areas where housing costs border on astronomical. Rent, share a house, or buy a duplex and rent half.

Pay yourself first. You are as valuable as your car, your house, and all the other things you pay for each month. So pay yourself each month, and do it first.

Another name for the money you pay yourself is savings. This is the money you invest in your future.

If you wait until the end of the month to set aside your savings, you might end up with only pocket change to spare. Instead, pay yourself as soon as you get your paycheck. Right up front, before you have a chance to spend it, put 10 percent (or more) of your take-home pay into an insured savings account or another safe place. Save this money first, and you may not even miss it.

Consider saving enough to have a comfortable cushion—six months' worth of your regular income. That way you can stay in charge of your money even if you lose your job; face a major, unexpected expense; or just want to take some time off.

After you've got a cushion, save for education, retirement, and other long-term financial goals.

Put on a lid on plastic. To keep your spending in line, use credit cards only as a substitute for carrying cash. Don't use them as a substitute for *having* the cash in the first place. If you pay for something with a credit card, set aside the same amount in cash. Then pay off the balance on your credit card each month.

If you have large credit card balances, remember that many banks offer "bill payer" loans. These are loans that you can use to consolidate all your debts and pay off your credit cards, often at a lower interest rate. Applying for these loans can be a wonderful reminder to curtail your credit card purchases in the future.

Buy it for less. You might be able to save hundreds of dollars on a sound system or thousands of dollars on a car by shopping around. Keep a lookout for sales, price wars, discount stores, coupons, and estate sales. If you're sending children to college, consider a public school over a private one. These are just a few examples of trimming your expenses with little extra effort and still getting the things you want.

Get the same benefit for less. Before plunking down your hard-earned cash, ask *What benefit will spending this money get me?* Go beneath the obvious payoff to the hidden benefit.

Say that you're attracted to a posh new car on the salesroom floor. Ask yourself *What's the benefit of owning this item?* The obvious answer is that you get a car to drive. Behind that payoff, however, is the true benefit, which is having access to a reliable source of transportation.

With that answer, you can brainstorm other ways to get the same benefit without buying that car. Going for a less expensive new car, a late-model used car, or a bus ride might deliver the benefit you're really after.

Don't buy it yet. If you're a procrastinator, use this habit as a tool to avoid spending. Keep putting off the purchase, and you might discover yourself living the life of your dreams without that precious item.

If this doesn't work for you, experiment with a cooling-off period before major purchases. Consider allowing one hour of waiting time for every ten dollars of purchase price. It's amazing how frivolous that new pair of pants might seem five hours from now.

Leave your cash in the bank. One way to spend less is to have less money in your pocket. Keep $100 dollars of spare cash in your billfold, and you're likely to spend it all over the next few days or weeks. Put a $20 bill in its place, and you might discover yourself skipping that extra ice-cream cone or twice-weekly dose of burgers and fries at Cow Kingdom.

Fix things yourself. Over the course of a year, bills for plumbers, carpenters, and mechanics can add up to hundreds or thousands of dollars.

Of course, it's often wise to hire out household jobs that go beyond your current skills. Another option is to increase your skills and learn to fix things yourself. You may not be able to do a full-fledged tune-up on your car, but you could learn to change the oil, rotate the tires, or replace the battery. That might save you the going rate for parts and labor at your local garage.

Look for the hidden expenses in eating. Many people would be amazed to find out what they spend on fast food and pizza during the year. Those extra doses of fat, calories, and cholesterol can drain your pockets with lightning speed.

You can avoid such unnecessary food expenses by cooking for yourself, shopping for food *after* you eat, bagging your own lunch, and avoiding snacks. The benefits of changing these habits are likely to show up in improved health as well as in decreased spending.

Match your values and money (JOURNAL ENTRY)

Begin this journal entry by gathering at least 100 blank 3x5 cards. On these cards, write expenses that you incurred during the last month. List one expense on each card— for example, "Rent: $600."

Next, create a list of your fundamental values. List these values on 3x5 cards also, one value per card. Examples of values include health, happiness, contribution, fun, integrity, and so on.

Now sort your cards. See if you can pair every expense card with a value card. For example, the $15 you spent on a health club membership last month could fit with the value of health. You might have to set up a miscellaneous stack of cards for expenses that do not fit under any of your values.

Afterward, in the space below complete the following sentences:

In comparing my values and expenses, I discovered that I ...

_____

_____

_____

To bring my future spending more in line with my values, I intend to ...

_____

_____

_____

LISTEN FULLY

It is the province of knowledge to speak, and it is the privilege of wisdom to listen.

OLIVER WENDELL HOLMES

Listening—a way of life

Most people think that listening is what we do when someone else talks. Actually, we can expand the meaning of the word *listen*. Listening in a larger sense means receiving everything at all times.

Listening can be a way of life, an attitude toward all things, an open posture to the world. We can listen fully to the joy and pain of other people, to our thoughts and emotions, to our bodies, to nature, to music, to circumstances, to the lessons of the past, to our dreams of the future, and much more.

The *American Heritage Dictionary* defines the word *listen* this way: "To make a conscious effort to hear; to pay attention; to heed...." Listening fully means paying exquisite, close attention.

When you pay attention, your world gets bigger. You can see this for yourself. Just put this book down for two minutes. Close your eyes and notice everything you hear at this moment. Next, open your eyes and notice all the colors you see.

Congratulations. You've just entered a new world, larger and far richer in sights and sounds than the world you inhabited two minutes ago. Of course, you didn't physically go anywhere—you just opened up your field of awareness. The difference between your former and your present state might be as sharp as the difference between waking and sleeping.

Listening means receiving whatever the world is "sending." And at any given moment, the world is sending plenty—thousands of tastes, sights, aromas, sounds, textures, ideas, and bits of information just waiting to be noticed. There's the shaft of sunlight streaming in the bedroom window, the sight of a full moon on a clear summer night, the fresh scent of the earth after a rainstorm, the sound of a sleeping baby's breathing, the wave of pleasure that spreads through your body when you bite into your favorite food. If we're not careful and conscious, we might tune out this symphony of sights, sounds, and sensations. Then there's listening to our intuition— a way of knowing that goes beyond logic and evidence. Using our intuition means tuning in to the still, small voice inside us as we make choices. Often we call that voice a hunch, lucky guess, inspiration, discovery, or *aha!* When people who face a major decision talk about "sleeping on it," they're allowing time for their intuition to speak.

We can also listen for guidance from deeper inside us or beyond us. For many people, spirituality means listening to God, Nature, the Creator, a Higher Power— whatever you wish to call the force that helps you see the sacred in the everyday and moves you to care about others.

When we adopt listening as a way of life, we create an invitation for the world to "speak" to us. When people sense that we're receptive to their ideas and feelings, they feel safe to open up.

Of course, we can always offer a literal invitation. We can ask them to speak about anything from their last vacation to their most intimate concerns. And we can deepen that invitation through listening with full attention and full acceptance—that is, full love.

When we understand that listening means receiving everything, we discover that there's a lot to hear.

wake up to the world (JOURNAL ENTRY)

For one minute, make an effort to list everything you see, hear, smell, feel, and taste. On a separate sheet of paper, write as quickly as you can, jotting down notes in single words or short phrases. Don't worry about making a complete or accurate list. Simply capture in words whatever you can in the available time.

After one minute is up, pause briefly and relax. Then review your list. Circle any sights, sounds, or other sensations you do not normally notice. After doing this and waking up to a new world, complete the following sentences:

I discovered that I …

_____

_____

_____

_____

_____

I intend to …

_____

_____

_____

_____

_____

_____

Strategies for full listening

Full listening springs from a mind that says *I don't know it all* and *There is more for me to learn*. Listening in this way can be an adventure.

Full listening can also be scary. Listening fully means putting all our opinions on the line and asking if they are accurate or useful. Listening fully means opening up to the ideas of others and being willing to change. When we listen fully, we let go of the way we think things are supposed to be. For the moment, we let go of everything we think we know.

It's no wonder that full listening is so rare. Many people are so comfortable with and committed to their opinions that they simply shut down and stop listening.

By refusing to risk full listening, these people miss the potential rewards. Most of us want satisfying relationships. And the quality of our relationships is directly tied to the quality of our listening. People feel acknowledged, appreciated, and affirmed when we listen fully to them. Listening also gives us access to countless new ideas and options for solving problems. Listening well is one of the best ways to get what we want.

The strategies that follow can help us break through to the dimension of full listening.

Remember—communication at best is challenging

Few people devote serious energy to improving their communication skills. Unless there's an obvious barrier—a hearing impairment, a language barrier—people often take communication for granted.

Consider a simple word like *chair*. Upon hearing this word, some of us immediately think of the standard four-legged object sitting next to a kitchen table. Others think of a large stuffed recliner. Then there are rocking chairs, folding chairs, swivel chairs, highchairs, antique wooden chairs, leather chairs, poolside aluminum chairs, and electric chairs. Let's not forget the person leading a club meeting or taking charge of the board of directors. She's a *chair*, too. The deluxe second edition of *Webster's New Universal Unabridged Dictionary* gives us yet another definition of *chair:* "an iron block used to support and secure the rails of a railway track."

If simple words like *chair* can be misunderstood, it's easy to see how more complex concepts— such as happiness, health, wealth, love, justice, and freedom—can wreak havoc.

Given the frequency of misunderstanding, it is best *not* to assume that listeners and speakers automatically share the

same message. Remembering this can help us pay closer attention and raise the quality of our listening.

Commit to full listening

Walk up to the self-help shelf at almost any bookstore, and you'll find a row of titles about how to listen better. Many of these books are full of techniques, and many of the techniques are useful.

When it comes to listening fully, something important comes *before* technique. That "something" is commitment—an intention to fully receive what others say. Commitment involves a willingness to completely surrender to the person who's speaking, and this willingness comes into play before we do anything else as listeners.

Be a sender or a receiver

Each of us has an agenda. When we're talking, *our* personal concerns—what *we* want, what *we* need, and what *we're* interested in—are usually on the front burner. The problem is that during most conversations, other people are giving *their* items top priority.

It's no wonder, then, that genuine listening is so rare. We want to cover all the items on our agenda, and others want to do the same with theirs. We're all trying to step up to the podium at the same time. Everyone's talking; no one is listening. Everybody's sending; nobody is receiving. Typical result: confusion.

Effective communication is a two-way street. People take turns sending and receiving. When one person is talking, the other just listens. Then they switch roles. This continues until they discover a shared meaning.

Listen only when you are willing to listen. If you realize you are not listening anymore, you have several options. One is to recommit to listening—to focus your awareness and listen. Another option is to tactfully leave the conversation. And still another is to make a direct request to switch roles and become the sender. If you do start sending, ask yourself how you can best use this precious gift—another person's listening.

In any case, either send *or* receive. Trying to do both at the same time can strain relationships. When you're listening, be quiet 98 percent of the time. The other 2 percent of the time, you can ask occasional questions for clarification or make comments that encourage the speaker to continue.

Wait before responding

Consider a typical conversation. Moments of silence are rare. As soon as person A takes a breath, person B jumps in. While person A was still speaking, person B was not really listening. Instead, he was preparing his remarks— "listening" with his answer running.

One strategy that can prevent this fate is the almighty pause. Before sending your message, allow a few moments of silence.

This strategy springs from a commitment to listen. When we are truly intent on listening, we usually digest what's being said and *then* choose what we'll say. We postpone our response until *after* the sender has come to a complete stop and we've taken time to understand her message.

In some cases, you can promote the speaker's full self-expression by postponing your response for more than a minute or two. If you found the message difficult to receive—or if you sense that the speaker found it difficult to send—then consider waiting several hours or even several days before you respond. The more difficult the message, the longer the optimum waiting time.

Postponing your response slows down a conversation. It helps ensure that conversations include both a sender and a receiver. This can cool tempers and increase understanding.

Ask for more

You might come to points in a conversation at which the sender stops speaking for the moment. But that doesn't always mean she's done sending her message. Perhaps she's just pausing and has more to say.

To promote full listening, make a habit of listening until you're sure you've heard everything the speaker has to say. Then permit even more speaking. Ask, "Is there anything else on your mind?"

Listen actively

One way to promote accurate communication is active listening. When we listen actively, we repeat in our own words what we *thought* the speaker said. At that point, the speaker can make any corrections that seem appropriate: "No that's not quite it. What I really meant to say was...." Or "You got it. Couldn't have said it better myself."

Active listening can be particularly useful in defusing arguments. When emotions run high, be sure to verify that you received the speaker's message. Summarize what you heard without judging it. Then fully allow any correction the speaker might make.

If we pay close attention as we practice active listening, we're likely to notice an almost universal signal of understanding. After we sum up their message, people nod their heads and say, "Yeah."

Listen through a filter

While listening actively, you might find it useful to listen through a filter—that is, to focus on certain aspects of the speaker's message.

For example, instead of focusing on the speaker's problems, you could listen specifically for any solutions he proposes. Instead of focusing on the speaker's past, you could listen for that person's vision of the future—what he wants and how he intends to get it.

Those are just two examples. You could also listen for the speaker's values, joys, strengths, confidences, requests, contributions, or anything else you choose to notice.

Listen as if you're the only listener

When you're in a group conversation, imagine that there are only two people in the room: you and the speaker. You're sitting front row, center—an audience of one. Your listening skills could rise to new heights. You'll automatically apply many of the listening techniques explained in this chapter.

Handle distractions

Even when you're fully committed to listening, you can find your thoughts wandering. If possible, write the distraction down. This can be useful when your thoughts involve an errand to run, a call to make, or something else to do later. Then you can return your focus to the conversation.

You might explain what you're doing so that you don't seem rude: "Excuse me just one moment. I'm distracted and need to make a note about something. Then I can pay attention to what you are saying."

Often you can handle distractions simply by noticing them and gently bringing yourself back to full listening.

Listen with two minds

First, listen with a receptive mind. Such a mind is still, calm, and open to fresh ideas. Full listening begins when we dip into this mind, keep our mouths shut, and channel all our effort into understanding another person.

When listening with a receptive mind, we simply assume that what we're hearing is the truth—from the other person's point of view. If we hear an idea that shocks or disturbs us, we ask ourselves *What if that's true?* and explore the possibilities.

There's another kind of mind that comes into play later. This second mind is questioning and critical. When we listen with this mind, we ask ourselves *What does this mean? What's the evidence? Is this idea logical?* We separate ideas that are inaccurate from those that are accurate and useful.

Listening fully calls for both of these minds. One without the other is incomplete. Just separate them in time. First, listen fully without judgment. When you're confident that you've received and understood the message, then you can take time to think critically.

Focus on the message, not the messenger

Most of us find it easy to stop listening when something about a speaker irritates us. If the speaker wears a lime-green leisure suit or has multicolored neon hair, we might become so busy judging his appearance that we stop listening.

One solution is to listen beyond the speaker. We can focus on the content of the message rather than the speaker's style, age, or appearance. When we do this, we might discover that the person who stutters has something important to say, or that the kindergartner who's too young to "know" anything has a fresh and useful outlook.

We can listen for kernels of wisdom from the people we disagree with the most. These might include Democrats, Republicans, lesbians, Christians, atheists, career army officers, pacifists, or anyone else. The person we loathe the most might actually have something useful to say to us.

Remember that understanding is not agreeing

Understanding and agreeing are two different things. As full listeners, our job is to totally understand the other person's point of view. Listening means receiving an accurate version of the message the other person is sending to us. Once we understand that message, we're free to respond in any way we choose. And one possible response is to disagree.

In confrontational situations, when they feel defensive, people often act as if careful listening is a sign of weakness. They fear that taking the time to understand another's viewpoint means giving up their own. That's a mistake.

It is a challenge to put our own ideas on the shelf so that we can listen carefully, showing a genuine intention to understand a new point of view. Yet skilled listeners do this routinely. Successful debaters can argue their opponents' point of view as well as or better than their opponents. This does not mean that they agree with their opponents.

Avoid "piggybacking" and counterpointing

Soon after my mother died, a friend came up to me and asked, "How are you?" I was still very emotional and thought that his question was an indication that he would listen to my response. So I said, "Thanks for asking. My mom died, and it's been hard for me. I was very close to her."

"Oh, I know just how you feel," he said. "When my father died, it was so traumatic. Let me tell you about it...."

That's an example of piggybacking. It happens when a listener suddenly stops listening, jumps on the speaker's topic, and starts talking.

Piggybacking can also happen when you talk about things you enjoy.

One of my daughters tried out for a prestigious dance school and was accepted. "Dancing is the love of her life," I said to another friend of mine, "and I actually didn't think she'd make it. But she did, and when it happened I felt...."

"Wow," my friend said. "You must feel great. I know that when my kids achieve things, I feel so good! In fact, I remember a time when...."

Many people might intend for their piggybacking to be a way to communicate their empathy with the speaker. Too often, however, piggybacking simply interrupts people and discounts their experience. To listen fully, avoid piggybacking.

Also notice counterpointing. This happens when a listener suddenly stops listening to state her disagreement with the speaker. Often this happens in the middle of the speaker's message—before he has had a chance to fully express his point of view.

To avoid piggybacking and counterpointing, simply wait until it's your turn to speak. Pick up on the speaker's topic or state your disagreement only after you've listened fully and you're certain that this is the most important thing you want to say.

Be careful of advice

As we listen to others, we might feel tempted to give advice. Giving advice, however, is not listening.

Trust people to arrive at their own solutions without your guidance as a listener. Consider offering advice only when people specifically request it, and then present your ideas as possibilities, not prescriptions.

Be careful of questions

Questions are often useful. For people committed to full listening, questions also have serious potential drawbacks.

Questions can be used to guide conversations and pull them in a certain direction—a direction that the speaker might not want to take. When listening fully, we ask questions rarely—only to clarify a speaker's message. When questions steer a conversation or smuggle advice into a conversation, they hinder listening.

Listen without obligation to act

When people talk about what they desire, they're not automatically asking for a response on your part. If your partner says that she'd like to vacation in Hawaii sometime, that doesn't mean you have to book tickets tomorrow. She might just want to speak her desires, sort them out, and explore possibilities.

When we listen to people's desires, we don't *have* to do anything about them. Knowing this frees us to listen fully. If we feel obligated to leap into action every time people open their mouths, we could feel overwhelmed and actually avoid listening.

Often people don't *want* us to do anything in response to their speaking. They just want to think out loud, or they simply want to be heard. We can grant them the gift of full listening.

Once in a while, people do want us to respond by moving into action. When that's true, they'll usually say so.

If you're not sure, you can always check it out: "You've told me something that you want. Can I do anything to help you get it?"

Listen with your body

People gather a great deal of information by observing our facial expressions, gestures, and posture. Remembering this can open a new dimension in our listening. We can use body language that invites other people to speak. When we make eye contact and face the other speaker directly, we're usually saying, "I'm awake, I'm here, and I'm interested in what you have to say."

Eyes, in particular, have been referred to as windows to the soul. Often we gain insight into what other people really mean by noticing their eyes. Eyes that meet ours squarely and directly usually mean one thing; eyes cast downward or to the side can mean quite another.

To get the most from this suggestion, temper it with some cultural sensitivity. Many of us find intense prolonged eye contact uncomfortable. And in some cultures, direct eye contact is sometimes considered offensive or a sign of disrespect. While paying attention to people with our eyes, we can act appropriately.

Allow and encourage emotion

Some listeners are uncomfortable when the person speaking expresses strong emotion. A person might be talking about his sadness and start to sob uncontrollably. Someone listening with an intention to comfort him, might say, "Please don't cry. It will all turn out OK."

Another speaker might be so enthusiastic that she celebrates her feelings with total abandon. She might laugh loudly, sing, or even break into a dance. Her friends might become embarrassed by this level of celebration and ask her to control herself.

Full listening means allowing and even encouraging others to express whatever they feel. We can tell them that it's fine if they laugh, shake, sing, sob, or express any other emotion, no matter how intense. When we grant this permission, we allow people to celebrate pleasant emotions and move beyond unpleasant ones. Both can be healing experiences.

Say your thanks

One effective way to follow up on full listening is to say, "Thanks for telling me. Now I know what you think and how you feel." This affirms the speaker and grants him permission to speak even more.

We can speak our thanks even when we disagree with people or feel threatened by what they say. By saying thanks, we put our judgments on hold and step away from antagonism.

The way we send thanks is important. If we say, "Thanks, I'm glad to know how *you* see the world," others might hear that as a subtle put-down.

To be present when people speak their fears, dreams, desires, and commitments is to stand on sacred ground. When people ask us to listen, they honor us. We can respond with gratitude.

Send or receive (EXERCISE)

This exercise helps to slow down conversations and ensure that genuine communication is taking place. It is especially useful when there's a potential for arguments or misunderstanding.

Find a partner who is willing to participate in this exercise with you. Then get two 3x5 cards. Label one card "sender" and the other "receiver." Ask your partner to take one card; you take the other.

The person with the "sender" card gets to speak first. While the sender speaks, the receiver's job is to just listen fully.

Next, trade cards so that you switch roles. But do this only after the original sender feels she's been fully understood.

You can switch cards—and roles—as often as you'd like. The point is to be conscious of your role in any given moment—to simply send *or* receive without trying to do both at the same time.

After doing this exercise, reflect on your experience with separating the roles of sender and receiver. Writing on a separate sheet of paper, describe what you learned about yourself as a listener. Also describe what it was like to receive the gift of full listening.

practice listening (JOURNAL ENTRY)

Enter into your next conversation with an intense commitment to full understanding.
For the moment, forget about listening techniques or exercises. Just aim to understand
another person's viewpoint as skillfully as you can. Do not worry about criticizing
or responding to this viewpoint.

After the conversation, consider your listening skill. Perhaps you created some new listening
techniques on the spot—simply from your commitment to understand. Describe in the space
below how well you listened and specifically what you did while listening. Also describe
any ways you intend to listen differently in the future.

I discovered that I ...

_____

_____

_____

_____

_____

I intend to ...

_____

_____

_____

_____

_____

Befriend criticism and complaints

Almost anyone who suggests a new idea, challenges the status quo, or takes action to meet goals will get criticized.

It's a good bet you will face criticism and complaints at some point—and you won't like it. Fortunately, you can work creatively with both types of feedback.

Treat criticism as feedback, not failure

If we keep our egos out of the way, we can accept criticism as an opportunity to evaluate ourselves. When we find truth in the criticism, we can learn ways to improve. We can move from thinking *How dare she say that!* to *How can I use this comment to become more effective?*

Imagine hearing someone say, "You're always late to our club meetings." Instead of taking that comment as an insult, we can hear it as the front end of a suggestion: "If you want to support the group, then be on time." We can use the comment to promote our success.

When we experience criticism in this way, we can actually be thankful for the gift it offers. Leo Tolstoy used to read drafts of his novels to his hired workers, seeking to make sure that his writing was clear. He received so much constructive criticism that he became one of the world's greatest novelists. Advertising executive David Ogilvy used to circulate drafts of his memos to colleagues with the note, "Please improve." His willingness to receive criticism built him a business empire and a fortune.

Put criticism into perspective

Blowing criticism out of proportion is self-defeating. Putting criticism into perspective allows us to hear it with more clarity.

One way we inflate the significance of criticism is to identify with the criticism. We hear the comment "You screwed that up," and translate it to mean "You *are* a screw-up." The difference is subtle but significant. The first comment points out that we *made* a mistake. The second one implies that we *are* a mistake. Remembering this distinction can help us put criticism into perspective.

We can also acknowledge and accept what we do well. Imagine that you give a performance and 100 people evaluate it. Seventy-nine of the reviews are positive, thirteen of them are neutral, and eight of them are negative. Many of us will spend more time remembering the negative evaluations than celebrating those that are positive. We might even lose sleep over those eight negatives.

Putting criticism into perspective means telling the truth. And telling the truth means celebrating what we've done well and acknowledging where we can improve.

The purpose of receiving criticism is to learn and grow. We do not need to use it as a weapon to berate or punish ourselves.

Avoid defending with denial, anger, or humor

Many people react to criticism by denying it, by becoming angry and attacking the person who is criticizing, or by making jokes. These strategies are designed to defend against attack. They compromise our ability to accept criticism as a gift.

There are two main problems with denial, anger, or evasive humor. First, they prevent honest reflection and self-evaluation. We cannot defend ourselves from criticism and engage in honest self-reflection at the same time.

Second, when we react with denial, anger, or jokes, we decrease the chances of receiving useful feedback in the future. After people run into our defenses, they're less likely to speak candidly next time.

Choose your response to criticism

Ultimately, we get to decide what to do with criticism. If we find some value in it, we can choose the next step to take in response. If we find no value in the criticism, we can thank others for their concern and let the comment go. The point is that we always have a choice.

Instead of being critical of criticism, we can develop a new habit of listening fully and absorbing it. We can take what we find useful and leave the rest behind.

Listen for the feeling in a complaint

When a person who is complaining feels that he's fully heard and understood, his upset often decreases. He's more likely to hear other points of view and discuss solutions. As listeners, we can help this happen by heeding the feelings that underlie the content of the complaint.

Consider a woman who says to her husband, "You spend most of your weekends watching sports on TV."

"So you're saying I shouldn't watch any sports?" he responds.

"That's not true," she fires back. "You're missing the whole point."

All the ingredients of an argument are coming together here. She feels ignored. He feels confused and defensive.

The problem can be avoided if he responds to the feeling in her complaint: "I understand that you're upset about me watching sports. You seem hurt."

"Right," she says. "The truth is, I really don't mind you watching sports. I'd also like it if you would spend some time with me and the kids on the weekends. Could you find a way to do both?"

Now the conversation is moving toward a resolution—one in which everyone in the family wins. What made the difference was listening for the feeling in the complaint.

Listen for the request in a complaint

In addition to finding feelings in a complaint, we can discover hidden requests as well.

"We never go out for romantic evenings any more" can be translated into "Can we go out for a romantic evening?"

"We always run out of money at the end of the month" can be heard as "Let's budget our money and find a way to increase our income, reduce our expenses, or both."

Complaints often contain requests. When people forget this, complaints become dead ends that create discomfort and perpetuate discontent.

Hearing the request in a complaint allows us to produce a new result. After extracting the request from a complaint, we might grant the request and promise to fulfill it. Or we might deny it, make a counteroffer, or suggest another way for the speaker to get what he wants. Any of these responses can be far more productive than the usual agreement, judgment, or sympathy that follows complaints.

When we hear a complaint, we might get defensive. If we listen for the request in a complaint, we can pave the way for solutions. One measure of excellence in listening is our ability to move from complaints to requests and then to action. By listening carefully for requests, we can turn even casual complaints into powerful commitments.

Find the request in a complaint (EXERCISE)

The next time you hear a complaint, see if you can find the request embedded in the complaint. In the space below, summarize the complaint and rephrase it as a request. If appropriate, also note how you intend to respond to the request.

Accept compliments

Some of us are just as uncomfortable receiving compliments as we are receiving criticisms. Many believe that they must discount the compliment in order to avoid appearing conceited:

> "Oh, it was really nothing."
> "It wasn't that good. I goofed up in several places."
> "This old thing? It's such a mess."
> "If you really knew the truth, you wouldn't think what I did
> was so great."
> "Well, thanks, but I really don't deserve it."

As a result, compliments get shut out, and the person who gave the compliment feels discounted.

Accepting a compliment acknowledges both ourselves and the person who offers it. One of the most simple, effective, and graceful ways to accept a compliment is to say, "Thank you. I appreciate that."

Often we receive a compliment for a result that others helped us achieve. When that's true, we can acknowledge the fact. This does not mean dodging the compliment or suggesting that we're unworthy. It does mean telling the truth about others who helped achieve the goal.

We can accept a compliment and at the same time share the credit with others who deserve it.

Success Strategy #8

CHOOSE YOUR CONVERSATIONS

Each person's life is lived as a series of conversations.

DEBORAH TANNER

Our conversations create our world

Right now each of us is awash in a sea of conversations. Our day might start with a conversation with our spouse or children about the fact that it's time to get up. Then we have conversations with coworkers, friends, neighbors, and relatives. We also converse with store clerks, bank tellers, teachers, supervisors, and many others.

Expand your definition of conversation

Now, think about the word *conversation*. This word can mean more than listening and talking to other people. It can just as well apply to the way we interact with books, magazines, movies, television programs, advertisements, and radio programs—any source of ideas or information.

For example, reading a book is like having a conversation. The author is putting across her point of view in words, even though they're written words and not spoken words. As we read, we have reactions to that point of view. (*What a genius. She thinks exactly like I do.*) We might even be so moved that we write the author to initiate a more direct conversation.

Magazines provide another example. The ads start conversations about how we can spend our hard-earned money. Articles beg for our attention. Editorials start conversations that aim to mold our opinions. And in some publications we'll run across "personals," ads from people who want to start a more intimate conversation.

Then there are the conversations that take place inside our own heads. These consist of the constant stream of images and words that flow through our minds. Even though these conversations don't directly involve other people, they can be just as powerful as any other conversation.

So conversations are happening all around us and inside us, just about every moment we're awake. And if we want to think of dreams as a form of conversation, then we're having conversations even when we're *not* awake.

We human beings—always and everywhere— are participating in some form of conversation.

Recognize the power of your conversations

Some conversations serve us well, and others don't. Perhaps you've had some ineffective conversations while standing around the water cooler at work.

"Sure looks like rain today," your coworker says.

"Yup," you say, rolling your eyes. All this guy ever talks about is the weather—and even then, only bad weather.

"I hate rain," he continues. "Rain makes me depressed. Always rains this time of year. And I always get depressed."

Think about how we feel after listening to gripe sessions like this. Or recall how it feels to eat lunch with a bunch of depressed people who complain constantly. Afterward, we probably won't feel empowered or enlivened, ready to sprint back to our desks and do our best work. Some of us might feel more like settling into a blue funk, attacking a punching bag, or taking a nap.

Then think about other conversations we've had—times when we walked away feeling energized, optimistic, and fueled for effective action. Compare those conversations to the blues-at-the-water-cooler conversations. There's a significant difference.

We can spot this difference in other types of conversations, such as movies and television programs. Some of them ignite powerful conversations. Others leave us feeling dulled and spoon-fed or dazed by violence. When we find these conversations insulting or offensive, we have the right to speak our minds to those who are responsible. And we can choose whether to enter those conversations in the first place.

Conversations have a power far beyond what we normally consider. Our words create our consciousness—what we pay attention to and think about. Our consciousness creates our actions, and our actions create our circumstances. The result is the world as we experience it.

So conversations have power. That's an amazing thing to consider, given that most people let themselves drift haphazardly from one conversation to another without much thought, as if none of them mattered.

Enter conversations by choice

Instead of falling into conversations by accident, we can choose them. Knowing that different ways of talking, listening, and thinking lead to different results in our lives, we can start taking charge.

This strategy is especially powerful when we choose conversations that steer us toward our goals and values. If we want to lose weight, we can start conversations with people who want the same result. If we want to exercise regularly, then we can talk with people who have the same objective. It sure beats complaining about the weather.

Sometimes taking charge of conversations calls for diplomacy. If we're in a conversation that goes in a negative direction, we can switch the topic. If that doesn't work, we can make a direct request to talk about something else. And if that still doesn't work, we can often leave the conversation without making a fuss. Even if we do make a fuss, that's probably better than staying in a useless or destructive conversation.

Note: Not all worthwhile conversations have to be lofty. Sometimes chatting about the weather or other small talk puts people at ease. It breaks the ice. It lubricates the conversation so that it can move into other areas.

Manage your community to manage your conversations

By choosing our conversations, we also choose our communities—
the groups of people whose attitudes and behaviors color our lives.

Every community has its own conversations. If we hang around
bowlers, we can reasonably guess that they're going to talk about bowling.
If we hang around people who are training for a marathon, we'll probably
talk about running. And if we hang out with dieters, we'll have conversations
about calories.

If you want to manage the conversations in your life, then manage
your communities. This is one of the main ideas behind alcoholism treatment.
People who stop drinking will tell you that if you want to stop drinking, then
quit going to bars. If you want to stay sober, then hang around other people
who want to stay sober. You can apply the same principle in getting anything
else you want: Just hang around people who have or want the same thing.

You have an infinite variety of conversations and communities to choose
from. You can complain or celebrate. You can criticize or compliment.
You can be in superficial conversations or intimate conversations. You can
be in materialistic or spiritual conversations. Your communities and their
conversations give you your life. And what's cool is that you get to choose.

As a conversation chooser, you might even want to shake things up once
in a while. Experiment with bringing new conversations to your community.
And if the people in your community don't want to be in those conversations,
then you can find a new community.

Ask "What else could I say?"

At any moment, you can choose your conversation. Before speaking,
simply ask yourself *If I choose not to say this, what else could I say?*
At any moment, you can look for something to say that's more fun,
more loving, more generous, or more aligned with your purpose.

You can apply this suggestion to any conversation. Before turning
on the radio or playing a CD, you could ask yourself *If I choose not to listen
to this, what else could I listen to?* And before turning on the television,
you could ask *If I choose not to watch this, what else could I watch?*

You might find it hard to change your internal conversation—that is,
your thinking. If so, just start speaking your thoughts. You'll probably find
it easier to control your lips than to control the constant stream of thoughts
in your head. You can also whip out a pen and start writing. By changing
the content of your speaking or writing, you can also change the content
of your thinking.

Moment by moment, we get to choose our conversations and community.
What's at stake is enormous—everything that we say, hear, watch, listen to,
read, and see. No choices are more powerful than these.

Choose your next conversation (EXERCISE)

Consider the following list of questions as starters for empowering conversations:

What are the three most important things you've learned about getting along with people?

If you could read only 10 books during the rest of your life, what would they be?

Who was your favorite teacher in school, and what was the most important thing you learned from that person?

If you were healthy and financially secure but only had six months to live, what would you do?

What do you want your obituary to say about you?

What is the single most important thing you could do to eliminate world hunger? (Or lower the crime rate? Or ease the threat of nuclear war? Or improve our schools?)

What are the three most important things you want your children to learn?

If you constantly feel pressed for time, then imagine that someone would pay you $10,000 to free up four hours during the next week. The only condition is this: You have to find those extra hours without skipping meals, losing sleep, avoiding major responsibilities, or taking time away from your family and friends. Could you find the extra time? How?

If you constantly feel pressed for money, imagine that your salary was cut by 10 percent. How could you live on the reduced income without sacrificing your overall quality of life? Could you live happily on 25 percent less? 50 percent less?

Another strategy for shifting conversations is to ask people to complete the following sentences. Use them as a springboard to new conversations.

A place I would like to visit is …

The thing I like most about my job is …

My most valued possession is …

One of my secret ambitions is to …

My greatest strength is …

One thing in my life I want to change is …

Advertising—enter the conversation with care

Advertising is an international conversation backed by billions of dollars. And the purpose of this conversation is to change your thinking and your behavior.

The average American is exposed to hundreds of ads per day. On television we see celebrities sipping wine and consuming high-sugar breakfast cereals. We see young men swigging beer, flanked by women in bikinis. Advertisers know that such images can be powerful. By linking their products to scenes of glamour, sexual conquest, and affluence, they hope to alter our everyday choices and actions.

The message underlying much advertising seems to be this: You are not complete unless you own the right deodorant, the right liquor, the right jeans, or the right car. Success is not a matter of who you are or what you do but what you *own* and how you *look.*

For example, many ads imply that happiness means having a young, athletic, thin, tall, gorgeous body. This "body beautiful" conception of happiness excludes millions of people—older people, people with chronic illnesses or disabilities, and anyone who doesn't look like a fashion model.

Advertising agencies might object to these points, claiming that their function is to provide information that helps consumers choose among thousands of products. That can be true. And yet much advertising offers little relevant information that helps us distinguish one brand from another.

Separate fluff from facts

There's an old saying, *caveat emptor,* which is Latin for "let the buyer beware." We can apply this ancient wisdom by entering the advertising conversation with care. You can use the following strategies to separate fluff from fact in advertisements:

- Practice healthy skepticism and critical thinking. While being open to new ideas, also look for the evidence that supports any advertising claim.

- Notice the source of the information. If a study that disputes the addictive property of nicotine comes from a major tobacco company, that's a signal to check out other research. Also beware of reports that quote only one "expert" or celebrity.

- Turn to print as well as television or radio. Many broadcast news shows claim to offer "in-depth reporting." Yet these shows are

often little more than headline services, devoting only a few minutes to any single story. To get the rest of the story, consult books and periodicals. When it comes to conveying detailed, factual information and opposing points of view, print is hard to beat.

• Read letters to the editor. The people who write these letters often provide contrasting opinions and dispute the claims that advertisers make. They can be your allies as you search for information.

Create your own advertisements

You can manage the conversations in your life—and have some fun— by borrowing the high-powered techniques of advertisers. Create words and pictures to reinforce the messages that matter to you.

There are many ways to do this. You can post inspirational quotations on your refrigerator. You can write your goals on 3x5 cards and tape them to your bathroom mirror. You can write your life purpose on a Post-it note and put it in your car. And you can create reminder cards to review daily, weekly, or monthly.

Keep exploring the possibilities. Through screen savers, bumper stickers, posters, billboards, and more, you can create timeless symbols to remind yourself of your core values— what you truly want in life.

Stay aware of conversations (EXERCISE)

In the space below, describe two conversations you've had that were empowering and two that were not.

Now write about how you can choose more powerful conversations today.

Balance your conversation space

Conversation space—if this term is new to you, don't be surprised. It's not common. Yet this term points to a practice that can re-create your everyday conversations and your life.

Conversations occupy many of our waking hours. They take up a lot of space in our lives. And we can make a conscious effort to balance the way we fill that space. To achieve balance, we can experiment with the following five options.

Balance the tenses of your conversations

We can classify conversations according to their focus in time. At any moment, we can ask about the tense of a conversation: *Where is this conversation resting right now—in the past, present, or future?*

Many people fill most of their entire conversation space with the past. They talk about what happened at work or school, about what they did yesterday or the day before. They focus on events that took place minutes, weeks, years, or even decades ago. The same can be said of our mass media. Most television programs, radio shows, newspapers, and magazines dwell on events of the past.

There is a second way that we can occupy our conversation space—focusing on the present. This is the domain of artistry, excellence, and joy. This is the focus of the tennis player at the moment of a great swing, the musician giving a great performance, the mountain climber ascending a sheer cliff. Deep friendship, intimate romance, good meals, enjoyable massage, and great sex occur when we savor the present moment.

Another option is to fill our conversation space with the future. This is the time we spend thinking, writing, reading, listening, planning, and speaking about what's yet to come in our lives.

For many of us, conversations about the future usually focus on what we *predict* will happen or what we *worry* will happen. Talk is seldom about the future that we *want*. Instead, conversation dwells on our fears or on the kind of future we will have if present trends continue.

The way we balance our conversations about the past, present, and future offers potential benefits—and potential problems. For example, people who talk and think mainly about the past might neglect to discuss what they want in the future. People who talk mainly about the present can have the same problem. At the same time, people who dwell on the future could miss talking about lessons from the past or the joy of the present moment. As a person who writes and teaches about creating the future, I sometimes get carried away. I find myself writing so many 3x5 cards about what I want next that I forget to enjoy what I've already created.

The point is that you can balance your conversations about the past, present, and future. And when you are in a conversation about the future, you can devote most of that conversation to creation. Instead of worrying about the future or predicting the future based on current trends, start changing the trends. Write, speak, and think about the future you *want*, the future you *choose* to have.

For most of us, balancing our conversation space means making a concerted effort to dwell more in the future. The following strategies can help:

- *Speak about the future.* Consider adopting a goal: *When I am with people, I will assist them to speak about the future.* We can meet this goal in many ways. One is to set an example—to model the possibility by speaking about the future ourselves. Another strategy is to shift conversations into the future: "For the last hour, we've focused mainly on the past. Can we shift gears for a while and talk about the future instead?"

- *Write about the future.* It's almost impossible to think about the past while writing about the future. When you write, your thoughts can trail your pen into the future.

- *Immerse yourself in the future.* Since many conversations are dominated by the past, you can usefully go overboard in speaking about the future. During the next 24 hours, for example, you could focus most or all of your conversations on the future.

- *Describe your distractions.* When you find yourself distracted with thoughts about the past or worries about the future, write each thought or concern on a 3x5 card. Perhaps you're filled with regret about a mistake you made. Describe that mistake on a card. Perhaps you're worried about an upcoming task. Write that task down. In summary, use cards to capture the distracting conversations you're having with yourself at any given moment. Doing this can help you refocus on the conversation of your choice.

- *Handle your distractions.* Once you've described your distraction on a card, you have several options for what to do next. One option is to file the card away and handle the matter later. You can also destroy the card; this works well with thoughts you don't want—worries, regrets, resentments, and so on. Another option is to flip the card over and write an action plan: Describe, step-by-step, how you will handle the distraction or complete the unfinished task. Or read your card to someone else. See if your distraction goes away when you report it.

- *Balance the long-term future with the short-term future.* Goals that we intend to achieve in five, 10, 20, or more years can start sounding hazy, distant, and vague. To give these goals more immediacy, bring them closer to the present. For example, spend 15 percent of your conversation on a long-term goal and 85 percent on the next step toward that goal— a step you could take today.

Balance the topics of your conversations

So far I've discussed ways to balance the *tenses* of your conversations. In addition, you can balance the *topics* of your conversation. For instance, you can talk about:
- Things (such as jobs, money, houses, books, and ideas)
- Other people (friends, family, politicians, and celebrities)
- Self (your opinions, fears, hopes, dreams, discoveries, and intentions)
- Us (the kind of relationship you have with the person you are conversing with)

Many conversations are dominated by "things" and "other people." Intimacy increases as we move from these topics to "self" and "us."

Balance problems with solutions

When I listen to people, the bulk of their time is spent talking about their problems. They spend only a small fraction of their conversation space talking about solutions. Check this out and see if it's true for the people in your life. Also listen to yourself and see if it's true for you.

Sometimes people move the conversation away from problems to solutions. When that happens, they tend to talk about the *one* solution to a problem. As soon as they create one decent solution, they start talking about other problems.

You can change these habits. Spend some time talking about your problems. Then devote the bulk of your conversation space to talking about solutions—*lots* of solutions. For any single problem, create at least 20 solutions before choosing one to implement. Your second, tenth, or twentieth solution might be the best.

If the solution you choose doesn't work, just go back to your list and pick another one. Since you've generated multiple solutions, you'll have more to choose from.

Balance complaints with celebrations

People constantly point out what's *not* working in their lives. They point out what's not working with the government. They point out what's not working with the movies they see or the books they read. And they point out what's not working with their relationships with colleagues, friends, and family members.

It's useful to talk about what's not working. And at any point, we can also choose to devote more conversation to celebration. We can celebrate what *does* work about the government, about our relationships, or about any other aspect of our lives. And as we shift more of our conversations from complaints to celebrations, we might find ourselves filled with more appreciation and more joy in life.

Balance content with process

The strategies in this book are processes—habitual ways of acting and thinking that can help you get more of what you want in life. This fact brings up another way to balance your conversation space—shift from content to process. Instead of focusing exclusively on *what* you do, also talk and think about *how* you do things.

You can use the Success Strategies as starting points for this shift in conversation. For example, talk about ways you focused your awareness, told the truth, or practiced moving toward love in many areas of your life. Also talk about new ways to apply these processes in the future.

Ask for help

Changing the way you fill your conversation space is not something you have to do alone. Enlist the help of others. Ask them to point out when you're speaking about the past or losing yourself in worry or prediction about the future. Also ask them to monitor the topics of your conversations and listen for the ratio of problems to solutions, complaints to celebrations, or content to process. This can lead to many intriguing conversations about your conversations.

In my office, I have a cartoon that shows a hiker standing at the intersection of two paths in a forest. One path is marked "Scenic Path." The other is labeled "Psycho Path."

This cartoon reminds me of the choices we can make when entering conversations. If we don't stay alert, we can easily find ourselves going down the "psycho path." We can join communities that focus on problems and complaints. We might spend hours with magazines that focus on the lives of celebrities. And we can dwell on advertisements that equate success with owning a new car or drinking the "right" kind of wine.

As an alternative, we can make the extra effort to stay awake to our conversations. We can join communities that focus on solutions and celebrations. We can create more intimacy with friends by talking about "us" instead of the things we buy. And we can increase our satisfaction with life through regular conversations about changing our habits and experimenting with new strategies.

Begin choosing now. The longer you travel the "psycho path" by hanging around people who have unbalanced conversations, the harder you might find it to return to the scenic path. And the more you start balancing your conversation space and managing your communities, the more often you will find yourself on the scenic path. Your friends might appreciate it when you start tuning up your conversation space. They might even seek you out as someone who restores balance and points the way down the scenic path. That's a compliment worth winning.

Tune up your conversation space (JOURNAL ENTRY)

During the next 24 hours, observe how you fill your conversation space. Gain some clarity and awareness about the typical focus of your speaking, writing, listening, reading, and thinking.

At any given moment, check to see where the tense of your conversation rests: in the past, present, or future. Also observe the topics of your conversations. In addition, notice the balance between problems and solutions and between complaints and celebrations. If you like, also notice how often you talk about content and how often you discuss processes.

To make these distinctions most useful, avoid judgment or blame. If you're speaking about the past when your aim is to dwell in the future, simply notice it. Any regret or self-reproach might only keep your conversation about the past more firmly in place.

At the end of this 24-hour period, describe in the space below the ways you filled your conversation space. Express your discoveries as percentages, such as: "I discovered that I spent 70 percent of my time talking about the past, 20 percent about the present, and 10 percent about the future; 50 percent of my conversation about the future had to do with worries, and 50 percent involved prediction."

I discovered that I spent ...

_____

_____

Now consider expressing these percentages in visual form. For example, your diagram might look like this:

Next, consider any changes you'd like to make. Think about ways to change the typical tense, topic, or other aspects of your conversation. Again, express your intentions as percentages. For example, "I intend to spend 10 percent of my conversations with my spouse on problems and 90 percent on solutions."

I intend to ...

_____

_____

Also consider expressing your intentions in visual form. For example, if your intention is to balance the tense of your speaking by allowing equal time for the present, past, and future, your diagram would look like this:

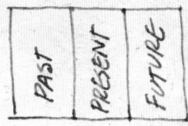

Below, create similar diagrams to express your intentions about other ways to balance your conversation space.

Turn problems into questions (JOURNAL ENTRY)

The word "problem" comes from the Greek word "proballein," which means to "throw forward." Given this definition, we can see problems in a new light. Instead of avoiding them, we can accept them as opportunities to grow—to "throw" our lives forward.

One way to shift conversations from problems to solutions is to restate any problem as a question. This technique offers several benefits. For one, it helps us step back and get some perspective on the situation. Suddenly the problem is not just "my" problem any more; it's a question that anyone could face. Also, a question by its very nature invites answers—possible solutions that can lead us into action.

Apply this idea to your life by completing four steps:

1. First, describe a current problem in your life.
2. Next, rewrite the problem as a question to answer. For example, the problem "I don't have any money left at the end of the month" can be rewritten as "How can I bring my expenses in line with my income?"
3. Brainstorm as many answers (solutions) as you can to this question. List every idea that occurs to you, even if it seems wild and crazy at first.
4. Finally, choose one solution that you intend to implement.

Play with this four-step process by writing in the space below.

The problem I want to examine is …

I discovered that I can rewrite this problem as the question ...

_____

_____

_____

_____

_____

Some possible answers/solutions include ...

_____

_____

_____

_____

I intend to ...

_____

_____

_____

_____

Success Strategy #9

CHANGE YOUR HABITS

Habits are powerful factors in our lives. Because they are consistent, often unconscious patterns, they constantly, daily, express our character and produce our effectiveness ... or ineffectiveness.

STEPHEN R. COVEY

Maybe it's just a habit

Consider an expanded definition of the word *habit*. Imagine for a moment that many of our emotional problems, basic character traits, and even "genetic defects" are just habits.

That fit of depression we blame on a childhood event—perhaps it's just a habit.

That roll of fat we blame on our mother's cooking—maybe that's just a habit.

And that fit of rage we blame on our hormones—maybe that's just a habit also.

Stress, fear, rage, antagonism, racism, procrastination, high debts, money shortages, and a whole host of other problems might be habits, too—nothing less, nothing more.

Likewise, happiness, health, loving relationships, or wealth might be habits. The same could be true for personal qualities we admire so much—playfulness, compassion, attentive listening, and others.

Change small habits to create huge results

Perhaps any aspect of our lives that we like or dislike is merely the tip of an iceberg—the last event in a chain of simple habits.

For example, the state of being depressed involves a series of minute behaviors. People who appear depressed might slump their shoulders, mumble, avoid eye contact, and isolate themselves. These people might also have disempowering beliefs, such as *Since I made this huge mistake, then I'm a failure* or *Things just never work out for me*. All these beliefs and behaviors are habits.

Optimistic and effective people display a constellation of habits, too. Often they stand erect, make eye contact, use animated gestures, laugh, and seek out the company of other people. Chances are that they have a whole different set of beliefs than people who often feel depressed.

Even something as large as contentment or profound inner peace could be just a habit. Some people will draw the line here. "Peace is something you get when you find God or fall in love," they might argue. "Someone or something outside myself has to change before I can feel more peaceful." That might be true. And it's also possible that we can experience more peace by adopting habits such as regular prayer and meditation.

In suggesting that we examine the role of habits in emotional problems, I am *not* saying that we should ignore the biological factors that help create conditions such as clinical depression. I *am* suggesting that even when we account for biology, we'll find that repeated behaviors—habits—play a large role in creating or sustaining these conditions.

Keep it simple

If all this is true, then solving problems and getting what we want from life might be as simple as learning to fasten our seat belts or substituting herbal tea for coffee. Taking charge of our lives might be as simple as taking charge of our habits—making simple, small changes in our behavior.

This viewpoint makes the task of getting what we want in life a doable job, one that we can begin today. When we view life as a series of habits, we take the mystery out of personal transformation.

Three steps to changing a habit

There are many possible approaches to changing a habit. The three-step strategy that follows has the advantage of being simple—and powerful. You can use these steps to take any intention out of the realm of New Year's resolutions and make it a reality.

Commit

If you want to adopt a new habit, then make a deep, soulful, and authentic commitment to change. The following steps depend on this one, so check out your level of commitment up front.

One key to commitment is your use of language. See if you can move from obligation ("I probably *should* become smoke-free") or passion ("I *want* to become smoke-free") up to the level of a promise ("I *will* become smoke-free").

Also, state the habit positively. Focus on what you want rather than what you don't want. For example, saying that you intend to become smoke-free is more positive than saying that you want to quit smoking.

Another key is going public with your commitment. Tell all the important people in your life about the change you want to make. Put that change in

writing. Make a formal contract with yourself and post it where your family can see it. Pledge to keep this promise with the same level of commitment you'd use in promising to tell the truth in court.

Monitor

Next, find a way to measure how well you're keeping your commitment. Set up a feedback system to keep track of how consistently you're succeeding in changing your habit.

For example, you could create a chart with spaces for each day of the week; just note how many times during the week you practice your new habit. You could make a similar notation in your calendar.

You can create other visual ways to display the occurrence of a behavior over time. One common format is to draw a graph that represents time on the X-axis and events or actions on the Y-axis. Say that you want to acquire a new habit of saving 5 percent of your take-home pay each month. Using a graph, you could visually display your progress in acquiring this habit.

We can find other ways to set up a feedback system for hard-to-monitor goals. For example, a consultant who does most of her work over the phone could tape-record her business conversations (with her clients' permission). Then she can review the tape to monitor her speaking habits. Teachers and trainers can videotape their presentations.

Remember that simple lists can work wonders. If you want to drop the habit of complaining, just list the number of complaints you utter each day in your journal. If you want to become more skilled at making promises, then log each promise in your daily journal. Once each day or week, review the list to see how well you're keeping these promises. Along with this, you can give yourself a daily "grade" on your overall progress in changing the habit.

We can also ask key people in our lives to observe us closely and share their observations, verbally or in writing. I had a habit of slouching forward as I walked. When I committed to change that habit, I asked friends and coworkers to give me daily feedback on my walking posture. I don't have the habit of slouching any more.

You could give your feedback system more teeth by building in rewards and penalties. When you practice the habit of exercising three times during the week, you could schedule a massage on Sunday. Or you could promise to pay your daughter $1 whenever she catches you driving without your seat belt fastened.

Practice

As usual, I forgot to exercise today.

I lost my temper with the kids again, even after I promised I wouldn't. No wonder they don't trust me.

I had a third cup of coffee today; yesterday I promised I'd only drink one. I can never trust myself when it comes to changing a habit.

Kicking ourselves with comments like these when we fail to keep our commitments consumes a lot of time and energy. That's energy we could channel into adopting a new habit instead. When our behavior falls short of our intentions, we can simply note the fact without reproach. Then we can get back to practicing the new habit.

Reproach kills many a New Year's resolution. For example, people make a resolution to exercise daily. On January 1, 2, and 3, they do. Then on January 4, they forget to exercise, slap their foreheads and say, *I missed a day. I'm such a failure.* Instead of reproaching themselves, they could simply recommit to the habit and just keep practicing.

When we notice ourselves falling into self-reproach, we might slip into reproaching our reproach: *Not only did I skip exercising today—I got really angry about it. I'm so disappointed in myself for having that reaction.* Comments like these just add another layer to the problem and impede our efforts to change. Self-reproach at any level is simply another habit that we can choose to release.

So the third step is to practice, practice, practice—without reproach. And remember that success in changing any habit has a lot to do with persistence. Some habits will change in a few hours, while others might take weeks or months. Be willing to hang in there and monitor your progress over time.

Begin now

Some people might not be content with these three steps to change a habit. They might argue that they need to hear a motivational speaker, get some counseling, or read another self-help book before they start exercising daily, or skipping that extra cup of coffee, or balancing their checkbook regularly.

Maybe not. Perhaps there's nothing you need to do first before you start exercising daily, balancing your checkbook regularly, or adopting any other new habit. Perhaps it's just a matter of three simple steps that you can begin now.

Many people will buy this idea when they want to change a relatively minor behavior, such as balancing a checkbook. They might not buy it when seeking to make a major change, such as releasing sadness or maximizing happiness.

Play with the three steps I recommend and see what works. You might find that commitment, feedback, and practice are enough to start living the life of your dreams.

cross off your excuses (JOURNAL ENTRY)

Describe any new habit that you'd like to adopt. Then list every explanation you can think
of for not practicing this behavior. Begin writing in the space below and use additional
paper if needed. Be sure to include all of your favorite excuses.

The habit I'd like to adopt is ...

_____

My excuses for not adopting this habit include ...

_____

_____

_____

_____

When you're done, scrutinize your list of excuses for one minute. Then literally and boldly
cross out each excuse. Cross off "being tired" as an excuse. Cross off "not wanting to"
as an excuse. Do the same for "I didn't feel like it," "I guess I'm too old to change,"
or any other excuse.

If you're unwilling to give up an excuse, that's OK. You can keep the excuse.
That means releasing any ideas about changing the habit for now.

Follow up with more writing. Describe what you learned about yourself by laying your
excuses out in the open. Ask yourself if you're truly willing to give up each excuse. Describe
in detail the benefits of doing so. Then declare the specific habit you intend to adopt.

By listing and crossing off my excuses, I discovered that I ...

_____

_____

By giving up my excuses, I discovered that I could gain benefits such as …

_____

I intend to …

_____

_____

change the habit (JOURNAL ENTRY)

In the space below, list something about yourself that you'd like to change, even if you're sure it's not just a habit. Then write a detailed plan describing how you will adopt a new habit as a means toward achieving your desired change.

I discovered that I'd like to change …

_____

_____

The specific habit I'd like to adopt is …

_____

_____

_____

To adopt this habit, I intend to …

_____

_____

_____

practice the habit of happiness (JOURNAL ENTRY)

Experiment with applying the three recommended steps for habit changing as ways
to immediately experience more happiness.

In the space below, describe a habit you intend to adopt as a way to routinely experience
more happiness. For example, declare your intention to exercise regularly, attend a weekly
support group, meditate daily, or begin releasing your resentments.

I intend to ...

_____

_____

Now create a feedback system. You can experiment with many options. One possibility is
to carry a 3x5 card with you; use this card to record how many times per day you practice
the habit. You could make similar notations in your calendar or journal.

Or you might choose to give yourself a daily "score" that summarizes your mood—anything
from −10 for extreme sadness to +10 for ecstasy. The simple act of monitoring your moods
might be enough to raise your level of happiness.

Describe your feedback system in the space below.

I intend to monitor my behavior or attitudes by ...

_____

_____

Finally, review your experience. After one month of practicing your new habit, come back to
this journal entry. Describe how habit changing worked as a path toward greater happiness.

If you noticed any examples of self-reproach, also summarize them here. Putting self-critical
statements on paper might help you release them.

I discovered that I ...

_____

_____

Turbocharge the three steps

One of the main points of this chapter is that changing habits can be simple. And *simple* does not always mean *easy*.

Habits are highly efficient. We've repeated our habitual actions many times and experienced benefits from them. Naturally, we resist changing these behaviors.

Remember, though, that people *do* change. Many of us know people who've made dramatic improvements in their habits. These people stopped smoking, started buckling seat belts, shed dozens of pounds, overhauled their diets, or succeeded at changing some other habit.

So you *can* do it. Experiment with the following strategies as ways to supplement and strengthen the basic three-step method for changing habits (commit, monitor, and practice).

Be willing to change

Changing a habit is a lot like replacing a car. To begin with, we give up on the old car. We're willing to put the old car out to pasture—to sell it to someone else or junk it. If we continue to entertain plans for repairing the old car and driving it again, we'll probably never get around to replacing it.

In the same way, people often continue a habit until they truly give up on it. Until then, they might persist in their old ways of thinking and acting. That's understandable, since the old ways are often comfortable and deliver some benefits.

At the same time, it's not reasonable to expect new results from repeating the same old thoughts and actions. Once people see the ineffectiveness of the old habit and become truly willing to let it go, they've set in motion a powerful force for personal change.

Remember the power of awareness

Destructive habits thrive on unconsciousness. People who smoke may have no idea how many times each day they light up. People who overeat often have no clue about how many times they snack each day. Keeping detailed logs of a behavior can help us see the benefits of changing that behavior. In some cases, awareness alone might be enough to produce a change of habit.

Celebrate small gains

Give yourself rewards for any success, no matter how small. For instance, consider seeing a movie after losing a pound or taking a day off from work after exercising daily for one week.

Take some time off from a behavior

For some selected period of time, you can shift gears from changing habits to just taking a break from a current behavior. For example, in January avoid sugar for one week. In March, take a 10-day break from seeing any relatives. In April, avoid all television for three weeks. And in May, be celibate for two weeks. June might be the month you choose to eat only vegetarian meals.

These breaks offer an opportunity to experience life with fresh eyes and to explore new habits you might like to adopt.

Thank your habits—then wave goodbye

As a way to promote behavior change, we can thank our old habits before bidding them goodbye.

Many habits that people adopt—from biting fingernails to mainlining heroin—have costs ranging from inconvenience to addiction. However, each habit offers a payoff as well. If the habit offered no benefit, people probably would have released the habit long ago.

Begin by distinguishing between a behavior and the *intention* of that behavior. Even when a habit creates problems, the intention behind it can be positive. Drugs might help us see the world in new ways. Smoking cigarettes can deliver a sense of ease and comfort. Pumping ourselves full of caffeine might boost our productivity for a while. There's nothing inherently wrong with feeling pleasant sensations or getting more things done. These could be the worthwhile intentions behind "bad" habits.

To change such a habit, we can first acknowledge the powerful resource it has been. This opens up space for a new behavior that delivers the same benefit with fewer costs. For instance, the person who turns to alcohol to change her moods might choose to exercise instead. Exercise helps release chemicals in the brain that deliver a natural "high."

Play with it all

The whole topic of changing habits seems to infect people with terminal seriousness. This only adds to the layers of guilt and anxiety that people bring to the subject of altering their behavior. Refusing to take ourselves seriously can help free up all that negative energy.

Look for ways to loosen up and have some fun with this strategy of changing habits. Go swimming at a public pool even if you're currently 30 pounds overweight. Dance for exercise even if other people are tempted to call 9-1-1 when they see you move on the dance floor. Actions like these demonstrate that you're changing habits with a light heart—and removing the layers of self-reproach that can sabotage your success.

Consider the costs and benefits of a current behavior (EXERCISE)

For purposes of this exercise, consider an *addiction* to be any behavior that satisfies an immediate desire to seek pleasure or avoid pain, even if the behavior results in serious, long-term harm.

Remember that not all behaviors conform neatly to the categories of "addictive" or "healthy." Many less-than-healthy behaviors are not addictive.

This exercise offers a chance to evaluate some of your current behaviors and to place them somewhere on a line ranging from "healthy" to "addictive."

Most of us have some behaviors that clearly belong on the "healthy" side of this line. We also have behaviors that fall toward the middle, such as occasionally eating more fattening desserts or watching more TV than we intend. And some of us have behaviors that belong on the "addictive" side, such as compulsive gambling or drinking.

Keep these distinctions in mind as you complete the following steps:

1. On a separate sheet of paper, draw a straight, horizontal line. Label the left end of the line "healthy" and the right end "addictive."

2. Now choose some significant behaviors in your life—behaviors that might fall anywhere in the entire range from "healthy" to "addictive." (You might not have any behaviors you consider addictive.)

3. At an appropriate place on the line you drew in step 1, place a dot representing each behavior and describe the behavior in a single, short sentence. To add value and perspective to this exercise, ask close friends or family members to look over your line. Ask for their perceptions about your behaviors. Perhaps there are some they would add to or delete from your chart.

4. Pick a behavior that you don't like, one that you would like to change. Describe that behavior in writing on a separate sheet of paper. Now give the part of you that wants to continue this behavior a voice. Let it speak. Converse with it. Have a dialogue (written or spoken) with that part of yourself. Ask that part of you what it is trying to accomplish, what benefit it is seeking to deliver. Write a description of the payoff for the "bad" behavior.

5. Now consider whether this behavior is costing you more than it delivers. If so, finish up by writing a goal to adopt a new behavior that delivers the equivalent payoffs with fewer costs. For example, instead of using alcohol to relax, you could breathe deeply or practice meditation.

Manage your associations

To get the hang of this strategy, consider two quick scenarios.

Scenario #1

Jason's family has just finished the main course of a huge, sumptuous meal. The turkey was mouth-watering and the dressing was even better. It's time for hot pumpkin pie with whipped cream. Most of the family is already savoring the sweet aroma of nutmeg and cinnamon wafting through the kitchen.

When Jason is offered a piece of pie, he says, "No, thanks." Everyone else at the table is curious. They're concerned that he doesn't feel well, or that he's on some crazy diet. "What's the problem?" they ask.

Jason explains that he doesn't eat sweets anymore. Everyone compliments him on the strength of his will power. It must be difficult, they say, to deny himself the pleasure of eating sweets. The truth is, it requires no will power at all. When Jason sees something sweet, he remembers how sick, uncomfortable, and lethargic he felt every time he overindulged in sugary foods. The thoughts and sensations he associates with pumpkin pie are unpleasant. Toughing it out or exercising will power is simply not involved here. His natural and immediate reaction is *No way*.

Scenario #2

Joanne used to hate exercising. When she was in junior high school, her gym teacher's favorite activity was forcing the class to run laps around the field. Joanne always finished last, and she has vivid memories of both the physical and mental discomfort she felt.

While in her mid-thirties, Joanne became close friends with Sara, a colleague at work. Sara, an avid runner, invited Joanne to join her for a morning's exercise. With some reluctance, Joanne agreed.

On the following Saturday morning the two friends met at the park. They enjoyed a rewarding conversation while walking around the lake, stopping twice to lean up against a tree and just laugh for a few minutes.

Soon they began walking together several times each week. Joanne looked forward to these times. She enjoyed the regular exercise and noticed that she felt more energetic during the day.

One day, Sara suggested that they jog for a brief stretch. Afterward they began jogging along this stretch every time they walked. Before long, Joanne asked Sara about doing 10-kilometer runs. Joanne's new associations with running—friendship, fun, and increased energy—led her to become a consistent runner without struggling to achieve self-discipline.

The point: Link what you want with what you like

One theme unites these homespun tales: Link what you want with what you already like. And link what you *don't* want with what you already don't like.

To change a behavior, we can simply change the associations that we link to the behavior. If we link a desired behavior to pleasure, we can succeed in doing it more often. If we pair a habit that we want to stop with pain or discomfort, we can watch that behavior start to disappear from our lives.

Be creative. For example, associate the idea of eating chocolate cake with adding a layer of brown, oily, wiggly fat tissue to your body. It all starts with the way you manage associations. Using the same strategy, turn three glasses of wine into a hangover...etc, etc.

The point is to consciously choose which behaviors we associate with pain and pleasure. Otherwise we live mechanically, merely reacting to external stimuli and random associations.

By learning to manage our associations, we approach living with more satisfaction and choice. Steely-eyed will power or superhuman motivation might be nothing more than the ability to manage associations.

Change a habit by managing associations (EXERCISE)

Describe in writing a habit that you'd like to change. Some possible examples are smoking, overeating, or reading the paper while your spouse is trying to talk to you. Describe your habit in the space below.

Now link this habit to a result that you find painful or undesirable. For example: "Drinking two beers a day adds fat to my waistline and makes me feel tired."

Next, describe a behavior you can use to replace the behavior you want to stop. Then link as much pleasure to the new behavior as you can. Write as if the change you desire has already taken place: "I drink fruit juices instead of beer. This leaves me feeling thinner and more energetic. I also end up with $10 more to spend or save each week."

Finally, put your new associations to work. Every time you think about the unwanted behavior, remember the costs involved. Then think about the new, desired behavior and visualize or affirm the benefits.

Review your experience
with managing associations (JOURNAL ENTRY)

In the space below, assess how effective the previous exercise was for you. If managing your associations worked, then describe how you will apply it to another habit you'd like to change. If the exercise didn't work for you, then consider ways to make it more effective.

I discovered that ...

_____

_____

_____

_____

I intend to ...

_____

_____

_____

_____

Go for substitution, not retribution (EXERCISE)

To shed an old behavior, we can replace it with a new one. Starting a new behavior can make it easier for us to stop an old one.

For example, substitute eating a carrot for biting into a brownie. Reach for a book instead of reaching for the TV remote control. Instead of lingering over dessert after dinner, linger over a tasty glass of fruit juice.

Right now, pick one behavior you would like to change. Describe it in writing in the space below, along with the times and places you typically engage in this activity.

_____

_____

_____

Now describe a new behavior you can substitute for the behavior you just listed. Be sure to choose an activity you can perform at the same time and in the same place as the behavior you want to stop.

_____

_____

_____

_____

Align habits with values (EXERCISE)

If you regularly align your actions with what's most important to you, you're more apt to get the results in life that you desire. Demonstrating this for yourself is the purpose of this exercise.

Begin by brainstorming a written list of your values. Start writing in the space below and continue on additional paper if needed.

_____

_____

_____

_____

Now choose habits that are consistent with each value you just wrote. Ask _If I were living consistently with these values, what would I do on a regular basis?_

For example, a person who values health could eat low-fat foods and exercise at least three times a week. A person who values wealth could make a habit of saving 10 percent of her income each month to make regular investments in a mutual fund.

Use the following space to begin listing habits that support your values.

_____

_____

_____

To get the most value from this exercise, keep your lists of values and habits as "alive" as possible. Review these lists frequently, using them as a tool for making choices in daily life.

Success Strategy #10

PERSIST

*Even if you're
on the right track,
you'll get run over
if you just sit there.*

WILL ROGERS

Stick with it

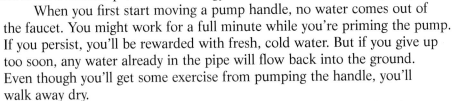

If you're looking for new ways to experience breakthrough in your life, take a cue from a humble piece of technology—the old-fashioned water pump.

When you first start moving a pump handle, no water comes out of the faucet. You might work for a full minute while you're priming the pump. If you persist, you'll be rewarded with fresh, cold water. But if you give up too soon, any water already in the pipe will flow back into the ground. Even though you'll get some exercise from pumping the handle, you'll walk away dry.

Persistence will also pay off if you ever intend to produce bamboo. A single plant can take up to 120 years to flower and produce seeds. But when your seed does start to grow, be prepared for huge rewards. Bamboo plants can grow one foot per day and reach a full height of up to 130 feet.

A far more complicated piece of technology—the rocket—offers another analogy for persistence. On a journey of hundreds of thousands of miles, rockets use most of their fuel during the first few miles to overcome the pull of gravity. Once they travel beyond Earth's atmosphere, rockets are no longer slowed by friction. They're free to soar through outer space.

Hang in there …

These examples suggest a useful strategy for overcoming obstacles to the life of your dreams: Persist. Continue. Sustain effort. Stay in action. Be patient. Hang in there. Give yourself time to overcome the pull of prejudice and the gravity of old ideas. When you're attempting to solve a problem, you could find that the last solution you invent is the one that works. If you stop inventing too soon, you could miss the payoff.

My father sold insurance, and the basis of his success was persisting in the face of customer after customer who said no. He expected that nine out of ten people would turn him down when he approached them about buying a policy. He actually celebrated when a prospective customer said no, figuring that each no was one step closer to the next yes. Many people in sales will tell you that they use the same approach.

If you persist, you'll find parallel examples in other fields.

For instance, Robert Pirsig wrote a novel inspired by a cross-country motorcycle trip he took with his son. Pirsig submitted the manuscript to 120 publishers—all of whom rejected it. Finally a far-sighted editor saw value in Pirsig's work and agreed to publish it. The book succeeded with both critics and book buyers, making Pirsig a millionaire. Had Pirsig given up on the manuscript after the 119th publisher, we would never have seen that book—*Zen and the Art of Motorcycle Maintenance.*

The game MONOPOLY® was developed by Charles Darrow, an unemployed heating engineer. Darrow presented his first version of the game to a toy company in 1935. That company originally rejected the game for containing 52 "fundamental errors." Darrow persisted, and today the game is so successful that its publisher, Parker Brothers, prints more than $40 billion of MONOPOLY money each year. That's twice the amount of real money printed annually by the U.S. Mint. Persistence pays.

Look for ways to experience the power of persistence in your own life. For example, it might take weeks of research to find the company you want to work for and the person who can hire you. But with that careful preparation, you could walk away with a new job at a substantially higher salary after just one interview.

Or you might endure years of living with a chronic illness, seeking out every specialist you can find. Armed with persistence and all the knowledge of health care that you've gained, you might uncover a nontraditional treatment that finally helps.

... and choose when to hang it up

Like any idea in this book, the suggestion to persist is just a tool. And no tool works for every job. You won't be able to build a house if the only tool you have is a hammer. Likewise, if the only tool you use is persistence, you might not succeed in creating the life of your dreams. You'll want to have other tools on hand.

One of those tools is: When you're done, you're done. If you aren't continuing, then don't pretend. There is a time to call it quits and move on to the next project, the next career, or the next relationship.

Sticking with it is not the same as making the best of a bad deal. People forget this distinction. Couples stay married long after they've truly stopped caring for each other. Bands stay on the road long after they've lost any interest in performing. Employees stay in jobs long after they've stop caring about their work. Instead of giving notice, they sometimes just mark time until retirement.

When you look for ways to stick with it, also look for times when it's appropriate to hang it up. Persistence is not a panacea—it's just another tool to keep in your hip pocket.

And when choosing whether to stick with it or hang it up, remember that most of the time we err on the side of quitting too soon.

Keep looking for answers

This book is based on questions: How can human beings live abundant lives? How can they become happier, healthier, more loving, more wealthy? *Falling Awake* is a collection of possible answers to those questions.

Answers are wonderful, especially when they relate to our most persistent and deeply felt questions. Yet answers can get in the way, too. Once we're convinced that we have *the* answer to a question, we might stop looking for other answers. When that happens, we stop learning and short-circuit our options. And if the one answer we found *doesn't* work, then we are stuck with our problems.

Stay in the inquiry

Faced with a difficult problem, you might feel tempted to grit your teeth, forge an ambition made of steel, fasten on to one solution, and declare: "I'm going to just get through this with will power." Yet the problem may not be lack of will power. It may just be that your chosen solution doesn't work in this particular situation. If that's true, then there's little virtue in trying harder.

Suppose a person wants to stop biting his fingernails. His first strategy is to use will power and just force himself to stop biting his nails. That fails. Instead of trying harder, he could:

- Provide a small punishment every time he notices he's biting his nails. Something simple would do—snapping a rubber band on his wrist or putting a quarter in a jar that he'll later give to someone he doesn't like much.

- Keep a written log, making a small tick mark every time he finds himself biting his nails. Faced with the stark facts in black and white, he might find his nail biting decreasing naturally over time.

- Wear gloves all the time. (Well, some ideas are better than others! Keep reading.)

- Replace his habit of nail biting with another one. Every time he feels an urge to bite his nails, he could snap his fingers, massage his palm, rub the tip of his finger with another finger, file his nails, or shout something nonsensical like "all's well in the world of Zog tonight." In fact, he might choose to do almost anything that's safe and legal—as long as it's not biting his nails.

- Stop and repeat an affirmation: "I am changing this habit and learning to be successful at what I choose."

- Get a manicure. That way, he knows he's destroying something beautiful when he bites his nails, and wasting money besides.

- Stop biting his nails one finger at a time. After all, success breeds success. As soon as he realizes that he can avoid biting one fingernail, he might realize that he can stop biting each other nail.

- Wear bright fingernail polish as a reminder to stop nail biting.

- Dip his fingertips in a harmless but noxious-tasting solution many times each day.

- Reward himself at the end of every hour that he stays free of nail biting.

The point is this: Instead of latching on to one answer, we can look for more. Instead of being content with the first solution that comes to mind and using it past the point of effectiveness, we can keep searching for options.

Even when we're convinced that we've finally handled a problem, we can brainstorm and refine our thinking until we create at least five more solutions. The last option might be the one that finally pushes us to breakthrough.

Ask "What if that's true?"

When presented with a new idea, many people pride themselves on being critical thinkers. They look for problems. They doubt until there's clear proof. They probe for weaknesses. Their main question seems to be "What's wrong with this idea?"

This approach can be useful at times. And if it is the *only* tool we use, we can come up short. When we constantly look for what's wrong with new ideas, we can miss what's useful.

A different and potentially more productive approach is to ask "What if that's true?" Doing this opens all sorts of new possibilities and variations. Rather than looking for what's wrong, we can look for what's potentially valuable. Faced with a new idea, we can look deeper, go further, and stay in the inquiry. The airplane, the light bulb, the transistor, the geodesic dome, the computer chip—these and countless other advances exist today because their inventors practiced staying in the inquiry. They tested explanation after explanation that failed; they built prototype after prototype that flopped. They persisted, played with the data gathered from each failure, and finally created something that enriched our lives.

Some people reject this suggestion to stay in the inquiry. They fear getting fooled: "If we thoughtfully consider every new idea that comes our way, we'll waste lots of time and money on worthless adventures, crazy ideas, and wacky products. We'll end up with a closet full of slicers, dicers, gizmos, procedures, strategies, and ideologies we'll never use."

Generally, this fear is unfounded. Asking "What if that's true?" doesn't mean letting others dupe us or take advantage of us. Staying in the inquiry does not mean automatically believing everything we see and hear. It *does* call for a willingness to experiment and play with new notions.

When faced with an idea that truly is foolish, we'll find that asking "What if that's true?" does no harm. Under the spotlight of calm and impartial investigation, unsound ideas have a habit of revealing their true nature. In the meantime, considering even the craziest ideas can lead to unexpected benefits.

Staying in the inquiry and asking "What if that's true?" sometimes calls for courage. When we consider fundamental questions about life and come up with answers that differ from mainstream thinking, we might bump into people who resent this fact. Jesus experienced this in his time; so did Mohammed, Siddhartha Gautama, Martin Luther King, and Nelson Mandela. People's tendency to suspect *any* new idea is a major source of religious persecution, racism, and prejudice.

An alternative is to tolerate and even seek out people who champion the most "offbeat" causes and the most "outlandish" ideas. Besides reducing hate and antagonism in the world, our tolerance paves the way for the next great innovation or the next world-changing idea.

Expand your options (JOURNAL ENTRY)

Think of a problem that you now face. The problem could exist in any area of life—professional or personal. It might be a problem you've never considered before. In the space below, complete the following sentence.

I discovered that I …

_____

_____

_____

Now describe a solution to this problem—perhaps one that you've considered or are already using.

_____

_____

Finally, create other solutions that might work. On a separate sheet of paper, write down at least five other ways to solve this problem.

Don't give up. Stay in the inquiry long enough to give this exercise a fair chance. If you keep drawing blanks, ask others for suggestions. Be willing to experiment with ideas that contradict your current solution and ideas you're "sure" won't work. Persist until you find alternative solutions.

Now that you've explored a variety of options, choose one that you will use to start solving your problem.

I intend to …

_____

Think clearly

Creating the life of your dreams is an exercise in thinking clearly. Writing down goals calls for thinking precisely about what you want. Assigning priorities to your goals means distinguishing between what is most essential to your vision and what is least essential. Meeting any goal requires you to identify plans that work and those that don't. Clear thinking supports each of these skills and countless others involved in creating the life of your dreams.

Take a moment to think about thinking. Sometimes thinking can be logical and powerful, leading to useful distinctions and clear guidelines for action.

At other times, thinking can be confused and muddled, leaving us with illogical conclusions, unsupported assertions, unworkable plans, and even unwarranted feelings of distress. For example, if we compare our standard of living with only the top one percent of the world's richest people, we might feel poor. But if we compare our personal income with that of most people who are alive on the planet today (and most people who ever lived), we could see ourselves as fabulously wealthy. The difference between these two outcomes is not in our bank accounts—it's in our thinking.

Clear thinking has little to do with IQ. Instead, clear thinking is largely a matter of persistence—taking care to make assertions that are clear, logical, coherent, and supported by evidence.

See clear thinking as a skill that anyone can acquire with practice. The following suggestions offer ways to begin.

Take time to be thoughtful

When faced with a major choice, most people see value in taking time

to reach a thoughtful decision. Faced with other issues, however, people often take the path of least resistance and jump to the first conclusion that occurs to them.

One example involves romantic relationships. Most of us don't think planning plays much of a role. We just wait, watch, and react. If someone we like shows up, we start a relationship. If not, we continue to wait and watch.

An alternative is to be thoughtful and plan. You can take the time to describe the specific qualities you consider vital in the next person you come to love. Possibilities include financial stability, a sense of humor, and willingness to be intimate, both physically and emotionally. Even if you are already married, you can use this same line of inquiry to create long-term goals for your relationship.

Whether we face a minor question or a life-changing issue, taking time to be thoughtful can raise the quality of our choices and our lives.

Look for errors in logic

Logic is a field of study that defines principles for making sound statements about the world. Experts in this field look for fallacies—ways that people trip themselves when they start down the path toward clear thinking.

One logical fallacy is called *either/or thinking.* Many people find safety in certainty. They want to know once and for all that certain activities are either safe or unsafe, that certain people are either friendly or unfriendly, that certain actions are either right or wrong. That's either/or thinking at work.

This kind of thinking comes at the cost of accuracy. People cannot be accurately described as all good or all bad. Most questions have multiple answers. Few actions are either right or wrong in all circumstances.

Like either/or thinking, *generalizations* help us see the world as familiar and predictable. If we knew that all border collies were friendly, we could always relax around them. If we knew that all people with pierced ears and leather jackets were thieves, we could ensure that they were arrested on sight.

You can think more clearly when you see these and other generalizations as suspect. For example, "All birds fly" is a generalization—and also untrue. There are many exceptions to this generalization, including penguins, which do not fly. Looking for exceptions can save you from many errors in your thinking and mistakes in your behavior.

These are just two examples of fallacies in thinking. If you poke around in the library for good books about logic, you'll learn to recognize many more.

Examine the evidence

Human beings are notable for their ability to manufacture nonsense. Examples come from many of the things people have believed at one point or another in human history: If we get too close to the edge of the world, we'll fall off. Women cannot be trusted to vote. Certain races of people, due to their genetics, are less intelligent than others.

To avoid nonsense, be alert for assertions that are offered without evidence. Look for reliable facts, figures, and examples that support the claims being made.

Balance logic with emotions and values

Logic is only one of several tools we can use when making choices. Other tools include our intuition and deeply felt values. Relying on logic alone is like trying to play a game of golf with only a putter.

Say that you're considering investing in a new business with the potential to make you a millionaire. You can begin by thinking logically—reviewing the facts, figures, marketing plans, and income projections. If you forget to consider these factors, you could lose a lot of money. You can also listen to your heart and ask whether this business is consistent with your values. If the bottom line adds up to fantastic profits but the product harms the environment, then the cost to your peace of mind might far outweigh the perceived financial benefits.

To have the life of your dreams, create specific plans with clear timelines and logically consistent goals. Also create a vision that inspires your passionate commitment and leaves you feeling great about what you contribute to others.

Put it in writing

Writing is a way to become conscious of your thinking, a way to transform the thousands of thoughts you have every day into something that you can see. It takes time to write, and that fact invites you to go more slowly and inquire more fully.

Writing offers another benefit. When the products of your thinking are sitting quietly on the page for your inspection, you'll find it easier to spot gaps in logic, fuzzy language, and assertions that have no evidence.

As you write, remember that you can do more than simply look for errors. You can also be creative and have fun. Through writing you trace the trail of your thinking and create a visible record of your brilliance—key ways to promote clear thinking.

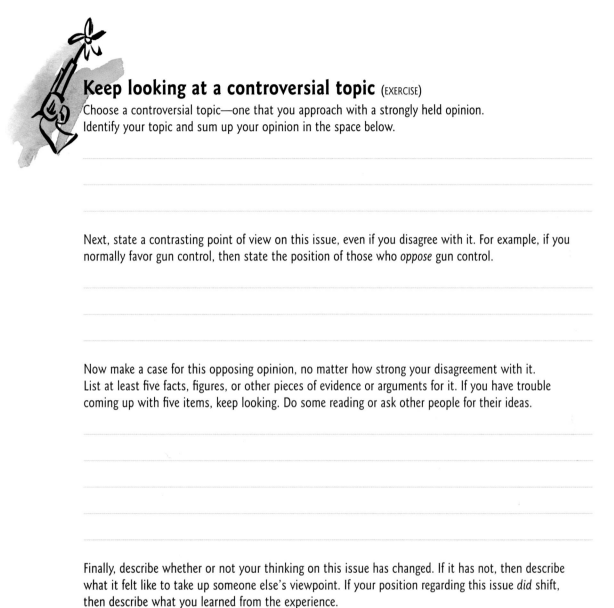

Keep looking at a controversial topic (EXERCISE)

Choose a controversial topic—one that you approach with a strongly held opinion. Identify your topic and sum up your opinion in the space below.

_____

_____

_____

Next, state a contrasting point of view on this issue, even if you disagree with it. For example, if you normally favor gun control, then state the position of those who _oppose_ gun control.

_____

_____

_____

Now make a case for this opposing opinion, no matter how strong your disagreement with it. List at least five facts, figures, or other pieces of evidence or arguments for it. If you have trouble coming up with five items, keep looking. Do some reading or ask other people for their ideas.

_____

_____

_____

_____

_____

Finally, describe whether or not your thinking on this issue has changed. If it has not, then describe what it felt like to take up someone else's viewpoint. If your position regarding this issue _did_ shift, then describe what you learned from the experience.

_____

_____

_____

Create motivation

"I'm low on motivation today."
"I've got a bad attitude."
"I just don't have the will power
    to get it done."
"I never had much self-discipline."
"I just lack dedication."
"I'm feeling lazy today."
"Guess I'm not very ambitious."

People say these things when they feel
that something is missing from their lives.
They often call that mysterious thing
motivation. The lack of it is their reason
for not getting what they want in life.

Pretend that motivation is a myth.
Pretend that you don't need motivation
or any other mysterious quality to start
creating the life of your dreams.

To some people, this idea might seem
like bad news. They might have to give up
hoping that someone or something outside
them—something they lack—can magically
infuse them with energy, enthusiasm, vigor,
or vitality. If motivation is a myth, people
might have to give up the idea that finding
a new boss, new spouse, or new self-help
book will provide the inspiration to create
useful plans, focused action, and new results.

Actually, seeing motivation as a myth
could be good news. It means that we don't
have to depend on anything outside ourselves
to motivate or inspire us. We don't have to
wait to develop motivation before we act.
We can generate immediate, consistent,
and powerful action by ourselves, relying
on our own choices and creativity.

Find a motive

Instead of talking about an abstract quality
like motivation, you can simply find
a worthwhile motive for anything you do.
Remind yourself about the long-term benefit
of your planned action. The next task on your
to-do list could be one step toward a degree,
a promotion, or improving a relationship. It
could mean satisfying your curiosity or solving
a problem that's persisted for decades. Remembering these benefits can provide all the
motivation you need to get started.

See how completing the task will bring
you closer to a goal you've freely chosen,
something that you ache for with all your heart.

What people call motivation often springs
from being clear about what we want in life.
Following the lead of our passions can give us
all the energy we need to play life full out.

Manage the gap

A standard piece of advice from motivational
speakers is to take a big project and break
it up into smaller steps. Then stop thinking
about how big the project is. Just complete
the next step, and the next, one at a time.
That's a useful strategy.

Remember that problems can arise
when the steps are too big *or* too small.
If your to-do list for the first day of a project
has 20 tough, time-consuming items for
you to complete, you could quickly feel
overwhelmed. But if your list has only one
easy item, you might feel "underwhelmed"—
bored or ineffective. There's a huge gap
between these two options.

An alternative is to manage the gap—
to create steps that are challenging *and* realistic.
Create steps that are doable yet ambitious
enough to maintain your interest.

Use community
to back up commitments

One of my favorite bumper stickers says
"Community is more powerful than
commitment."

Most of us have had the experience
of committing to change a habit, giving it our

best shot, and watching the whole effort fizzle long before we have achieved our goal.

When this happens, people usually resort to a tempting explanation: "I just don't have any motivation."

One possibility is to replace motivation with *community*. It's usually easier to follow a plan when we're in the company of like-minded people who have the same objective. If we want to stop smoking, lose weight, quit drinking, exercise regularly, or change almost any other behavior, we can harness the support of others and succeed more often. Doing it alone is the hard way, and motivation is no match for the support of a community.

Group support can take us further down the road toward achieving our goals than all the teeth-gritting determination and "I'll never turn back" motivation we can muster. Besides, sharing our goals with others is usually a lot more fun.

Fan the flywheel

Consider for a moment the flywheel, a humble and powerful mechanical device. A flywheel can be difficult to get started. Yet once it's moving, the flywheel is difficult to stop. The secret is giving the flywheel periodic boosts of energy, such as a small push.

We can apply the same principle whenever we feel unmotivated or un-inspired. One way to get past this feeling is to do just one task toward a goal, no matter how small the task is. This alone may not yield sudden excitement or in-spiration. Yet doing almost anything can take us one significant step away from feeling stuck. We can follow this small task with another, then another, and even more. Often the combined effect of these small tasks is all we need to fuel our motivation.

Action itself inspires more action. Motion creates motivation. Success breeds success. We might even catch ourselves having fun.

Just give your word—and keep it

If we wait for motivation to strike us before we change our lives, we could wait forever. Instead, we could give our word and mean it. We could promise to start exercising, get that reading done, complete that report, stop eating desserts, or follow through on any other goal we set. We could promise these actions to other people and ask them to hold us accountable. When we know that key people are counting on us to keep our word, we can move into action quickly.

Perhaps people don't have various amounts of will power. Maybe they just have different habits about giving their word and keeping it. Perhaps motivation is no more complicated than a promise: "I will get it done; you can count on me."

End procrastination

If you've never put anything off until the last minute, then skip ahead to the next article. The rest of us can benefit from considering the following suggestions.

Befriend your discomfort

Sometimes persisting means doing tasks that lead to discomfort. And discomfort can easily translate into procrastination.

You can start by befriending your discomfort. Notice the thoughts running through your head—*This is the last thing I want to do right now; I'd rather walk on a bed of hot coals than complete this task*—and speak them out loud.

Also observe what's happening with your body. For example, are you breathing faster or slower than usual? Is your breathing shallow or deep? Are your shoulders tight? Do you feel any tension in your stomach, neck, or jaw?

Once you're in contact with your mind and body, stay with the discomfort a few minutes. Don't judge it as good or bad. Resisting thoughts and body sensations allows them to persist. Accepting them robs them of their power; then they might stop being a barrier for you.

Choose authentically

When we're authentic, procrastination often disappears. If we repeatedly put off a project, that's a clue to look deeply within ourselves and see if the project aligns with what we truly desire.

For example, a single mother decides to change careers and go back to school. She has more energy and ambition than her current job merits. She also wants to provide her children with more financial security. She is willing to make temporary sacrifices—paying tuition and studying for long hours—in order to improve her long-range job prospects.

If she is not authentic about her decision to go back to school, she can let doubts foster procrastination or even stop her cold. She might worry about appearing foolish or irresponsible, knowing that she'll take on some hardships for the next several years. She might question her academic abilities and mentally rehearse failure. She could doom her adventure before it even begins.

If, on the other hand, she is authentic about her decision, her internal struggle disappears. She's aware that she'll face challenges: managing her time; applying for financial aid; budgeting her money; balancing her life between work, school, and children; perhaps letting go of a romantic relationship for now. Yet her commitment is so strong that she's willing to take it all on and end procrastination.

When a choice leads to sustained internal struggle, we can take a second look at our authenticity. If we're not fully committed to a goal, we can check out other options.

Take a break

One antidote to trying harder to get started is to stop trying for a while. Just take a break. Besides supplying some much needed rest, taking a break might loosen up your thinking and help you find another way to begin.

This is one of the most fun aspects of getting past procrastination. Do something mindless. Walk. Call a friend. Nap. Watch a TV show. Do an easier part of the same job. You might tap some reserves of hidden energy and overcome procrastination in an unexpected way.

Do it now

Carry out your plan. Act on your intentions. You don't have to wait until you're motivated before acting. In fact, moving into action might create all the motivation you need. Just do it now.

Don't do it

You often have the option to let a task go. Instead of struggling with procrastination, you can choose *not* to do the task that you've been putting off.

Some tasks are better left undone. These low-priority tasks contribute little to our overall purpose or goals. They may be tasks that we keep on our to-do lists through habit, or solely out of a sense of obligation. We can benefit by putting them off— perhaps forever.

Feel the feeling—then do it anyway

Courage is an old-fashioned word for an old-fashioned virtue. Traditionally, people have reserved that word for acts of the high and mighty: the campaigns of generals, the missions of heroines, the selfless acts of rescue workers during a disaster, the steely will of a surgeon who undertakes a risky operation to save a life.

This concept of courage is fine as far as it goes. Yet it has some potential problems.

The conventional definition of courage excludes too many of us. Everyday life is about ordinary people who demonstrate tremendous courage in their daily adventures and struggles.

Courage is the kindergartner whose heart is pounding with fear as she waves goodbye to her parents and boards the bus for her first day of school.

Courage is the 40-year-old man who registers for college classes after a 20-year absence from the classroom.

Courage is the woman who leaves her secure job with a public relations firm to work from home as a freelance writer.

We gain a powerful perspective when we see courage as what we *choose* to do even when we feel afraid. Courage means accepting our feelings and sticking with our planned, purposeful action.

Recall times you acted courageously

Even people who ascend to the top ranks of their field feel fear. A famous actor can quake in his boots with stage fright before the curtain rises. A concert violinist can find her hands trembling and her armpits dripping with sweat before she sounds the first note of a concerto. A skilled teacher can dread the first day of school even after 30 years in the classroom. These people feel fear and choose to do what they do anyway.

Most of us have had this kind of experience. We've gone for job interviews, scared so silly that we're not sure if we can remember our name. Yet we go through the ordeal anyway—and even get hired. As students, many of us entered exam rooms praying for divine intervention. And we plodded through and even passed the tests.

If we comb our personal histories, most of us can recall scores of times when we acted independently of our fears and still did what we planned to do. These times demonstrate a larger meaning of courage.

Permit action independent of feeling

When we remember acts of courage, we learn that we don't have to fix our feelings before taking constructive action. That's great, since feelings seem to be as fickle and unpredictable as the weather.

Also, feelings can be unrelated to external circumstances. People can have thousands of dollars in the bank and still feel poor. They can have a stack of party invitations and still feel lonely. They can have a wall full of diplomas and still feel ignorant.

Actions are much different than feelings. While we can't always choose our feelings, we can usually claim full responsibility for our actions. We can feel depressed and still choose to do the laundry. We can feel homesick and still choose to do homework. We can feel lazy and still choose to mow the lawn.

The ability to act independently of our feelings is a gift. It means we don't have to be pushed around by our feelings. We can fully experience our feelings, know all the details about them, and even celebrate them. And we don't have to obey the pushes and pulls of our feelings all the time.

What's so remarkable about this ability to act independently of fear is that we already possess it. There's nothing we have to do first in order to gain courage—nothing we need to learn, and no one we need to pay to teach us this skill. Courage is a gift each of us already possesses. We've demonstrated this quality in the past and can act with courage again—whenever we choose.

Play full out

Some people spend vast stretches of time in activities they call "boring": their jobs, their hobbies, their relationships. They find themselves just going through the motions, doing the same walk-on part day after day without passion or intensity.

This way of life can become so habitual that people get resigned. They expect the majority of their days to be as dull and dry as cracked cement.

The suggestion to "play full out" holds up another possibility— that we can "go for it." We can live life as if it matters. We can spend much of our time fully focused and involved. We can experience enthusiasm and efficiency as natural parts of our daily routines. Energy and vitality can accompany many of our activities.

When we play full out, we set goals that do justice to our potentials. We love what we do, and we do what we love. We're awake, alert, and engaged. Instead of letting projects slide, we handle tasks immediately. And if for some reason we're unable to get a job done promptly, we make a specific plan to handle it in the near future.

Playing full out means living your life as if your life depended on it. The challenge is finding ways to bridge the gap between desperation and adventure. Even when we're feeling as listless and limp as a wet noodle, we can get back to playing full out. The following suggestions can help.

Pursue excellence

People sometimes forget about excellence. They dwell on the same task for weeks, months, or years. They find it easy to accept slow declines in quality. They leave houses uncleaned, debts unpaid, degrees unfinished, and books unread. And even if they complete tasks, people often settle for meeting low standards.

When playing full out, we seldom settle for results like these. We raise our standards. We habitually look for new and more effective ways of doing any task that matters. We approach major problems with the attitude that no stone will remain unturned until a solution is achieved.

Make it urgent

One powerful way to play full out is to bring a sense of urgency to whatever task is at hand. We can choose to view any activity as important, seeing if this mental shift helps us have more fun and become more fully involved.

For example, we can take notes at a meeting as if the fate of the company hinged on our records. (It can happen.) We can drive to work as if our lives were at stake. (Often they are.) We can listen carefully when our children speak, believing that the quality of our attention in that moment makes a real difference in their lives. (Often it does.)

When this mind-set becomes a habit, we find that tasks we once labeled as routine take on a new luster.

Work smarter, not harder

Playing full out does not necessarily mean working harder or longer. There's a difference between efficiency and effectiveness. As the old saying goes, efficiency means doing things right; effectiveness means doing the right thing right. Efficiency can include working hard; effectiveness means being smart about what we choose to do in the first place.

The executive who spends 65 hours each week at the office and does the work of three people is certainly determined and long-suffering. She might even be efficient. But if she skips meals, avoids exercise, and forgets to take vacations, she can burn out in a year. By pacing herself, delegating tasks, and focusing on high-priority projects, she can be effective as well as efficient. She can contribute mightily to the company and still keep her sanity.

Hard work is no substitute for brains. When playing full out, we can balance efficiency with effectiveness—and have a ball at the same time.

Pair feelings with new actions (JOURNAL ENTRY)

This journal entry offers you a chance to explore the idea that you're in charge of what you do, even when feelings—like fear, loneliness, rejection, sadness, and inadequacy— seem overpowering.

On a separate sheet of paper, complete the following sentence with as many examples as you can think of from your own life. Enter a specific feeling in the first blank and describe a specific action in the second blank. Example: When I feel anxious, I discovered that I usually eat.

When I feel _____, I discovered that I usually _____.

Now write goals that allow you to free your behaviors from your feelings and to create new behaviors. Using the same feelings that you described earlier, choose different behaviors. Example: The next time I feel anxious, I intend to take a short, brisk walk.

The next time I feel _____, I intend to _____.

Experiment with acting on your intentions and reflect on how well this journal entry worked for you.

In pairing feelings with new actions, I discovered that I ...

_____

_____

_____

Practice playing full out (EXERCISE)

Think of something you do every day—a task you think is a bit boring. Examples might include doing the dishes, reading textbooks, vacuuming, or sorting mail.

Next time you do this activity, pretend that every detail is crucial and you must act with great precision and care. Even if you're feeling bored, move into the task with enthusiasm and animation. Aim to play full out.

Using your imagination might help. For example, become an actor. Pretend that you're someone who's truly passionate about this task. Really play the part. Or pretend you can win a $10,000 cash prize as your reward for a perfect performance at this task.

On a separate sheet of paper, describe specifically what you will do and how you will practice playing full out.

After doing this activity, describe what was particularly effective in helping you play full out, even if you didn't feel like it. Also describe your feelings about the task after doing it full out.

Success Strategy #11

CONTRIBUTE

We tire of those pleasures we take, but never of those we give.

JOHN PETIT-SENN

Fill yourself up and give yourself away

This book describes a process of filling your life with daily ecstasy, vibrant health, deep intimacy, full celebration, or whatever else you want. I offer the Success Strategies as ways to determine what you want and meet any goal—ways you can create paradise on earth.

As you fill yourself up by living the life of your dreams, consider giving it all away.

This might seem like a self-contradictory or even silly suggestion. So let me explain what I mean.

You're constantly exposed to messages telling you how to live the life of your dreams by having a more wonderful life. Buy this car and have a more wonderful life. Change your career and have a more wonderful life. Have better sex and have a more wonderful life. Or gain better health and have a more wonderful life.

Well, much of that works. And something else that works is to contribute. Give your time. Give your money. Give your love. Give your attention. Give your compliments. Give your creativity. Just look around and see what people

want and give it to them. The more you get what *you* want, the more you can give others what *they* want.

Then life truly becomes paradise.

It's difficult to imagine a person who becomes so joyful that he decides to isolate himself from others. Such a person who jealously guards his happiness by not sharing it with others makes himself a prisoner of his own joy.

Instead, we can spread the light. When contributing consistently to our own happiness, the natural next step is to contribute to the happiness of others.

We can start by seeing everything we do and say as a potential contribution. And we don't have to stop there. Most of us have received letters and phone calls from charities and nonprofit groups—everything from the local animal rescue society to Amnesty International. And many of these communications boil down to one request: Will you donate some money to us? At times, these groups want more than our money; they want our time, too. They ask us to knock on doors, circulate petitions, stuff envelopes, or make a few fund-raising calls ourselves. We can do all these things and more.

Contribution can become a way of life. Explore this book as a whole for ways to fill yourself up and this chapter in particular for ways to give yourself away—day by day, moment by moment.

Review a past contribution (EXERCISE)

Recall a time in the past when you contributed. Perhaps you volunteered time to a charitable organization. Perhaps you listened to a friend's problem and offered a suggestion that made a real difference. Or perhaps you performed a simple act of kindness that had an immediate effect: pausing to open a door for someone in a wheelchair, mowing a neighbor's lawn unasked, or filling the gas tank in a friend's car.

Write about your contribution in the space below.

Plan to contribute again (JOURNAL ENTRY)

Review what you wrote for the previous exercise and explore this act of contribution
a little more. In the following space, describe any feelings of pleasure or satisfaction that
accompanied this act of contribution. Be specific.

I discovered that I …

_____

_____

_____

_____

Now consider that you can enjoy contributing again. If you choose this option,
state something that you will do within the next week as an act of contribution.

I intend to …

_____

_____

_____

_____

Take on bigger problems

Something usually happens when we focus on contribution: We start to take on bigger problems. In the process, other problems shrink. Sometimes they even disappear.

Imagine that you wake up one day with two things on your to-do list: mow the lawn and write to your mother. Tasks like these have a way of expanding to fill the time allotted to them. You could spend the whole morning wiping off the mower blades, going to the service station to buy gas, checking the oil, and even taking the mower into a local small engine shop for a tune-up. That leaves the afternoon for finding paper, scrounging up a pen, schlepping to the post office to buy just the right stamp, drafting that letter to your mother, and getting it to a mailbox.

Now consider what happens when your to-do list expands by just one item—an item that includes contribution. In addition to mowing the lawn and writing to your mother, you promise to put in a two-hour volunteer shift at the local homeless shelter.

With some friendly pressure from that commitment, you can go about your other tasks with more focus and intensity. Instead of taking the entire morning to mow the lawn or the whole afternoon to write your mother, you could do these tasks with more efficiency, saving enough time to make that volunteer shift. And at the end of the day, you can cross all three items off your list.

Of course, it's possible to overdo this strategy. We can saddle our schedule with so many commitments that we sabotage ourselves with impossibly long to-do lists. The idea here is to stretch our limits gradually and discover what we're truly capable of accomplishing.

The point is that problems are like gas: They expand to fill the space we give them. So one way to shrink our current problems is to simply decrease the amount of space we give them in our lives.

From this perspective, a strategy for dealing with problems is not to rid ourselves of them. Instead, we can take on bigger problems. We can contribute our time and money to projects that make a real contribution to the happiness of others and the health of our planet. Problems are always going to be with us, so we can tackle the kind of problems that lead us to bigger adventures.

Some people insult themselves by taking on problems that are too small. Instead, these people could choose bigger problems that are more worthy of their talents and energy.

By the way, this is not a suggestion to ignore everyday problems. Instead, I'm suggesting that you consciously choose the amount of time and attention you give to any problem, big or small.

Some of the wisest members of the human race have suggested taking on bigger problems as a path to happiness. Most of the world's major spiritual traditions say that we achieve fulfillment in life by devoting our energies to something that transcends us—a community of people or a project that's larger than ourselves.

Contribution is a win-win process. Other people and organizations win when we bring to them the skills we've gained while filling ourselves up. And we win, too. There's lasting joy in merging our own efforts with a cause that's bigger than we are, one that will outlast us.

Contribution makes solid, practical sense. We can start taking on bigger problems immediately. And we don't have to do this because it's noble or moral to do so. Instead, we can take on bigger problems as ways to fill our day-to-day lives with more fun, energy, and ecstasy.

Open up to bigger problems (EXERCISE)

Brainstorm a list of big problems. As you do this, expand your horizons. Look for challenges to the well-being of your family, neighborhood, community, city, country, or world. Consider national and international problems—for example, world hunger, human rights violations, or depletion of the ozone layer. For a moment, enlarge your sphere of concern, moving from the hassles of your daily life to the problems of the planet.

Begin your list of problems in the space below and use additional paper, if needed.

Take on a bigger problem (JOURNAL ENTRY)

Review your list of problems from the previous exercise. Describe any feelings that surfaced during this exercise—for example, sadness about a major problem or excitement about the idea of contributing toward a solution.

I discovered that I ...

_____

_____

_____

_____

Now choose one problem from your list and consider taking it on. Think of a specific thing you could do as a step toward solving that problem. For example, you might donate money or time to a charitable organization. You could even consider changing careers so that you can work to solve this problem on a full-time basis.

I intend to ...

_____

_____

_____

_____

Strategies for contributing

Get past blocks to contributing

People experience at least two major barriers to contributing.

One is feeling overwhelmed or resigned. People put off or give up on contributing, saying, "My efforts are so futile," or "There is just too much to do."

Well, of course there's too much to do. If we ever think we've finally solved all of our local and global problems, then we've fallen asleep to what's possible. Our goals for contribution are far too limited.

In the name of contribution we can bump up against a second barrier: reproaching ourselves and others. We might judge ourselves harshly for not contributing enough. Or we might scold others for the way they spend their lives, demanding that they contribute more. Judging ourselves and others adds a layer of upset to our lives that drains our energy and distracts our focus from contribution.

The ways we respond to these barriers can fan the fire of worry and hopelessness—or take us more deeply into contribution. Instead of sinking into resignation about the fact that there's always more to do, we can see this fact as a stimulus to move into action. And instead of sliding into reproach, we can celebrate our current successes in contribution. By contributing with a sense of lightheartedness and fun, we can set an example for others to follow.

Say yes!

Start contributing by responding to what others ask of you. Grant both spoken and unspoken requests. Make more and bigger promises and work like mad to keep them. This is one way that you can naturally generate enthusiasm. Whenever possible, grant other people's requests.

Connect with your passion

When looking for specific ways to contribute, begin by asking *What is my abiding passion in life?* Many times the answer will light a path to contribution.

For example, your passion might be loving animals. If so, then you can choose to work for an animal rights organization. Or your passion might be helping people overcome suffering. That can lead to helping drug addicts get sober, getting kids off the streets and back into school, helping youngsters master reading skills, or assisting dying people to live out their last days with dignity and insight.

You contribute even with passions that seem "selfish." If your passion is woodworking, you can contribute beautiful objects to the world for others to enjoy. Or if your passion is to make money, you'll likely realize that providing goods and services that others find useful is a path toward wealth.

Notice what really contributes to others

Helping others is not the same as deciding what they need or imposing our personal agendas on them. To contribute to others, we can spend time listening to them and following their lead. Our efforts to help can be much more effective once they're in tune with what people really want.

We can also beware of using contribution so that we look good to others. This motive can lead to superficial results and even resentment from the people we want to help.

Caution: Giving others what they want might not always be the most useful contribution. One obvious example is giving drugs to an addict. Another is continually loaning money to people who go into debt carelessly. Sheltering others from the consequences of their behaviors deprives them of the chance to learn.

Give an optimal amount

I have a cartoon that shows a man on the street begging for spare change. He's carrying a sign that reads, "I used to be a philanthropist but got carried away."

You can avoid such a fate by giving an optimal amount. If you want to make a difference when you contribute money or time, then consider this guideline: Give so that it's more than a token gesture and less than a sacrifice. Give enough money to generate excitement about what you're doing—and not enough to drain your account. Give enough time to generate your enthusiasm—and not so much that you drain your energy.

Champion your cause without antagonism

While contributing, we can promote our favorite causes without being condescending to others. Instead of berating others for failing to contribute— or for failing to take on *our* pet projects—we can let people contribute in their own time and way. We can share our ideas about ways to contribute while listening to others' ideas, remembering that there are many paths to solving any problem.

See conflict as a chance to contribute

If you avoid conflict—well, welcome to the human race. Many of us don't like what happens when we experience conflict with other people. So we avoid it. Some people even develop this avoidance into an art form.

"Be nice to people." "Be polite." "Be kind." These ideas enjoy wide circulation in our culture. The trouble is that people think being nice and polite and kind means avoiding conflict at all costs.

Precisely the opposite can be true. Being kind, nurturing, and supportive can mean facing conflict head on. By avoiding conflict, we can miss an opportunity to contribute to the happiness of others.

We can turn conflicts into exercises in problem solving and achieve outcomes that create a "win" for everyone involved.

Hang around skilled contributors

To apply Success Strategy #11, we can learn from skilled contributors. Seek out people who regularly donate their time, money, and talents. These people teach contribution by one of the most effective means possible—their example.

Form a support group

A well-organized support group offers one powerful way for people to contribute to each other. The "technology" of effective support groups— their strategies for success—has been well explored. You can take advantage of what's been learned.

Working in mutually supportive groups is not a new idea. In fact, it's quite old-fashioned. In the recent past, farmers enlisted the help of neighbors to raise barns, plant seeds, and harvest crops. Today, students form study groups and executives find mentors to teach them business skills. Group support is becoming a popular strategy for anyone.

One purpose of a support group is to create a setting where you are willing to "put it all on the line." The group can be a place where you feel safe, accepted, and supported—a place where you're willing to take risks and say anything. You might be able to practice this level of candor with people from your home or work environments. And you might find it easier to begin with a group that brings new people into your life.

To keep your support group effective, consider these suggestions:
- Be open to changing group members, and be flexible about how long the group lasts.
- Decide on a format for your group. You can use a book such as *Falling Awake* when creating the agenda for group meetings. Read and discuss the articles in this book. Do the suggested exercises together. Write journal entries and share them with the group. Assign yourself "homework" to complete before the next meeting, and ask other members to hold you accountable for getting it done.
- Elect one person to keep track of the time, keep the group on task, and mediate conflict. This role can be rotated among all group members.
- Help each other articulate problems, brainstorm solutions, set goals, and create action plans.
- Invite guest speakers or special one-time group leaders.

Practice contributing in everyday ways

A popular bumper sticker urges us to practice "random acts of kindness and senseless acts of beauty." You can easily find ways to act on this suggestion: Pay someone's dinner bill or double the tip you were going to give. Shovel someone else's sidewalk or put money in a stranger's expired parking meter. Compliment a clerk on what a good job he is doing. Open the door for another person or let someone move in front of you in a line. Pass a book or magazine you have finished on to a stranger. Offer directions to someone who looks lost, or send someone an anonymous gift.

Finding small ways to contribute, moment by moment, can be more challenging than giving away large amounts of money and time. I've given away millions of dollars—more of my net worth than anyone I know. And one of the things I found hardest was to give something simple to my wife, Trisha. She had a habit, which I used to find annoying, of picking food off my plate. Finally, I asked her to stop doing that, and she did for a while.

Then Trisha started *asking* if she could have a bite from my plate. Now, I love this woman so much that I'd give my life for her. But, somehow, I still had a problem with giving her a bite from my plate.

Finally, I saw that I had a chance to contribute. I realized that I could just give Trisha my food. So I started telling her that she could have anything on my plate. I even gave her permission to ask for the last bite that's going into my mouth; to this day I'll joyfully give it to her. My willingness to contribute to her in this small way added something wonderful to a relationship that was already tremendous.

Don't worry about how

Very little contribution results when we wait until we're sure how to contribute. One of the most powerful steps we can take is to promise to contribute, even before we know how. Specific strategies will spring from the promise. Commitment moves us from hopelessness to excitement and then to specific plans and actions.

The whole point of contributing is to commit ourselves to something beyond ourselves. Outrageous satisfaction begins as we rise to a calling that transcends us. We can stay in the inquiry, remain alert, and trust that opportunities to contribute will make themselves known.

Begin now

Any of us can practice contributing, even if we feel pressed for money or time, or worry that we lack the necessary skills.

This is where some people object. "There's no way I can do anything for others at this point in my life," they say. "I'm up to my eyeballs in alligators. I'm barely staying afloat." Even when that's true, we can often find a small way to give to someone else. It can be as simple as preparing a meal for someone, picking up the garbage in a neighbor's yard, giving directions to someone who is lost, giving a larger tip to a waitress who provided good service, or slowing down in heavy traffic for someone who is trying to change lanes.

Giving to others in modest ways, even when we're feeling down, can put our personal problems in perspective. Contributing to others in small ways can help us feel better and open us up to additional opportunities for giving ourselves away.

It helps to be selfish

Serving others is not the same as being a servant. People who care take care of themselves. While practicing contribution, we can avoid becoming martyrs, sacrificing our own health and sanity in the quest to make life better for others.

To contribute without burnout and frustration, we can pursue the path of enlightened selfishness. Remembering the following strategies can help us stay on that path.

Stay in touch with your desires

Leaders are filled with desires. Often these people are the first to articulate a widely held desire.

Martin Luther King Jr. was filled with a desire for racial justice. He had a passion, and his desire changed the world.

Elizabeth Cady Stanton and her fellow suffragettes wanted women to have the right to vote. That desire turned them into leaders.

Muhammed Yunus has a passionate desire for a world without abject poverty. He started a bank to make small loans—as little as $100—to people in Bangladesh. Today this bank has over two million borrowers. These people use loans to start their own businesses and rise above the cycle of poverty. By creating a model for micro-lending, it's possible that Yunus has done more to end poverty on the planet than anyone in history. Yunus's passion has made him a leader.

This is one way you can lead your family, your coworkers, your community, and your world: Tap into the universal desire pool. Look to the long-term future of humanity. Discover what you passionately want for other people over the next decade, the next century, and beyond. You'll find plenty of other people who want the same things.

When contributing to others, there's no need to sacrifice your wants.

Instead, follow the lead of your passions. Stay in touch with your deepest desires.

Know that you can contribute— and you don't have to

While exploring the strategy of contribution, you might discover that you can join an organization with a huge humanitarian goal— anything from stopping child abuse to ending world hunger—and make a tremendous difference in that organization's work.

When you truly taste your power to make a difference in the world, you might feel wonderful. And you might feel obligated to use that power, whether you want to or not.

We live in a culture that sends the message "If you *can*, then you *should*." If you can help end child abuse, then you should. If you can help end world hunger, then you should.

The problem is that few of us want to do anything just because we feel obligated. There's no freedom in obligation—no sense of passion or play or fun.

Patrick Henry spoke for all of us when he said, "Give me liberty or give me death." We desire liberty, choice, and freedom. If discovering that we have a huge potential to contribute saddles us with a huge obligation, then it's no surprise that we're tempted to go underground and run away from that potential.

There is another operating principle that allows both contribution and freedom: "You *can*—and you don't *have* to." Realize that you can contribute to the end of child abuse, world hunger, or any other problem— and you don't have to.

If you want to succeed at contribution, then contribute only if you know you'll have a ball. If you'll have more fun by sailing a boat for six months than by contributing, then I say go for fun. Of course, after sailing for those months, you might discover that you want to sail for another six months. Or you might discover that you're ready to start contributing. You might *want* to join an organization that's committed to making a difference in the world. You might relish the thought of taking on a huge problem and helping to solve it. You might even discover a way to contribute to the world *and* continue sailing.

When you move into action from a desire to have fun rather than from a feeling of obligation, you'll be far more effective at whatever project you take on.

Model the possibility of ecstasy

One school of thought says that if you're helping yourself, then you're not helping others. If you're focused on ways to lose weight, make more money, have a passionate sex life, or get whatever else you want in life, then you're self-centered.

There's another viewpoint: When we succeed at losing weight, we discover ways for others to do the same. When we enjoy high-voltage sex in a loving, long-term relationship, we discover ways for other couples to meet the same goal. When we achieve financial independence, we model this possibility for others. When we create lives of daily ecstasy, we discover ways all of us can be more serene and more free.

By helping ourselves get more of what we want in life, we light a path for others. We can give away what we've learned and actively share our strategies for success.

One path to contribution is to make our struggles public. We can reveal our secrets, tell the truth about our problems, and let others in on our solutions. When we do, we give others a gift—the chance to learn with us as we rise to new levels of happiness, health, love, and wealth.

Human history is the story of great people who did great work on themselves. It's the story of Jesus who fasted forty days in the wilderness to overcome temptation. It's the story of Buddha who vowed to sit in meditation until he discovered a way out of suffering—even if that meant sitting for years. What we remember about Jesus, Buddha, Gandhi, Mother Theresa, and other spiritual leaders are the personal problems they took on and the solutions they discovered. When we learn what they learned, we too are helped.

So it can be with us. Our story is the human story, and our paths to happiness can become everyone's path to happiness. Our struggles—and our successes—can become the common property of humanity. By contributing to ourselves, we can contribute to everyone else.

Success Strategy #12

CELEBRATE

*If the only thing
you ever said
was "thank you,"
that would be enough.*

MEISTER ECKHART

Practice the art of appreciation

Success Strategy #12 is about living our whole lives from a stance of "thank you." Our lives can be an occasion for constant celebration. And we might forget this while we're busy determining what we want in life and taking action to get it.

Lighten up

This business of success—setting and achieving goals—can get pretty serious. I know that *Falling Awake* is a book about solving problems and transforming our lives. But none of us is going to make it out alive, even though most of us act as if we are. We're all going to die at the end—even after the most wonderful life imaginable—and we don't know when it's going to happen. Remembering this, we can just lighten up a little and start appreciating what we already have.

I offer this reminder for my own benefit as well as yours. I spend too much of my time looking for ways to create better circumstances and too little time appreciating the wonderful circumstances I've already created. I tend to spend too much time looking for a new show in life that will give me more pleasure and too little time enjoying the show that I already have.

Several years ago I created a 100-year plan. It took up seven single-spaced pages filled with written goals. I even planned to die graciously. Not long ago, I also set a goal to die with laughter and celebration. I don't want to have just a funeral—I want a "fun-eral."

I'm not the only person with this goal. Recently, I saw an advertisement for a workshop by Patch Adams on dying with fun. Now, that's celebration!

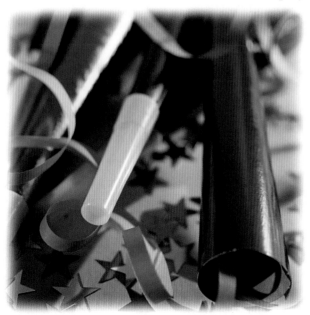

Celebrate often—and authentically

Of course, you can start celebrating long before you die. You can celebrate anything you like about your life. Any time you meet a goal, celebrate that. Any time you solve a problem, celebrate that, too. Celebrate your brilliance and the brilliance of others. Celebrate your family, your friends, your home, or your career. Just pick something and celebrate.

If you start celebrating a lot, people might wonder what's happened to you. They might think you're a little strange and ask you what's going on. If you say that you just chose to start celebrating, they might not buy it. So make up a reason to celebrate. Tell them that something big just happened to you—for example, that you just read a wonderful book about creating the life of your dreams—and that you just want to celebrate.

When suggesting that you celebrate often, I am not advising you to become a positive thinker. I'm not suggesting that you celebrate everything, or that you fake celebration. I *am* suggesting that you look around and celebrate whatever you authentically can.

For example, you can celebrate your outrageous wealth. At first, you might object that you aren't wealthy. But being wealthy is not the same as having a million dollars in the bank. Wealth means having more than enough—and enjoying what you already have. The vast majority of people in Canada, the United States, and Europe *are* truly wealthy. For most of human history, even the richest people lived with far fewer luxuries than the average middle-class wage-earner does today.

Wealth is just one of many things you can appreciate. If your intention is to celebrate, you'll open up your imagination and find much more.

Celebrate in any circumstance

When I visited Bangladesh in 1994 and India in 1996, I spent time with people who lived in abject poverty. Most of them had little to eat. Often they had no chimney for their indoor fires and no clean water. Most didn't even have toilets, indoors or out.

My initial reaction was to feel miserable and sorry for people living in these conditions. Strangely, my feelings quickly turned to a sense of celebration. In part, I celebrated the fact that I wasn't dying and that I wasn't hungry. But there was more. I saw that people who seemed to have nothing often laughed. They took pleasure in the moment, enjoying the simplest and most universal things—their children, their families, their daily tasks. And my hosts were gracious and pleasant. In many moments they were even lighthearted and joyous.

Against a background of such extreme poverty, I saw these moments as precious. I realized more deeply than ever the sacredness of life and the human capacity for joy in almost any circumstance.

End up with paradise, no matter what

In Success Strategy #1, I suggest that you create four times as many goals as you think you want to achieve. Then you can fail to meet three-fourths of your goals and still create the life of your dreams. Given the games you and I get to play, we can lose 75 percent of the time and still end up with paradise.

So imagine that your search for happiness is over. Imagine that you've already found what you're looking for. Imagine that your major problems have already been solved and your most important goals have already been met. Discover something you love about your life, and then just celebrate.

Go for fun

The motto "No pain no gain" can easily lead us astray. Struggle and sorrow are not prerequisites for excellence, and maximum productivity can come from maximum fun.

When I suggest creating a life filled with pleasure and celebration, some people object that this might kill productivity. If people just went around enjoying themselves all of the time, then no one would get anything done.

Perhaps the opposite is true.

I work with people who are dedicated to solving serious problems in the world. For the last several years, I've provided life coaching to three leaders of international, nonprofit organizations. All three people are dedicated to ending poverty and hunger within our lifetime. And one of the goals they have for their organizations is to end poverty and hunger while having a blast.

You might ask what's so fun about poverty or hunger. That's an understandable reaction. Nearly 30,000 people die every day from lack of food. People who are committed to solving this kind of problem tend to get a little serious. My purpose in working with these organizations is to help people bring joy to their work. I think they'll end poverty and hunger sooner if they structure their jobs so that they love what they're doing.

Telling people to go for fun is a little like ordering them to be spontaneous. By their very nature, fun and spontaneity are almost impossible to command. Yet we can set up conditions that favor fun and set the stage for laughter. Play with the following suggestions.

Discover everyday pleasures

Often we can discover enjoyment even in the most mundane tasks. For example, washing dishes can be a sensual experience—a chance to enjoy the pleasurable sensation of warm water contacting your skin. Mowing the lawn can be an excuse to get outdoors and exercise on a summer day. And buying groceries offers the chance to gather ideas for delicious new meals. Keep looking and you'll find pleasures waiting to be had in the midst of daily life.

Celebrate more, produce more

Compare two work environments. The employees in one office barely speak to each other. During lunch time they huddle at their desks for a solitary sack lunch. By mid-afternoon these desperate people start watching the clock. They're silently waiting for the time when they can slink out the door, unnoticed, to drive home. Despite the nose-to-the-grindstone atmosphere that prevails here, the company is barely profitable.

In contrast, the people who work at the second office see each other regularly. At the beginning of each meeting, they "check in" with each other and socialize for a few minutes. This practice paves the way for enduring friendships that extend beyond working hours. In addition, their cubicles and hallways occasionally reverberate with laughter. The prevailing spirit of cooperation and teamwork leads to sustained growth and low employee turnover.

This is not just a hypothetical example. For a decade I owned a consulting and publishing company that often created an atmosphere of fun. We set aside regular times for the purposes of deepening our relationships and celebrating our successes. And the company was highly profitable. My goals in starting this company were to work with people I love, to make a difference in the world, and to have a ball.

People who enjoy their work are more likely to excel. Ask almost any skilled artist, executive, teacher, or musician to explain what drives them in their chosen profession. They might tell you about long years of study or hours spent in practice rooms. They'll also tell you how much they love their work and look forward to getting up each day. We can follow their example and find ways to bring a spirit of passion and play to our own work.

In any environment, including those in which productivity counts, we can take time to celebrate. We can celebrate the beginning, middle, and end of a project. When someone proposes a brilliant idea or develops an innovative product, we can celebrate. When the company meets a goal, we can celebrate. And when the company misses a goal, we can celebrate what we learn from the mistake.

Just laugh

It seems logical to laugh when we have reason to laugh—a hilarious joke, a slapstick gag, a comic stunt. We can also create humor from nothing, even when there's no "reason" to laugh.

For example, you can buy recordings that consist solely of people laughing. Almost no one who hears these can resist the urge to join in. Laughter truly is contagious.

Sometimes just laughing means noticing your usual tendencies and then doing the opposite. For example, one common response to getting laid off is to weep. Well, if you lose your job, you can weep and then use another strategy: throw a no-holds-barred party.

Some people will object that this action makes no sense. Tell them that celebrating with friends at such a time makes at least as much sense as isolating yourself and feeling miserable.

While promoting laughter, we can also practice dropping antagonism. Much humor is unloving, cutting, or cruel. Comedian W. C. Fields said it: "I never saw anything funny that wasn't terrible. If it causes pain, it's funny; it if doesn't, it isn't."

Perhaps Fields was wrong. We can look for humor that is inclusive and kind. This kind of humor underlines our common problems and shared humanity. For example:

"So you think that money is the root of all evil? Have you ever asked what is the root of money?" (Ayn Rand)

"When you come to the fork in the road, take it." (Yogi Berra)

"Lord grant me patience, and give it to me now." (Alcoholics Anonymous saying)

The benefits of laughter are so great that it pays to cultivate humor systematically. We can scan the comic pages for our favorite cartoons and clip our favorite strips. We can watch situation comedies and collect recordings by our favorite comedians. Regularly raiding our humor stash can be a life-saver.

Zoom out for instant perspective

Remember the situation that once seemed so disastrous and now seems so funny? You know the one—the time you took off your shoes while visiting a friend's new home and noticed a large hole in one of your socks. Or the time you got home from a date and realized that your fly was unzipped all night. The passage of time has a way of bringing out the humor in what was once an embarrassment.

You can learn to compress time: Start laughing as soon as a screwy event occurs. With practice, you can mentally zoom out from the situation to gain perspective. Ask yourself *How will I view this situation twelve months from now?* If you're going to laugh at yourself then, why wait? You might as well start now.

State what you like about yourself and others (EXERCISE)

Find another person to be your partner for this exercise. Then complete the following steps:

1. Choose one person to do the talking. For purposes of this exercise, this person is the "speaker." The other is the "listener."

2. Allow the speaker five minutes to complete the following sentence in as many ways as possible: What I like best about me is …

3. As this speaker talks, remember that the listener has only one task—to simply receive what the speaker says without making any comments. (The listener can offer simple phrases of acknowledgment, such as "Uh-huh" or "Okay.")

4. Next, switch roles. The person who spoke will now listen, and vice versa. Do this step for another five minutes.

5. Now start again. Choose one person to be the speaker and another to be the listener. This time, let the speaker complete the following sentence for five minutes: What I like best about you is …

6. As the speaker talks, remember that the listener can only respond with phrases such as these: "Thank you; you sure know quality when you see it." "Thank you; you're very perceptive." "Thank you; I know."

7. After five minutes have passed, switch roles again.

This exercise has several purposes. It offers you and your partner a chance to practice listening and giving the gift of attention. It also invites you to practice giving and receiving compliments.

Do this exercise with your spouse, lover, family members, old friends, recent acquaintances, and people with whom you're currently in conflict. You might find this to be a quick and powerful way to practice celebrating with anyone in your life.

Laugh three times daily
and call me in the morning (JOURNAL ENTRY)

Laughing changes our whole physiology and psychology, even if just for a few moments.
Few stress management techniques are as powerful as a good, gut-busting guffaw.

Assess how often laughter is a part of your life. Review the past week and recall the times
and places you laughed. Then complete the following sentence in the space below.

I discovered that I ...

_____

_____

_____

_____

Consider taking specific steps to cultivate laughter in your life. Some possibilities are:
Watch funny films. Read funny books. See stand-up comedians. Start a joke stash, and
practice memorizing and telling jokes. Smile at random and watch your mood change.
Or stand in front of a mirror and laugh as loudly as you can, straight from your belly.
If you don't feel like laughing, just fake it; notice the effect on your mood.

Choose one of these strategies to use on a regular basis. Or use another strategy that you
remember or invent. In the space below, describe specifically how you will bring more
laughter into your life.

I intend to ...

_____

_____

_____

_____

choose your ways to spell "fun" (JOURNAL ENTRY)

Quickly list what you do now for fun, or would like to do—walking, reading, golfing, partying, listening to music, whatever. In the space below, list as many items as you can. Use additional paper if needed.

I discovered that I can have fun by ...

_____

_____

_____

Now create two variations on each activity and plan to enjoy them regularly. For example, you might enjoy preparing and tasting new foods. A variation and a way to savor this pleasure is to invite people to dinner so that they can share your next culinary experiment. Another variation is to form a recipe exchange with neighbors.

Write your variations below. Again, use a separate sheet of paper if you run out of room.

_____

_____

_____

Finally, pick one of the items you just listed and do it in the next week. Then pick a few more that you will do in the next month. Write a plan to ensure that you will do the things on your fun list. Consider scheduling your fun activity; it's as important as anything else in your calendar.

I intend to ...

_____

_____

_____

Create happiness NOW (EXERCISE)

We have far more choice in our level of happiness than most of us realize. In most situations, even those we label neutral or unpleasant, it's possible for us to generate an experience of happiness. We can be happy almost anywhere, anytime; there's no reason to wait. This might seem impossible for many people to comprehend until they experience it for themselves.

Do not do this exercise unless you want to be happy right now. Sometimes it seems appropriate to be unhappy. Feeling upset is a natural response to difficult conditions. And at any moment, in almost any circumstance, you can let go of upset and replace it with celebration.

This exercise suggests a strategy for creating happiness. Using these suggestions, you can begin creating happiness for a few seconds, then for a few minutes and even longer periods. Eventually, you might find that happiness is the predominant experience in your life.

Begin this exercise with a genuine commitment to be happy. Then continue reading.

Step 1: Create a few seconds of happiness without fixing anything

The first step in this exercise is to create the experience of being happy no matter what's happening in your life. Go for it right away. Just create an experience of happiness. Do it now.

Could you do it? If not, try again. Still didn't work? Then play with these ideas:

• Remember a time in the past when you were happy. Recall how you felt at that time. Re-create the experience as vividly as you can. If possible, re-enact the scene in the present.

• Picture a time in the future when you believe you will be happy. Imagine how you will feel at that time and capture that feeling for the next few moments. Picture an event that you anticipate with joy.

• Reflect for a few moments on the gifts others have given you. Focus on a single period in your life and be as specific as possible. Name the people involved and describe to yourself in detail the gifts they gave you.

- Plan to give someone a gift. Picture the recipient of your gift and choose specifically what you will give that person. Imagine how it will feel to give your gift.

- Look like a happy person. Position your body in a way that you usually position it when you're happy. Move like a happy person: Sing. Sit up straight. Smile. Laugh. Run. Jump for joy. Do with your body what happy people do with theirs, then let your emotions catch up.

- Fake it. Pretend you're happy. Think of yourself as an actress on stage, playing the role of a happy person. This is not lying—just prematurely telling the truth. Once you have artificially created the experience of happiness, take a small step and notice if you are actually being happy, if only for a few seconds.

Step 2: Expand moments of happiness to several minutes

Once you discover that you can create being happy for a few seconds in a row, see if you can extend the time. When you find a technique that works, practice creating happiness for one minute, then two, then three or more.

Step 3: Create happiness while doing something else

Many people can quickly achieve the first two steps of this exercise. These steps develop our ability to set other concerns aside for a short time and create a moment-by-moment experience of happiness.

Now practice creating the same level of happiness while you're doing some activity that's generally not linked to being happy. For example, if you're generally not happy when cleaning the house, then do this exercise at that time. While you are cleaning, practice generating the experience of happiness—first for a few seconds, and then for a few minutes in a row.

One qualification: This is not a suggestion to retreat from problems or ignore tough emotions when they are present. Dealing head-on with problems and fully experiencing all of our emotions promote our happiness.

This exercise has a different purpose. It raises the possibility that we can celebrate under many circumstances—far more often than we usually imagine. With sustained practice, we can develop the skill of generating happiness during almost any activity. Happiness is a choice we can make right now. Celebrate.

CONTINUE CREATING THE LIFE OF YOUR DREAMS

Too much of a good thing can be wonderful.

MAE WEST

Do this book again and raise the stakes (EXERCISE)

This whole book exists to convince you of one idea—that you can get whatever you want. The message behind every line in this book is that you can create the life of your dreams.

The cover of this book listed me as the author. That was merely a convenience for the publisher—a trick, really. What you bring to this book is far more important than what I put on the pages. What you get out of this book depends on you—how well you absorb its message, and what you do in response to that message.

Right now, I ask you to make a commitment: Please be willing to go through this book several times. And commit to getting a lot out of the book each time you use it. Make this book a force that enhances the quality of your life forever. Continue using the book to create the life of your dreams.

Caution: There are people who don't believe they can create the life of their dreams. They don't believe that they can co-create a book. This is a normal, reasonable, and sensible thought. Please suspend it.

One of the first exercises in *Falling Awake* asked you to write your own testimonial for this book and then to act in ways that made your testimonial come true. Experiment with this strategy again.

Right now, consider the benefits of reading and doing this book a second time (and a third, fourth, fifth, or more). Take a few minutes to write a new testimonial for your next experience of *Falling Awake*. Consider raising the stakes by creating an even more powerful testimonial than you wrote the first time.

Again, here are some possible examples:

> *Every hour of every day I can make the choice to have my life continue to be outstanding.*

> *Several years ago I read this book and made remarkable changes in my life. I still use strategies from the book. And as hard as it is to believe, my life continues to get better and better.*

> *After I read this book, I transformed the quality of my life—dramatically— in just a few days.*

> *After reviewing parts of this book, I realized that I totally missed many tremendous ideas. As my life continues to get better and better, I'm eager to go through the whole book again and find even more ways to be happier, healthier, wealthier, and more loving.*

Write your testimonial on a separate sheet of paper.

Pick any topic and apply each Success Strategy (EXERCISE)

This exercise has four steps:

1. List three of the biggest problems in your life or three of the biggest goals you want to achieve. Do this now on a separate sheet of paper.

2. From your list, select the biggest problem or the toughest goal and write about it here.

_____

_____

_____

_____

3. Now write down every wild and crazy solution you can come up with. List every action you could take to meet your goal, even if that action seems impossible.

_____

_____

_____

_____

_____

_____

_____

_____

_____

_____

_____

_____

4. Now, on a separate sheet of paper, brainstorm ways to solve your chosen problem or achieve your goal by using each of the Success Strategies. Aim to create a list with at least twelve solutions or possible action plans. If you get to a Success Strategy that doesn't seem to fit, do a force-fit. Use your imagination. Some of the most outlandish ideas can yield the most practical real-life solutions.

Apply a strategy (JOURNAL ENTRY)

Please refer to the exercise on page 269 and select at least three of the many solutions you have created. Then, establish a timeline for when you will implement them. The idea here is that even great solutions are worthless if they are never implemented, and we are more likely to implement something when we have committed to it in writing with a timeline. Complete the following sentence several times:

I intend to _____ by (date) _____

I intend to _____ by (date) _____

I intend to _____ by (date) _____

I intend to _____ by (date) _____

I intend to _____ by (date) _____

I intend to _____ by (date) _____

In addition to a timeline, having partners also increases the likelihood of implementing solutions. Now review the intentions you wrote above, and add to them by listing people who might assist you to implement these solutions. Complete the following intention statement several times:

I intend to ask _____ to assist me with _____

I intend to ask _____ to assist me with _____

I intend to ask _____ to assist me with _____

I intend to ask _____ to assist me with _____

I intend to ask _____ to assist me with _____

I intend to ask _____ to assist me with _____

Take a First Step—
...again (EXERCISE)

One useful way to assess the difference that this book has made in your life is to repeat the suggested journal entries and exercises. In particular, you can derive value from repeating the "First Step" exercise, which was included in Success Strategy #2: "Tell the truth." The core instructions for that exercise are reproduced below.

Part 1

Set aside 10 minutes to complete the following sentence on a separate sheet of paper. Aim for at least 10 responses. And don't worry about whether your writing is wrong or silly. If an idea pops into your head, put it down. You can review and reflect on your responses later.

One of my strengths is that ...

Following are sample ways to finish this sentence. These are not prescriptions for what you should write—just examples:

I have a clear sense of the factors in life that I can control and also of the factors that I cannot control.

I periodically examine the quality of my thinking and choose beliefs that promote my happiness.

I take risks, even if it means making mistakes.

I use an effective set of strategies for responding to stress.

I listen attentively and with skill.

I communicate my thoughts and feelings without blaming others.

Part 2

Take another 10 minutes to complete the following sentence. List as many responses as you can—at least 10. This will be a rough draft, so don't worry about the quality of what you write. Just get as many ideas down on paper as you can.

Things don't work well when ...

Again, some examples follow:

I discover my relationships are not working and avoid conflict with the people involved.

I spend more than I earn and accumulate large balances on my credit cards.

I break agreements with the people closest to me.

I think I'm unlovable.

I stop listening to people I dislike.

Part 3

Once you've finished the first two parts of this exercise, take a short breather. Also celebrate the difficult and potentially rewarding work that you've done so far.

Now take another step to solidify your insights. Review the two lists you've created. Cross off any ideas that don't make sense. Add any new ideas that come to mind. Put an asterisk next to statements that really ring true. Look for ways to reword any of these statements to make them clearer or more accurate.

Part 4

Here's your chance to follow up on what you've learned about yourself.

First, review your list of strengths regularly, especially when you feel discouraged or just plain stuck. You might want to post this list in a prominent place so that you'll see it often.

Next, look again at your list of problems from Part 2. Take your most limiting problems and rewrite them as goals. Move from problems to possible solutions.

For example, *I run low on cash at the end of each month* can be transformed into *I intend to decrease my spending so that I have cash left over at the end of the month.*

If any of your intentions bring up outrageous possibilities or hold the promise of far-reaching change, that's great. Consider breaking these long-range goals down into simple, specific actions you can start taking immediately.

There's only one step left, and it goes beyond writing: *Do* what you intend. Take action. Savor any positive new results in your life. Also, come back to this exercise periodically. Use it any time to spot-check for problems and take charge of your life again. You can make truth telling a habit.

Reflect on your First Steps (JOURNAL ENTRY)

Begin a new direction for the future by completing the following sentences
in the space below.

After repeating the First Step exercise, I discovered that my life has changed
in the following ways:

_____

_____

_____

_____

After reviewing my experience with this book, I discovered that the most important
things I can do to raise the quality of my life right now include . . .

_____

_____

_____

_____

To follow up on these discoveries, I intend to . . .

_____

_____

_____

_____

Keep the Success Strategies alive

People who attend lots of personal growth seminars know about the "workshop syndrome." It goes something like this:

On Friday night at the first workshop session, they feel excited about meeting new people and learning new ideas.

On Saturday they feel inspired.

By Sunday night, they feel that they've achieved a breakthrough in their lives.

Throughout the next week, they feel the weight of their everyday routines on all that newfound enthusiasm. And by Friday they're so worn down by the daily grind that they need another workshop.

Please don't let anything like this happen to you after reading this book. Keep your goals, dreams, and vision of a wonderful life alive. Keep your understanding of the Success Strategies in working order. Use the following suggestions to keep determining what you want in life and choosing ways to get it.

Display your dreams

Make your own advertisements as reminders of the Success Strategies. For example, write the names of Success Strategies on 3x5 cards or Post-it® notes. Then post those reminders on your bathroom mirror, on your desk at work, or in your car.

Create a clay sculpture, drawing, or painting that symbolizes your vision. Design screen savers for your computer that display your goals. Rent a billboard!

Get a coach

Consider hiring a life coach—someone who will listen fully and support you as you talk about the life of your dreams in all areas. Professional life coaches exist in many cities, and they might be willing to take you on as a client. Some psychotherapists offer services similar to life coaching.

You can also set up informal coaching networks where you trade services with people who are willing to coach you. In turn, you offer to coach them, and no money has to trade hands.

Make it a habit

Success Strategy #9 suggests ways to change habits. Use these suggestions to apply the Success Strategies. Each of them consists of a set of habits that you can practice. Using the core steps—commitment, monitoring, and practice—adopt one new habit at a time. Then savor the results in your life.

Share the Success Strategies in a group

Reread this book and share the ideas with others. Whenever you get a chance, talk about the Success Strategies and ways you can use them.

Consider starting a support group. Ask other people about a dream they have that's not currently fulfilled. Then, as a group, brainstorm ways to achieve it.

You can use this book as the "textbook" for your group. Do the exercises and journal entries together.

Share ideas and strategies. Support each other in getting what you want in life. Hearing ways that other people apply the Success Strategies can inspire you.

To experience the full support of other people, take some of your goals all the way up the ladder of powerful speaking and turn them into promises. Ask people in the group to assist you in keeping your word.

Schedule time for visioning

Add a date in your calendar to review your responses to the journal entries and exercises in this book.

Reread your discovery and intention statements.

Review your goals and write new ones.

And of course, schedule time to act on those goals.

Celebrate success

Every time you achieve a goal, celebrate. "Success breeds success"—you've probably seen this slogan or something like it on a bumper sticker. Well, many of the things you see on bumper stickers are true. So celebrate any success, no matter how small.

Explore many roads to ecstasy

In this book, I enthusiastically promote twelve Success Strategies. These are the most effective ways I know to create the life of your dreams. But an idea that I am even more enthused about than these Success Strategies comes from the lyrics to one of my favorite songs by Libby Roderick. The song starts, "There are many roads to ecstasy, the shortest is your own." That idea captures the essence of *Falling Awake.*

Please be creative and discover your own road to ecstasy. Use this book as a stimulus and then be willing to think what you have never thought, say what you have never said, feel what you have never felt, and write what you have never written.

Come up with dozens or even hundreds of new ways to create the life of your dreams. And remember that your path to ecstasy is unique. You might travel a different road than everyone else, and you might even choose to change directions from time to time.

I wish you many passionate hours of determining what you want, getting it, and celebrating the paradise that you create.

Index

Index

Index

Index

Index

G

H

I

Index

L

Index

O

Obligation, 46, 47, 233, 242
    in contribution, 252, 253
    in ladder of powerful speaking, 110
    and promises, 63
    to act when listening, 177
Observable behaviors, 64
Observations in "I-messages," 112, 113
Ogilvy, David, 181
Opinions, 90, 124, 172, 229

P

Pain
    chronic, 102
    loving the, 75
Parker Brothers, 221
Partners
    in doing *Falling Awake,* 17
    in meeting goals, 47
    See also Involving others
Passion, 30, 248, 259
    in ladder of powerful speaking, 110–111
    as moral guide, 24–25
Past versus future, 41–43, 194–195
Peace, 154, 204
Persistence, 219–239
    clear thinking, 226–228
    controversial topics, 229
    courage, 224, 234–235
    feelings and new actions, 238
    hang in there ... and choose when
        to hang it up, 220–221

motivation, 230–231
    options, 225
    play full out, 236–237, 239
    procrastination, 232–233
    stay in the inquiry, 222–225
Personal boundaries, 80
Personal growth seminars, 273
Personal transformation, 204
Perspective, 260
Petit-Senn, John, 241
Philanthropy, 25, 29
Philosophers, 125
Physical abuse, 94
Physical sensations of fear, 85
Physical tension, 138–140
    See also Relaxation techniques;
    Tension and compliments
Pictures (expectations), 128–130
Piggybacking, 97, 176
Pirsig, Robert, *Zen and the Art
    of Motorcycle Maintenance,* 220
Planning
    by creation, 41–43
    by prediction, 41
    in ladder of powerful speaking, 111
    vision for your life, 22–23
    zero-based, 41
Play full out, 236–237, 239
Play and fun, 212, 259
Positions versus interests, 91
Positive thinking, 256
Possessions, identifying with, 124
Possibility in ladder of powerful speaking, 110
Posture, 177
Poverty, 100, 252, 257, 258

Index

Index

Index

Recommended readings

Bach, Richard. *Illusions: The Adventures of a Reluctant Messiah*. New York: Delacorte, 1977.

Bandler, Richard, and John Grinder. *Frogs into Princes: Neuro-Linguistic Programming*. Moab, UT: Real People, 1979.

Dominguez, Joe, and Vicki Robin. *Your Money or Your Life: Transforming Your Relationship with Money and Achieving Financial Independence*. New York: Viking, 1992.

Driekurs, Rudolf, and Vicki Soltz. *Children: The Challenge*. New York: Dutton, 1964.

Elgin, Duane. *Voluntary Simplicity*. New York: Morrow, 1993.

Ellis, Dave, and Stan Lankowitz. *Human Being: A Manual for Happiness, Health, Love and Wealth*. Rapid City, SD: Breakthrough Enterprises, 1995.

Ellis, Dave, Stan Lankowitz, Ed Stupka, and Doug Toft. *Career Planning*, 2nd edition. Boston: Houghton Mifflin, 1997.

Ellis, Dave. *Becoming a Master Student*, 9th edition. Boston: Houghton Mifflin, 1999.

Ellis, Dave. *Creating Your Future: Five Steps to the Life of Your Dreams*. Boston: Houghton Mifflin, 1998.

Ellis, Dave. *Life Coaching: A New Career for Helping Professionals*. Rapid City, SD: Breakthrough Enterprises, 1998.

Gawain, Shakti. *Creative Visualization*. New York: New World Library, 1998.

Golas, Thaddeus. *The Lazy Man's Guide to Enlightenment*. New York: Bantam, 1993.

Johnson, Vernon E. *I'll Quit Tomorrow*. New York: Harper and Row, 1980.

Keyes, Ken, Jr. *Handbook to Higher Consciousness*. Berkeley, CA: Living Love, 1974.

Keyes, Ken, Jr. *The Hundredth Monkey*. Coos Bay, OR: Vision, 1982.

Porter, Sylvia. *Sylvia Porter's Your Financial Security*. New York: Avon, 1990.

Rajneesh, Bhagwan S. *Journey Toward the Heart*. New York: Harper and Row, 1980.

Robbins, John. *Diet for a New America*. New York: H J Kramer, 1998.

Sher, Barbara, with Annie Gottlieb. *Wishcraft: How to Get What You Really Want*. New York: Ballantine, 1986.

Sinetar, Marsha. *Do What You Love, the Money Will Follow*. New York: Dell, 1989.

Sign on...

As this book goes to press, the *Falling Awake* web site is evolving toward my goal of providing the most personalized, effective, accessible, and interactive life-planning process available on-line.

I want the web site to be a constant resource to anyone, any time, at any stage in the *Falling Awake* process.

Use it along with the book, instead of the book, before the book, after the book—however you wish.

Use the site to argue with me or make suggestions as to how the project could be improved.

Use the site to help organize or customize your process.

Use it to network with others who are "falling awake."

And, perhaps most importantly, use it to celebrate.

Celebrate your successes, victories, insights, even your confusion or frustration. I think we can celebrate anything and everything—it's all part of the process of *Falling Awake.*

Just log on at:
www.FallingAwake.com

Watch it

In addition to the website, you can also be involved with *Falling Awake* by participating in a video workshop. Several video tapes are available. You can find out more by signing on to www.FallingAwake.com or by writing to:

Falling Awake
PO Box 8396
Rapid City, SD
57709

DAVE ELLIS is an author, educator, and philanthropist. His book, *Becoming a Master Student,* is the best-selling college textbook in America. It has been translated into French and Spanish and is used by college students and faculty in the United States and several other countries to promote their success inside and outside the classroom. In addition to this book, he has authored or co-authored several other books on human effectiveness.

Dave is also a nationally known lecturer and workshop leader. He facilitates workshops and does most of his writing at a retreat center he designed in the Black Hills of South Dakota.

Dave taught computer programming at the college level for four years. He counseled students and worked as Assistant Dean of Student Services.

He also founded The Brande Foundation and has given away millions of dollars.

Dave is married and has four grown daughters.

Other books by Dave Ellis include:

Becoming a Master Student

Career Planning (with Stan Lankowitz, Ed Stupka, and Doug Toft)

Creating Your Future

Human Being (with Stan Lankowitz)

Learning Power (with Peter Lenn)

Life Coaching

These books as well as videotapes that accompany the books can be ordered by signing on to our website at *www.FallingAwake.com* or by calling toll free 1-866-FallAwake (1-866-325-5292).